The Church in Council

The Church in Council

E. I. Watkin

DARTON, LONGMAN
& TODD
LONDON

SHEED & WARD
NEW YORK

DARTON, LONGMAN & TODD LTD.
29a Gloucester Road,
London, S.W.7

SHEED & WARD INC.
64 University Place
New York 3

Nihil obstat : P. Leo Smith, O.S.B., Ph.D., Diocesan
Censor Deputatus.
Imprimatur : Cyril Restieaux, Bishop of Plymouth,
15th August, 1960.

PRINTED IN GREAT BRITAIN
BY CHARLES BIRCHALL & SONS, LTD.,
LIVERPOOL AND LONDON

To
my daughter
Magdalen

I wish to thank the Abbot and community of Buckfast Abbey for kindly allowing me the use of their library, indispensable for this book.

E.I.W.

CONTENTS

ABBREVIATIONS

Abp. — Archbishop
B. — Bishop
Bl. — Blessed (Beatus -a)
C. — Cardinal
E. — Emperor, Empress
K. — King
M. — Martyr
Pr. — Patriarch
P. — Pope
Q. — Queen

1

INTRODUCTORY

THE declared intention of the present Pope John XXIII to convoke an ecumenical Council invites the enquiry what precisely is
an ecumenical Council, how many such Councils have there been,
under what historical conditions were they called, what functions
did each perform, what work did it achieve. The purpose of this
book is to answer these questions by an historical study of
the twenty Councils recognised by the Roman Catholic Church
as ecumenical. Such a study in turn requires some knowledge of
the general historical background of ecclesiastical history in
so far as it explains the situation confronting the Council and
the issues on which it must decide. It is hoped that this sketch
will answer these questions with sufficient detail for human
interest yet not so much as to obscure the outlines of the
picture.

An ecumenical Council is a universal or general Council. The
word ecumenical derives from a Greek word meaning the habi-
table world, but in practice often restricted to the Roman
Empire. As understood by Roman Catholic theology, with which
alone this book is concerned, it is a council to which all diocesan
bishops of the church are invited.

Cardinals, whether bishops or not, are also members of an
ecumenical council. To these have been added the superiors of
some religious orders. Indeed at some of the earlier Latin
councils abbots were numerous, sometimes even outnumbering the

bishops. Moreover it became customary in the Middle Ages to invite representatives of secular governments, though they had no voice in framing or enacting conciliar decrees.

Substantially, that is to say, an ecumenical council represents the diocesan bishops as the divinely ordained rulers and teachers of their flocks—comprising what is termed the ecclesia docens or the teaching Church. According to present Canon Law, the law of the Church, it must be convened by the Pope and its decrees sanctioned and promulgated by him. Only then is it accepted as ecumenical and its doctrinal decrees as invested with the infallibility claimed by the Church as depository and interpreter of Divine Revelation.

Since the solemn definitions of doctrine by the Pope, for example Pope Pius IX's definition of Mary's Immaculate Conception[1] Pope Pius XII's of her bodily Assumption[2] are infallible without any confirmation by the Church, councils may appear superfluous. Certainly they are not indispensable. For the first three hundred years of the Church's existence there were none—they were indeed in practice impossible when the Christian religion was proscribed by the State. Between 869 and 1123 no general council was summoned. Nor was there any during the three centuries which separated the Council of Trent from the Vatican Council.

In the earlier centuries, however, though the supremacy of St. Peter's successor in the See of Rome was recognised, its scope was ill defined and in the Eastern churches its exercise was rare and frequently contested. Under such circumstances a General Council possessed in practice, though not by right, weightier authority than an unsupported Papal utterance. When the final schism between East and West in 1054 reduced the visible Catholic Church to the Western and Latin churches where the Pope's authority was more completely recognised and more regularly exercised, General Councils, when revived after a lengthy interval, were

---

[1] The doctrine that Mary's soul from the first instant of its creation possessed the supernatural union with God conferred on other souls by baptism.

[2] The doctrine that not only the soul but the body of Mary are in heaven and have always been united since she left the earth.

reinforcements and supports of Papal authority. The Council of Trent made it clear that the Catholic episcopate rejected the doctrines taught by the Protestant Reformers and formulated the Catholic teaching on the questions in dispute. Finally the Vatican Council showed that the Catholic episcopate recognises the Pope's doctrinal infallibility. Moreover the Pope does not define, and never has defined, a doctrine, relying on a personal inspiration to which he makes no claim. Though the assent of the Church is not required to render his pronouncement infallible, he always takes means to obtain it before the pronouncement is made. Before the definitions of 1854 and 1950[1] every bishop was consulted and behind the bishops the general belief of the faithful was explored.[2] Indeed the doctrine of the Immaculate Conception made its first appearance as a pious belief of simple Catholics, rejected by professional theologians. Later it won their assent[3] until it became the dominant doctrine in the theological schools. At the close of this process it received the solemn sanction of a Papal definition. If, however, it is a question not simply of one particular doctrine but of a complex of doctrines requiring careful technical formulation and to some extent disputed by Catholic theologians, as was the case pre-eminently at the Council of Trent, the most satisfactory method to discover the mind of the Church is through a general council of bishops who hear and weigh the arguments of theological experts, debate the most accurate formulae, and only then arrive at the doctrinal decrees submitted for Papal confirmation. That is to say, general or ecumenical councils, though not strictly necessary, have played a most valuable part in the history of the Church, at times even a part *practically* indispensable.

Not all the councils now recognised as ecumenical did in fact fulfil the conditions now laid down by Canon Law. The earlier

[1] The Immaculate Conception, the Assumption.

[2] This is not to say that the method of doing this practised recently, pressure put on individuals to sign petitions asking for the definition in question, is altogether desirable.

[3] St. Bonaventure tells us he had never heard it defended (in the theological Schools). Duns Scotus c. 1300 was the first Catholic teacher of eminence to teach and defend the doctrine (See Duns Scotus, *Doctor of the Immaculate Conception*, Julian Kaun, O.F.M. following Fr. Balic (*Theology Digest*, Spring, 1958).

councils were summoned not by the Pope but by the Emperor.
At the first general council at Nicaea the Emperor Constantine's
nominee presided and, so far as we know, Pope Sylvester was
not asked to confirm its decisions. The second ecumenical council,
confined to a handful of eastern bishops, met at Constantinople
without even the Pope's knowledge. The eighth general council
was not recognised as ecumenical for more than two centuries, not
in fact until the utility of its disciplinary decrees brought about
its tardy recognition by the Catholic Church.

Though all diocesan bishops are in principle invited to a general council, it is obviously impossible that all can attend. In
many cases only a small minority has attended—sometimes only
the bishops of a particular area. Out of at least 220 bishops at
the first Council of Nicaea the West sent only four bishops and
two priests representing the Pope. The 186 bishops present at the
1st Council of Constantinople (381) were all Eastern, as were
almost all the Bishops at Ephesus (431) and though the three
Papal legates presided at Chalcedon (451) its composition was
oriental. The same must be said of the later Councils up to the
eighth. Henceforward the General Councils have been Latin and
Western. The Council of Trent, though its membership was
greatly increased as it proceeded, opened with no more than four
Cardinals and 31 bishops. Indeed of all the General Councils the
last, the Vatican (1869) was the most universal in its composition,
774 prelates, about 70 per cent of the total Catholic hierarchy
—including some 50 Oriental bishops in union with the Holy See.
How then can all these councils be truly ecumenical, truly general? Because the Church and the Pope have recognised them
as such. This recognition, even if never explicitly formulated,
makes a Council ecumenical even when by its composition or the
circumstances of its summoning it would not qualify for this
status, and in consequence invests its doctrinal decisions with the
infallibility which the Church claims as the recipient, guardian
and interpreter of a revelation of Divine Truth to man.

Still less do irregularities, even scandals, in the conduct of a
council's proceedings—and some have been marred by unedifying

scenes of disorder and lobbying, by political pressure and political aims—invalidate the authority of this recognition. God, it has been said, writes straight with crooked lines. It is a truth not seldom exemplified in ecclesiastical, therefore in conciliar history. A Church not composed of saints, God's field in which tares and wheat flourish together, must inevitably display an all too human aspect. In the Church as a concrete historical fact it is impossible to separate the gold, the truly religious and the divine, from the dross, the earthly and the human. But as Baron von Hügel pointed out pure gold cannot endure the rough usage of human life but must be strengthened by the alloy which diminishes its purity. Students of the ecumenical councils will do well to bear this constantly in mind. They may otherwise succumb to the superficially plausible temptation to refuse gold and dross together. The student of church history must avoid two extremes, to pronounce the dross a product, substantially if not wholly, of deliberate wickedness on the part of the Church's rulers or to pretend that it is not dross but gold.

In particular two evils have persistently beset these ecumenical councils.

From the outset of Christianity doctrinal error has been attributed to a wicked will. All who accept, still more all who teach, a heresy are assumed to do so in bad faith against what they know in their heart to be true. They are therefore wilful enemies of God doomed, unless they recant their errors, to everlasting perdition. This unreasonable assumption, though it may in individual cases be justified, contradicts, generally speaking, the facts of human psychology. Man has, moreover, usurped God's prerogative of reading hearts. Its evil results would be difficult to exaggerate. It has embittered controversy, making calm and charitable discussion impossible. Persons have been anathematised and, even worse, persecuted when condemnation of their teaching was alone justified. When justice and charity might have reconciled opponents and effected agreement, personal condemnation has stiffened opposition. Breaches have been widened and in some cases presumably rendered permanent, when they might otherwise have been closed. The strength and persistence of this fatal error was evident so late as the Vatican Council. Bishop Strossmayer aroused considerable indignation when he spoke of the sincere love of Jesus manifested by so many Protestants.

The other evil is political interference. When the Roman Emperors embraced Christianity it was not to leave religion free of state control. The first certainly Christian Emperor, Constantine, regarded himself as the divinely commissioned protector of the Church entitled to intervene in disputes between her members. 'General Councils' says the 21st of the 39 Anglican Articles 'may not be gathered together without the commandment and will of princes.' As expressing what ought to be the statement is unacceptable to Catholics. But it is an accurate statement of fact in respect of all the earlier councils. Every council was convened by the Emperor who, present in person or by his representatives, supervised its meetings and procedure. As Dr. Dvornik observes, 'to convoke and direct' (the procedure not the decrees) 'a General Council was, according to Byzantine law, solely the Emperor's concern, a privilege that had been his since the time of Constantine the Great'. When the Church became restricted to the Latin West and secular governments were comparatively weak, the popes were in a position to convene and regulate their own councils. Later, however, when a large portion even of the West was in revolt and national sovereigns were powerful, the political rivalry between France and the Emperor delayed for many years the Council of Trent. Political troubles suspended the sessions of the Council and, when it had closed, it was many years before the French crown permitted the promulgation of its disciplinary decrees.

The secularisation of the modern state, in some cases its malevolence, enabled the Vatican Council to function with a healthy disregard of secular governments. When, however, the Pope lost his temporal sovereignty of Rome, it was impossible to continue the Council under the sway of an anticlerical Italian state.

Whatever the anarchist's amiable dreams, the government of human society, of sinners and fools, cannot dispense with force.

Force, however, has no legitimate place in a religion of divine love. To unite the Church, therefore, with the State is to defile her purity, degrade her dignity. It was the Church's misfortune that from the first the State was determined upon the ill-matched union. Caesar must persecute or patronise Christ. He offered no alternative. Henceforward the history of the Church will be largely an unceasing conflict waged with varying success between Caesar claiming the things of God and God's representatives claiming the things of Caesar. So intimate in fact became the union between Church and State that they were no longer regarded as *in the concrete* two distinct societies. Catholic Christendom was a society of which the State, the kingdom of this world resting on force was one aspect, the Church, God's supernatural kingdom founded on faith and love, another. Under these conditions the Church could not operate solely with the spiritual forces of faith and love, could not refuse the force employed by the State. So long as the political society was identical in membership with the religious, because its members were Catholics, but far from Christian in its aims and methods the ideal enunciated when Our Lord told Pilate that His Kingdom was not of this world, the ideal of a genuinely free Church in a free State, was in practice impossible. Even today it is only in some countries, Britain for example or the United States, that it has been achieved. The Church could but make the best of what at best must be a bad job. Silk purses cannot be woven of sows' ears. The ideal was unattainable. When Catholic truth can be imparted to an entire population, Christian holiness be made accessible only by the patronage of the State, the Church cannot reject it despite the evils it will inevitably produce. This inevitability is her historic tragedy.[1]

Nevertheless the evils arising from this inevitable intercommunion of Church and State are not the less evils or less serious evils on that account. A disease is no less painful and destructive if it is the product of inevitable conditions. Such an evil, for

[1] This is not to overlook the fact that the clergy are human. They appreciate Caesar's gifts, possessions or power and do not willingly relinquish them.

example, was the descent from Pope St. Siricius' denunciation
of the death penalty for heretics, St. Augustine's earlier condemn-
nation of all persecution, to the final establishment of the Inquisition with its torture chamber and stake. A consequence of this
evil is the conflict surviving today between two opponents equally
irrational, those who argue that what is true must be supported,
if possible, by persecution and those who argue that what is or has
been supported by persecution cannot be true.

Perception of these two evils may however, engender two radical errors. Because our forbears were mistaken in ascribing doctrinal error to personal sin, it does not follow, as the reaction of
a superficial enlightenment has concluded, that doctrinal truth
is a matter of indifference, its determination therefore the un-
profitable occupation of dreary bigots spinning theological webs
in a void. All truth is valuable for its own sake and the more important its subject matter the more valuable the truth, the more
worth while its pursuit. Scientific truth, for example, or historical
is more valuable and rewarding than the truth about our neigh-
bour's character or private life. If then religious truth, truth about
the first Cause and the meaning of the universe, about God's
purpose for man, the significance of his life, his ultimate destiny,
is in fact attainable and unless it is, unless God has revealed it, the
entire Christian religion including the doctrines debated and
determined by councils is an illusion, doctrinal decisions cannot
be unimportant. Sincerity, integrity, even personal holiness on the
part of a man who teaches or accepts religious error cannot make
that error other than the loss, however inculpable, of a value
beyond price. The subject matter therefore of this book is not, as
some readers may suppose, much ado about nothing but, on the
contrary, ado about supreme verity.

The other error attendant on perception of the political en-
tanglements of the Councils is one widespread and powerful
today, namely that religious beliefs and controversies concerning
them are but the ideological cloak of political, social and economic facts. Certainly these facts played their part—often a lam-
entable part. National dislike, for example, of the Byzantine

Empire decided the Egyptian Church and the West Syrian Churches to espouse the Monophysite heresy against the decree of Chalcedon, the East Syrian to espouse the Nestorian heresy against the decree of Ephesus. We all know the part played by nationalism in the revolt of the reformed states against the Catholicism reaffirmed at Trent. But the issues nevertheless, whether or not our Lord united two natures in one Person, whether his mother is truly termed the mother of God, whether we are or are not justified by faith only are not political or economic but religious, true or false irrespective of facts and ideas belonging to another order.

These considerations are after all commonsense. But unfortunately in the study of religious history erudition and commonsense have too often been divorced.

Another danger against which the student of history should be on his guard is to lose sight of the wood for the trees. The issues which are fundamental, profound, of wide scope and enduring significance may be overlooked by a too near-sighted scrutiny of particular facts, a too exclusive preoccupation with them. It is of course not only justifiable but indispensable to study such facts, to discover, so far as the evidence permits, the truth about them. But from time to time the student of history must stand back and survey the scene as a whole in the perspective of the entire historical process and theological development, must ponder the significance of the issues at stake, of the decisive facts, above all of a council's doctrinal decisions. What, for example, he should ask himself, is the significance for us of the Ephesine definition of Mary as God's mother, what light does it shed on the nature and destiny of man, on his history and the history of the world, on God and the relationship of man to God?

Such considerations may perhaps be made easier by the very restriction of this book to an outline in which there is room only for outstanding events and decisive issues. Any reader sufficiently interested by this view of the wood will not lack elsewhere views of the trees.

Finally we must remember that ecumenical councils, as indeed other public manifestations of ecclesiastical authority, can in the nature of things reveal very little of the interior holiness of the Catholic Church—the devotion of her children, their intimate commerce with God, nor yet the lives of loving service to God led by innumerable Catholics clerical or lay known to God alone. The conciliar history which makes it necessary for example to describe in detail the vacillations of Vigilius but must pass over with a sentence or two the contemporary achievement of St. Benedict continued by his spiritual children, achievement of prayer and achievement of a Christian culture inspired by prayer must of necessity distort the perspective and hide the reality of the Catholic fact. The prayer for whose sake the Church exists cannot be revealed by conciliar decrees defining the doctrines which prayer alone can realise in vital experience, reforming abuses which in one way or another render it more difficult, or less pure or actually set barriers to its efficacy. The Councils, that is to say, of their nature cannot display the interior life of the Church which they safeguard and serve. They inform us what the Church teaches but cannot show us how her children translate the teaching in their prayer and in their life. Those who would know the Church, cannot be content with ecclesiastical history or even dogmatic theology, indispensable though they are. They need ascetic and mystical theology, the lives of saints. This book, therefore, must be read in perspective.

2

BEFORE THE FIRST GENERAL COUNCIL

FROM the outset the Catholic Church was not a collection of like minded individuals sharing the same Christian experience. It was a society united by a common doctrinal belief and governed by the Apostles chosen by Christ and themselves acknowledging the supreme authority of St. Peter appointed by Christ Himself to feed His flock and be the rock on which the Church is built. Even St. Paul, though he owed his apostolic commission to a personal revelation, was careful to have it confirmed by St. Peter and the other "pillars" of the Church. A subordinate hierarchy was soon created to provide for the government of the rapidly expanding Church—first the seven deacons entrusted with the financial administration of the infant-Church of Jerusalem, later the presbyters ordained in newly founded mission Churches. Elsewhere we read of 'episkopoi', 'overseers', bishops in charge of local churches and of deacons. The precise relationship between these bishops and the presbyters is disputed. They were, it would seem, identical. Only in course of time did the senior presbyter or bishop become the sole and sovereign ruler of a local church. This monarchical episcopate, as it is termed, seems to have originated in the Mother Church of Jerusalem when after the Apostles' departure for the mission field St. James, a close relative of Our Lord, became its head—in fact a local bishop.

The Council held in Jerusalem (Acts XV 1-29) to decide the question whether Gentile converts should or should not be compelled to accept circumcision and observe the Mosaic Law might well have been reckoned the first ecumenical council. For St. Peter was present with other apostles and the assembly concluded by drawing up an official letter to determine the issue in favour of liberty. 'The Holy Spirit, and ourselves, have determined'—an evident claim that a Council of the Church possessed authority to decide disputed issues and the assistance of the Holy Spirit to decide them rightly. Already therefore in the Apostolic Age the General Council exists in principle. If this particular Council is not in fact counted among the number of General Councils, the explanation presumably is that its authority was, so to speak, regarded as merged in the authority accorded by the Church to Canonical Scripture.

Henceforward for roughly three hundred years a General Council was impossible. For Christianity was for the greater part of the time an unlawful religion under the ban of the State, whether or no there was active persecution. Doctrinal and disciplinary authority was mainly in the hands of the local bishops. But there was active intercourse between the Churches and above them all the supreme authority of St. Peter's successor at Rome, ill defined to be sure, exercised sporadically and sometimes opposed, but generally recognised nevertheless. For the Church of Rome was regarded as the sovereign Church. There St. Peter and St. Paul were put to death, there St. Peter had exercised his Christ given primacy, and there at latest from the middle of the second century shrines[1] marked the site of the Apostles' martyrdom. Before the first century closed Clement (93-101) in her name rebukes rebellious presbyters at Corinth, in Trajan's reign Ignatius of Antioch on his road to martyrdom salutes with a unique reverence the Church 'which in the country of the Romans presides' over the rest.

The apostolic missions were directed eastward as well as westward and it is possible, though far from certain, that St. Thomas founded a Christian Church in India. Nevertheless it was the

---

[1] St. Peter's tomb or cenotaph on the Vatican? Archaeology may yet give a decisive answer.

westward mission field, the Roman Empire which was the scene of a mission so successful that in the early fourth century the Roman Emperors became Christian.

The Roman Empire by the order and peace it established, by its excellent communications, by the common government it had imposed on so many different peoples—a government moreover which they finally accepted with a proud loyalty, presented the Church with a mission field providentially prepared. Centred on the Mediterranean Sea, its boundaries were the Atlantic, North Britain, the Rhine and the Danube, the Black Sea, the Euphrates, the deserts of Arabia and Africa. Beyond the Rhine and Danube indeed were Teutonic tribes, held at bay often with difficulty and destined finally to break through and submerge the western part of the Empire and to the East across the Euphrates Parthia first and later the more powerful Persia were a constant preoccupation. Nevertheless during these centuries of Christian growth the Empire appeared permanent, the final creation of human history. Nor presumably would barbarian pressure have proved so largely victorious had it not been for the internal struggles of conflicting legions who, during the greater part of the third century set up their commanders as rival Emperors—conflicts which impoverished and weakened the Empire and produced a succession of short-lived rulers, some of them never acknowledged universally. Moreover the later Emperors practised the disastrous policy of recruiting their armies, officers as well as men, from barbarian tribes who finally preferred to rule than to serve. The Empire was divided between the West, where Latin was the official language, and the East where the official language was Greek. Other languages were widely spoken, Punic for example or Celtic tongues. But those two alone were official. Since the Church began in the East, Greek was the language of the New Testament and all the earlier Christian writings. What is indeed surprising is the fact that the language of the Roman Church and her liturgy until the second half of the fourth century[1] was

---

[1] The change took place between 360 and 380, see Dr. Christine Mohrmann. *Liturgical Latin.*

Greek not Latin. The explanation must be that the Church of
Rome, though including some noble families, was mainly composed of groups, slaves, artisans, small traders, who spoke Greek.
It was apparently in Africa first that the services of the Church
were in Latin and Latin was the language of her writers, Tertullian and Cyprian in the third century.

As we should have expected, local churches became grouped
under the leadership, even jurisdiction, of the Bishop of a particularly important see, later to become Archbishop. In Gaul for
example the Sees of Lugdunum (Lyons) first, later Arelate (Arles)
were pre-eminent. In Africa the Bishop of Carthage was supreme.
Egypt was dominated by the Bishop of Alexandria. Traditionally
St. Mark, St. Peter's disciple, first evangelised Egypt and this
may be the explanation of the particularly close relationship between the Egyptian and the Roman Church. By the fourth century the See of Alexandria was recognised as one of the
three most important Sees in the Catholic Church whose occupant was entitled a patriarch—a super archbishop with jurisdiction over all the bishops in his patriarchate. The other Eastern
patriarchate was Antioch, held to have been St. Peter's first See
before he visited Rome. The third and always the only Western
patriarchate was Rome. The Pope, that is to say, is patriarch of
the Western and Latin Church.[1] When Constantine for strategic
reasons planted his capital at Byzantium on the confines of Europe
and Asia henceforward Constantinople, the hitherto insignificant See became a patriarchate which supported by the Emperor
and for his honour increased in extent and power until it was
recognised as the second greatest patriarchate after Rome. Reverence for its sacred sites led in 451 to the elevation of the See of
Jerusalem to patriarchal rank. But its area and power were small.

Disagreements arose from time to time between these churches
grouped around a dominant see and similar groups, notably the
refusal by Bishop Cyprian of Carthage and his African bishops
to accept a papal ruling that baptisms administered by heretics

[1] The patriarchates of Venice and Lisbon are purely honorific. Their occupants
possess no patriarchal authority.

are valid and must not be repeated if the subject is converted. But there was no schism between one group and another.

Already there were two or three anti-popes falsely claiming to
be the Bishop of Rome and supported by a group of followers,
notably Hippolytus who for doctrinal reasons revolted against
Pope Callistus (217(18)-222(3)) and a little later when the
Novatians, a body of rigorists put up their leader Novatian as
Pope. The latter continued for a considerable time as a schismatical body.

The Catholic Church moreover was confronted by heresies, beliefs held in defiance of her teaching and doctrinal condemnations—though these were not always officially formulated. During the first two centuries the Church was faced by the various
Gnostic sects, whose teachings are in some ways reminiscent of
modern theosophy. The Gnostic—his name means the man who
knows—looked for salvation not to the Christian faith but to
an esoteric knowledge (Gnosis). Between the supreme and true
God and the creator of the material universe were a number of
spiritual beings. One of these had fallen and in consequence a
spark of pure spirit had been imprisoned in gross matter. The
voluntary descent of a divine being into Jesus had brought the
saving knowledge whereby the Gnostic might be released from
material bondage and rise to the divine sphere. A heretic named
Marcion, son of a Catholic Bishop, though he did not profess this
esoteric Gnosis taught that the creator of the material universe,
the God of the Old Testament, was a tyrant and the matter He
created evil. His yoke had been broken by the true God manifest
in Jesus. Of the entire Bible Marcion retained only the Pauline
epistles, and even these as edited by himself. Condemned by the
Church, he founded a sect which endured several centuries.

In the second half of the second century Montanus in Phrygia
(Asia Minor) inaugurated the sect of the Montanists. The Holy
Spirit, he declared, speaking through himself and two prophe-
tesses, had promulgated a law more perfect than that of the
Church—second marriages were forbidden—in preparation for
Christ's return in the near future. This fanatical enthusiasm would

reappear in so many ecstatic and adventist sects down to recent times. The Montanists who streamed out to Pepuza to await the descent of the heavenly Jerusalem were the remote ancestors of the crowd of Irvingites who gathered outside their church in Gordon Square in confident expectation of the Second Advent. Tertullian joined the Montanists who survived for several centuries until finally destroyed by imperial persecution.

From the outset the Church believed that there is only one God. But she also believed that Jesus Christ is God.

It was not however easy—I do not say to explain the mystery involved and the apparent contradiction, for we are faced with a mystery which as such is above the understanding of human reason—but to find a doctrinal statement which will do justice to the totality of the revealed truth and avoid the pitfall of a seeming harmony achieved by denying or distorting any part, any aspect of that truth. The Church's profound intuition, though not always immediately registered on the surface of her conscious thought, is aware of the mystery in its integrity and sooner or later it will find expression. Two opposite solutions of the problem, each unacceptable, were widely current in the primitive Church.

One of these denied the personal distinction between Father and Son. Hence the name Monarchianism, belief in one divine principle, borne by its adherents. It was prevalent in Rome in the early years of the third century. The Roman Monarchian Sabellius has handed down his name to many future Unitarians. For a time he won over Callistus, probably before his accession to the papacy. Callistus formulated his tenets in a doctrinal statement. Jesus, he said, as Man was the Son but as God was the Father. Later however, presumably in consequence of the criticism of his opponent Hippolytus, he recognised his mistake and officially condemned Sabellius.[1] The Pope's final decision was orthodox.

The other solution pressed too far the distinction between Father and Son. The Son was regarded as inferior to the Father,

---

[1] Hippolytus cannot have attributed to Callistus a profession of faith which the Roman Christians would know he had not made. But even Hippolytus had to admit Callistus' change of belief, though he would not admit its sincerity.

produced by the Father from His own Being in view of creation and therefore not co-eternal. Some even spoke of Him as a second God. Such was the teaching of Justin Martyr in the second century and in essentials of Hippolytus. The great third century Alexandrian philosopher and Biblical scholar Origen held the Son subordinate to the Father and of less ample divinity, co-eternal however. This was indeed but one of several doctrinal errors which Origen incurred with no heretical intent by his bold but premature attempt to construct a synthesis of Catholic theology. He was the pioneer of the theological synthesis constructed more successfully by the great mediaeval doctors. Pioneers can hardly avoid serious mistakes. The nature of the Holy Spirit and His divinity were throughout this period in the theological background, Origen is uncertain whether He was created or, more probably, he thought, Divine in the third degree of Deity.

An outstanding dispute concerned not with doctrine but practice divided the churches. Whereas the majority kept Easter on a Sunday regardless of the day on which the Jewish Passover might fall the churches of Asia Minor, following a custom inherited from St. John the Evangelist, kept it on the Jewish Passover, the 14th of Nisan, whence their name Quarto-decimans, fourteeners. In the second century the future martyr Polycarp, Bishop of Smyrna, visited Rome to discuss the question with Pope Anicetus (c.155-c.166). They agreed to differ and when some years later Pope Victor (c.189-c.199) attempted to enforce his usage on the Quartodecimans on pain of excommunication, St. Irenaeus, Bishop of Lyons, himself a native of Asia Minor and Polycarp's disciple, dissuaded him from the execution of his threat.

Irenaeus was one of the most outstanding theologians of the primitive church. In his treatise against the Gnostic heresies he penetrated and expanded the teaching of St. Paul as no other primitive Christian writer. Jesus is the second Adam who has summed up humanity in Himself, His Mother Mary the second Eve. Their obedience made good the disobedience of our first parents. He insists on the doctrinal authority of the Church. 'We must not seek from other sources the truth it is so easy to accept from the Church—the storehouse into which the Apostles brought all truths' (all revealed truths) . . 'Wherever the Church there is the Spirit of God and where the Spirit of God there is the Church and every grace, even the Spirit of truth.' The apostolic descent of bishops guarantees the deposit of truth faithfully handed down. And in this connection he names the succession of popes from St. Peter to his own day for 'on account of her pre-eminence Christians "from all parts", would they preserve the integrity of their faith, must assent to the teaching of the Roman Church'.[1] If St. Cyprian, in the heat of controversy, departed from this agreement it was in defiance of the logic, if not the intention of earlier statements insisting on the Roman Church as the centre and keystone of Catholic unity.

The belief is still all too prevalent that between the persecution of Nero when for the first time the Roman Empire declared war on Christianity and the conversion of Constantine—roughly a period of two hundred and fifty years—the Church was subject to unremitting persecution. It is common to speak of the Church of the Catacombs as though Christians could worship only underground hidden in the recesses of the earth. In fact the catacombs were the local cemeteries of the Church of Rome used for burials and anniversary celebrations of the Eucharist in funerary chapels. During short spells of particularly active persecution they may have served for places of worship—this was certainly the case during Valerian's persecution (258) when Pope Sixtus II was arrested as he said Mass in the papal catacomb and decapitated on the spot. But they were never the normal places of Christian worship. Christians met for worship in the halls of wealthy and noble members of the Church. From the early years of the third century—probably first organised by Pope Callistus—there were Roman parish churches known as titles. Externally undistinguished from dwelling houses, they bore the name of the man or woman who gave them and was, generally speaking, the legal

---

[1] Adversus Haereses 332. This seems the only convincing understanding of an awkward Latin translation.

owner. But they were of course well known for what they were and could not have existed without the toleration of the State. Fifteen of these titles are known to have existed before the accession of Constantine.[1]

For in fact persecution was spasmodic and in the earlier centuries ill organised. Nero's persecution for all its hideous atrocities was confined to Rome or was intense there alone. Domitian's victims seem to have been usually distinguished either by their social position or rank in the Church. When under Trajan Ignatius, the Bishop of Antioch, is taken to Rome to be thrown to wild beasts in the arena, at every stage of his journey he is met by deputations from local churches who arrive and depart unharmed. And Trajan in reply to Pliny the Governor of Bithynia (Asia Minor) tells him that, although Christians denounced as such and persisting in their profession must be put to death, no search must be made for them. There were local outbreaks of persecution, notably at Lyons in the reign of the Stoic philosopher Marcus Aurelius, martyrdoms of individuals or small groups. But there was no general persecution. When Alexander Severus became Emperor (222) a devout man who revered all religions and set up a statue of Christ in his private chapel he officially tolerated Christianity. Though Pope Callistus suffered martyrdom under his rule, he was lynched by a pagan mob. A brief persecution by Maximin (235-238) was followed by some years of peace. The Emperor Philip (244-249) was possibly himself a Christian, certainly favourable to Christianity.

Decius (249-251) was the author of a persecution more general and more systematic than any hitherto experienced. Everywhere local commissions were to summon suspected Christians to offer sacrifice on pain of death for final refusal, if imprisonment and torture had failed to enforce conformity. There were many apostates, Christians unable to face the unexpected ordeal.

---

[1] Though Father Philip Hughes speaks of forty pre Constantinian titles I prefer to follow the Benedictine author of St. Sylvester's life. Confiscated under the persecution of Diocletian, Maxentius had restored the titles to Pope Miltiades. At a later date these titular patrons were venerated as saints, the patron of the title of Clement identified with the Pope and supposed martyr of that name.

Many others purchased from officials certificates of a sacrifice they had not performed. Even before the close of his short reign Decius acknowledged defeat and a few years of peace followed. Then Valerian (253-260), who was friendly at first but feared that the disasters and dangers confronting his Empire were due to the wrath of the gods, revived the persecutions. His son and successor Gallienus (260-268) however once more declared Christianity lawful and restored to the bishops cemeteries and churches confiscated by his father. Thirty-four years of toleration followed during which Christians might occupy even the most exalted posts in the imperial administration. Then out of the blue fell the most intense and prolonged persecution suffered by the Church in antiquity.

The aged Emperor Diocletian (284-305) hitherto well disposed to the Christians, more superstitious as his strength failed, yielded to the persuasions of his colleague Galerius and in the spring of 303 inaugurated a persecution which lasted many years. The administration of the Empire had been divided between four Emperors. In the Eastern half of the Empire the persecution was ruthless. In Phrygia an entire township of Christians was massacred. Fiendish tortures were inflicted. In the West the persecution was milder and in Britain and Gaul, where Constantine's father Constantius ruled, almost nonexistent.[1] When Spain passed under his rule (305) persecution ceased as a year later in Italy and Africa. Maxentius in Italy even restored to Pope Miltiades the titles and other property of the Church. In 311 an edict of the two supreme rulers Constantine, Constantius' son, for the West, Licinius for the East formally tolerated Christianity. On the turn of 312 and 313 the eve of his victory over Maxentius, in consequence we are told of a dream, Constantine was converted to faith in the Godhead of Christ. A second edict issued in conjunction with his pagan colleague Licinius confirmed the toleration in a more benevolent sense. Henceforward the Church was confronted

[1] In Britain so far as we know there were only two instances of persecution, the martyrdom of St. Alban at Verulamium (St. Albans), SS. Aaron and Julius near Caerleon.

by an Emperor no longer an enemy of her faith actual or potential but a patron and protector. The stage was set for the first ecumenical council.

3

THE FIRST GENERAL COUNCIL: NICAEA I 325
AND
THE SECOND GENERAL COUNCIL:
CONSTANTINOPLE I 381

SHORTLY after Constantine's triumph over Maxentius Pope Miltiades was succeeded by Pope St. Silvester whose pontificate lasted twenty-one years until 335. The Pope contemporary with the first Christian Emperor became a hero of legend. Constantine, so the story runs, is conducting a savage persecution of Christians which compels the Pope to go into hiding. Smitten with leprosy, his pagan priests inform him that he will be cured by bathing in the blood of slaughtered infants. At the last moment the lamentations of their mothers turn him from his purpose. The following night the Apostles Peter and Paul appearing in a vision bid him summon Silvester, who instructs and baptises the Emperor. Constantine in return enriches the Church with privileges. In the forum Silvester permanently banishes into its underground cavern a dragon, the Vestal virgins' pet, whose breath destroyed 6,000 victims a day.

It is unfortunate that of this fairy tale the Roman Breviary retains Silvester's alleged baptism of Constantine, though it is indisputable that he was baptised only on his deathbed and by Eusebius Bishop of Nicomedia.

A later development was the Donation of Constantine, an opportune forgery of the 8th century when the Papacy to secure its Italian territories was seeking the political support of the Frankish rulers. It attributes Constantine's transference of his capital to the banks of the Bosphorus to his desire to leave supreme political authority in the Western Empire to the Pope, as Dante summed it up, Constantine 'to leave room for the chief shepherd became a Greek'. In this particular the Donation does but refer back to Constantine's intention what was in fact the long range effect of the foundation of Constantinople. The absence of a resident Roman Emperor in the West which will soon result from the barbarian invasions will not only secure the Pope's spiritual independence of Caesar but will eventually produce not only his temporal government of the papal state, not finally lost until 1870, but a claim to political overlordship over Catholic rulers expressed by attempts, not always unsuccessful, to depose recalcitrant sovereigns.[1]

In fact of Silvester's pontificate (314-335) almost nothing is known. In the doctrinal controversy which culminated in the Council of Nicaea he played no active part, nor in defending it later from the insidious attacks of its enemies. The grant of the John Lateran. Silvester no doubt collaborated with these im-large and sumptuous basilicas very different from the inconspicuous titles of earlier days were the work of Constantine. Chief among these Constantinian basilicas was old St. Peter's erected on a most difficult site above a cemetery where a modest shrine dating from the second century marked the scene of the Apostle's martyrdom. On the Ostian way there was a similar shrine of St. Paul. Beside the Lateran palace rose the cathedral of the Roman Church the basilica of Our Saviour, known today as St. John Lateran. Silvester no doubt collaborated with these imperial undertakings and received gratefully the imperial donations. Otherwise it might be said of him what Gilbert said of his peers that he 'did nothing in particular and did it very well'. After all however, as Father Philip Hughes has suggested, this masterly inactivity was perhaps the best policy to adopt in face of an unprecedented situation fraught with danger to the independence of the Church, the appearance of Caesar as her patron and guardian. From the outset, even before Silvester's accession,

---

[1] This forged Donation, as indeed the majority of the numerous ecclesiastical forgeries, was not intended to make a claim known to be unjustifiable, but to support a claim of whose justice the forger was convinced.

Constantine had interfered in an ecclesiastical dispute to preserve the unity which was politically so desirable if a strong and united Church was to offer its religious support to the Empire. He was therefore ready to intervene in the Arian controversy which now broke out.

It was concerned with the doctrine of the Trinity which, as we have seen, was as yet ill defined. Arius, a priest of the church of Alexandria, pressed the subordinationist view of the Second Person so far as to teach that the Son, the Word was no more than a creature freely created by the Father to be His instrument in further creation. His deification by the Father entitled Him to be termed God. In Jesus the Word took the place of the soul in other men. Though this heresy bears his name Arius had not invented it. He learned it from a priest and teacher of Antioch, Lucian. After long excommunication Lucian had been reconciled with the Church, on what terms we are ignorant, died a martyr in Diocletian's persecution and is revered as such. But the error he taught lived after him in the teaching of his Egyptian disciple.

Twice condemned by his bishop Alexander presiding at synods of his suffragon bishops, Arius was not the man to retract the doctrine he had espoused. Nor did he disdain the advertiser's arts. He consigned his doctrines to a collection of doggerel verse in a rollicking metre—the Thalia—to be sung by the dockers and other labourers of Alexandria. When after his excommunication in 321 he was obliged to leave Egypt he betook himself to Nicomedia (in Bithynia) where Eusebius an old friend and fellow disciple of Lucian's was bishop, and proceeded vigorously with his propaganda. Soon the Eastern churches—the West had little taste for theorising—seethed with controversy. Constantine after a futile attempt to patch up a compromise—the politician's penchant to find a formula—on the advice probably of his friend Ossius (Hosius) Bishop of Cordova, summoned a council to meet at Nicaea in Bithynia. The facilities of the imperial postal service were placed at the bishops' disposal. It met in May 325, the first ecumenical council. Traditionally the number of bishops who assembled is 318. This number, however, the number of Abraham's retainers, had long been invested with an occult mystical significance and is probably artificial. Not more than 220 signatories are known. Ossius apparently presided. Constantine was present in his capacity of protector of the Church. But he did not presume to take part in the theological debates—nor indeed was he capable of doing so. Pope Silvester was represented by two priests Vitus and Vincent. In all only six representatives from the Latin West were present. The first eight general councils will consist of orientals. Not more than seventeen bishops defended Arianism, though there were a considerable body who disliked the language in which it was proposed to state the orthodox creed. Finally all the bishops except two signed a definitely Catholic profession of faith. It corresponded roughly with the first part of what is now termed inaccurately the Nicene creed.

'We believe in one God the Father almighty ruler of all things visible and invisible. And in one Lord Jesus Christ the Son of God begotten of His Father, the only begotten, begotten that is to say of the Father's substance, God of God, light of light, true God of True God, begotten not made of the same substance with the Father, by whom (the Son) all things were made alike in heaven and on earth, who for us men and for our salvation came down from heaven, was incarnate and made man, suffered and rose the third day, ascended into heaven and is coming to judge the living and the dead. And in the Holy Spirit.'

Five canons were appended condemning in detail the Arian doctrines. In subsequent councils down to the last, the Vatican, it has been customary to pass such formal canons of anathema, condemning heretical doctrines. The operative word in this creed is homoousios 'of the same substance, consubstantial'. The term however had on a past occasion been used with the Sabellian meaning of a complete identity between Father and Son and in that meaning condemned. Many therefore whose doctrine was entirely orthodox looked askance at it. Nevertheless it was adopted. The minutes of the Council have not come down to us. We

know however that some disciplinary canons (rules) were passed.
One condemned the Quartodeciman practice of keeping Easter on
a weekday, another the transference of a bishop from one see to
another. This rule, though soon broken, would not be abrogated
for many centuries. For the bishop was regarded as wedded to his
diocese—he still wears a wedding ring—and marriage is indissoluble. Finally however practical convenience triumphed over
symbolism and diocesan divorce and remarriage is now customary. There is no evidence that the decrees of the Council were
formally communicated to the Pope, still less that he was asked
to confirm them. Nevertheless such confirmation is implied by
the signatures of his legates never subsequently disavowed.

The Council of Nicaea should have been a deathblow to
Arianism. Unfortunately the malcontents led by Eusebius of
Nicomedia bishop of an imperial capital and increasingly the
Emperor's confidant and favourite, though for some years they
could not make a frontal attack on its decision, strove by indirect
means to undermine its authority. With imperial aid bishops
hostile to Eusebius and his friends were deprived of their sees and
replaced by an imperial nominee agreeable to Eusebius. The
great champion of orthodoxy against Arianism St. Athanasius had
attended Nicaea as Alexander's deacon and shortly succeeded to
his see. In 335—ten years after Nicaea—the Eusebians were in a
position to charge Athanasius before a council at Tyre with
trumped up offences. He had already been accused of murdering a
bishop triumphantly produced alive. An imperial court directed
the proceedings, excluded bishops favourable to Athanasius and
refused to examine the witnesses. Though for the time Athanasius
successfully appealed to Constantine a further calumny contrived his banishment and Constantine's death (337) found him
in exile. Arius himself, on signature of an ambiguous and unsatisfactory profession of faith, made his peace with Constantine who
commanded that he should be readmitted to communion with
the Church at Constantinople. The patriarch dared not refuse
but 'prayer was made unceasingly by the Church' against him.
On the day appointed for his solemn reconciliation Arius retired

from the excited throng to satisfy the needs of nature. He did not
emerge alive. Whether coincidence or divine intervention, for we
may confidently reject Gibbon's insinuation of poison, his opportune decease tells us nothing of Arius' spiritual state. Even the
most sincere heresiarch is ineligible for membership of the
Church. It was the Arian Eusebius who baptised the dying Caesar.
Though sincere in his profession of Christian faith, a man who
put to death his own wife and son was hardly the saint and 'equal
of the apostles' which Constantine has been made by servile veneration and misconceived gratitude.

Though Constans, the son who ruled first Italy then the entire
Western Empire, was a Catholic, the ruler of the East his brother
Constantius favoured the opponents of Nicaea and Constans' death
finally re-united the Empire in his hands. Unlike his father
Constantius interfered directly in doctrinal questions. Time and
again by brow-beating threats and the banishment of recalcitrants
he imposed on more or less reluctant bishops a series of credal
formulas differing one from another but none of them possessing
the unequivocal orthodoxy of the Nicene formula. For the Emperor, constant only in his rejection of Nicaea, changed with
the influences brought to bear upon him provided only he was
flattered in the persuasion of his imperial capacity to regulate
the government and even determine the doctrines of the Christian
Church. 'My will' exclaimed Constantius to a group of stalwart
orthodox bishops 'is Canon Law. Obey or go into exile'. This
usurpation by Caesar of the doctrinal authority committed by
Christ to His Church, 'Caesaro-papism,' would finally triumph
in the Byzantine church and more flagrantly still in the Anglican
church and the Lutheran, even some of the continental Calvinist
churches. With Charlemagne it would for a time hold sway even
in the Roman Catholic church and, if the ecclesiastical usurpations
of other western rulers were in the field of discipline rather than
doctrine, this may be due in part to the predominantly practical
temper of the western mind.

During the dark period of Arian victories, doctrinal confusion
and imperial tyranny, which extends roughly speaking from Con-

stantine's later days to the final re-establishment of the Catholic religion by the Emperor Theodosius, Athanasius stood firm as the pillar of orthodox faith. Many years banished, his see invaded amid scenes of violence and bloodshed by an Arian intruder and for many more a fugitive from the imperial officials, he never yielded. Hence the proverbial phrase 'Athanasius contra mundum'. 'Athanasius defying the world.'[1] From time to time he published writings against the Arians, écrits de circonstance rather than theological treatises but displaying a sure grasp of essential issues. The exiled Athanasius appealed to the Pope. His appeal awoke the papacy from its Silvestrine slumbers. Pope Julius I (337-352) convoked a local council which reversed his unjust condemnation and the Pope thereupon wrote to the Eastern bishops condemning the gross breach of canon law. The Protestant Professor Gwatkin describes the Pope's reply as 'one of the ablest documents of the entire controversy'.[2] But he could not restore Athanasius in the Emperor's teeth.

To conciliate his brother Constans, Constantius consented to a joint council of the Eastern and Western bishops to meet (342 or 343) on the frontier at Sardica (Sofia in Bulgaria). Ossius once more presided. In all there were 170 present, 76 from the West. Pope Julius sent two legates. The council might well have been the second ecumenical council. The Eastern bishops however demanded the immediate ratification of Athanasius' deposition and when this was refused, they excommunicated Ossius and the Pope, issued an ambiguous creed and decamped. The schism between the Western Church and the Eastern consummated 700 years later had thus begun with the first of a long series of temporary schisms.

The Latin bishops however persisted with their council and the Council of Sardica, one of the most important of the non-ecumenical councils, issued an orthodox profession of faith and passed a series of disciplinary canons among them canons recognis-

[1] St. Athanasius did not compose the creed which commonly bears his name. The earliest writer to show knowledge of the 'Athanasian' creed is a sixth century bishop in Gaul, St. Caesarius of Arles, who may indeed have composed it.

[2] *Arianism:* quoted by Professor Foakes Jackson in article on Arianism in Hasting's *Encyclopaedia of Religion and Ethics.*

ing the papacy as the Supreme Court of Appeal and thereby strengthening its jurisdiction in the Western Church.

In 346 Constantius permitted Athanasius to return to Alexandria. Ten years later imperial soldiery attacked him when holding a solemn vigil. Except for a brief interval Athanasius went underground for the seven years following. Wandering perhaps abroad, concealed in monastery, cemetery, even in the back room of an Alexandrian maiden celebrated for her beauty, once escaping his pursuers by a hair's breadth he suffered for the truth he taught.[1]

The groups opposed to Nicaea which successfully drew up creeds to be imposed by the Emperor were three. One of these were the true full blooded Arians who taught that the Son was unlike the Father (anomoios) and are therefore called the Anomaeans. Tragically the aged Ossius, he was 101, was tortured into signing a formula in this sense which however he recanted on his deathbed. Another and middle group consisted of those who sought to evade the doctrinal issue by an ambiguous formula that the Son is like (homoios) the Father. They were therefore called Homaeans. The third group were closer to orthodoxy. The formula they favoured was that the Son is of similar nature (homoiousios) to the Father. A little later a group attached to this party became distinguished for their denial of the Godhead of the Holy Spirit and in consequence the soubriquet Semi-Arian has been applied to the entire group. In fact very many of its members, St. Cyril of Jerusalem for example, understood homoiousios in the sense of homoousios (consubstantial, of the same nature) and objected to the Nicene term only because it had no scriptural authority and in their opinion it failed to make any distinction between the two persons of the Trinity. 'The profane of every age' writes Gibbon 'have derided the furious contests which the difference of a single diphthong excited between the homoousians and the homoiousians'. As Gibbon himself observes, the gibe is absurd. A proximity of sound may denote a chasm of sense. In this case however, as Gibbon also observes, the difference of meaning was not *in itself* significant. Homoiousios could be and

[1] See *inter alia* Maisie Ward's chapter on St .Athanasius in her *Early Church Portrait Gallery.*

was in fact understood in the sense of homoousios. Its inadequacy was its ambiguity.

Pope Liberius (352-366), banished by Constantius who intruded an anti-Pope, Felix II, was later allowed to return to his See. Under imperial pressure he signed one formula, possibly two, of this homoiousian type but made it clear that he understood homoiousios in the orthodox sense by adding a condemnation of all who denied that the Son is like the Father *in substance* and all else. But he also condemned Athanasius. This happened in 358. In the following year however delegates from an eastern council (150 bishops) held at Seleucia, and from a Western council (over 400 bishops) held at Rimini, met at Constantinople and under pressure from Constantius adopted a homoean creed. The world, St. Jerome would comment, groaned to find itself Arian. More truly it found itself suspended ambiguously between Arian and Catholic. In any case the decision was not as at Nicaea the free decision of the Catholic episcopate but the decision of too timid bishops—bullied by the state. Liberius moreover formally denounced the surrender. The accession of the pagan Julian (361-363) set all parties free to fight each other anew but also enabled the Latins led by St. Hilary of Poitiers to reject Arianism and re-affirm the Catholic faith. Julian excepted however the redoubtable Athanasius, once more a fugitive until the Emperor's death. The Western Emperor Valentinian I (364-375) was a Catholic, as were his sons Gratian and Valentinian II, though his brother Valens maintained an Arian supremacy in the East. Theodosius I, however, who began his rule in the East in 379 to which in 392 he added the Western provinces, was a convinced Catholic who from his baptism declared his allegiance to the faith taught by Pope Damasus of Rome (366-384) and by Peter, Athanasius' successor at Alexandria. St. Gregory Nazianzen was summoned from Cappadocia to restore Catholicism as patriarch of Constantinople.

It was the end of Arianism as an imperial creed though not universally. An Arian bishop Ulphilas had evangelised the Goths and in consequence the majority of the new barbarian and Teutonic kingdoms were Arian: the Ostrogoths in Italy until Justinian's reconquest c.554, the Burgundians until 517, the Spanish Visigoths until 589, the Lombards, latecomers until 671 and the Vandals in Africa until 533. Moreover whereas generally speaking these Arian rulers tolerated the practice of their religion by their Catholic subjects, the Vandal monarchs from time to time launched ruthless persecutions. This however is to anticipate.

This was, particularly in the East, an age of universal interest in theological controversy. At Constantinople the conflict between the Arians dominant hitherto and the Catholic restoration was an occasion of popular rioting. So would it continue for centuries in the capital of Byzantine Christendom. Even the sporting factions of charioteers paraded on occasion in addition to their distinctive colours different theologies. 'In nearly every doctrinal encounter the Greens and the Blues ranged themselves on opposite sides—the Greens mostly favouring the heretical tenets, the Blues championing orthodoxy.' To try to imagine two popular football teams, say Aston Villa and Arsenal, officially Baptist and Catholic is to gauge the distance between ourselves and Christian Byzantium.[1] This theological preoccupation provides the popular background to all the early Councils and, whatever its excesses, was far nobler and more worthy of humanity than the preoccupation of our contemporaries with sex, gadgets and the standard of living.

No sooner had Theodosius restored Catholicism in the East than he decided to summon a council to decide the remaining Trinitarian issue, the divinity of the Third Person, the Holy Ghost. Arius of course had denied the divinity of the Holy Spirit. But it was also denied by many Semi-Arians orthodox, in intention at least, in respect of the Son. The Council was not strictly necessary. For Pope Damasus whom the Emperor had recognised as a doctrinal arbiter, had already issued an official letter in which he taught the Godhead of the Holy Spirit. But, as Tixeront suggests,[2] Theodosius had become aware that the papal writ did

---

[1] Dvornik: *The Schism of Photius.*

[2] *Histoire des Dogmes* II, p. 63.

not run inevitably or even easily in the East. At that moment in particular, hostility had been aroused by misguided papal support for an uncanonical intruder into the see of Antioch.

In any case the Pope was not invited to the council which met at Constantinople in May 381. The first president was Meletius the Bishop of Antioch rejected by Rome. On his death the patriarch of Constantinople, St. Gregory Nazianzen replaced him. But not for long. Already wearied by his struggle with the Arians he found an environment of quarrelsome prelates a heavy burden. 'The younger bishops,' he complained, 'chattered like jays, buzzed angrily like a swarm of wasps, and their elders did nothing to check them.' Attacks were launched against his translation from the see of Sasima. The Egyptian bishops even refused his communion. Though Gregory could have pleaded that he had never exercised his episcopate of Sasima, his canonical position was weak. Nor did he desire to continue a distasteful office. He therefore resigned and was succeeded as patriarch and president of the Council by Nectarius. Only 186 bishops were present, all oriental. Thirty-six of those who denied the Godhead of the Holy Ghost refused to retract and withdrew from the Council leaving 150 members. The Council drew up a dogmatic statement of Trinitarian theology which however has been lost. Its tenor may be conjectured from the first of four canons which have been preserved. 'The profession of faith drawn up by the 318 Fathers assembled at Nicaea in Bithynia must not be repudiated. It must remain in full force. Anathema to all manner of heresy, in particular the heresy of the Anomaeans, the heresy of the Semi-Arians or enemies of the Spirit, of the Sabellians.[1] and Apollinarists.'

The Apollinarists were followers of Apollinaris, recently Bishop of the Syrian Laodicea.[2] Our Lord, Apollinaris taught, did not possess the rational soul which understands and chooses freely. Its place was taken by his Godhead, his human nature consisting only of his body and an inferior soul confined to the vital

[1] See above p. 20.
[2] Not the city of Asia Minor mentioned in the Apocalypse

functions common to men and animals. Apollinaris' teaching had also been condemned by Pope Damasus' letter. But no notice was taken of this. The latter part of our 'Nicene Creed'—the part concerned with the Holy Spirit and his operations—was ascribed to this Council when the Creed was first officially adopted by the Council of Chalcedon. No creed was in fact formulated by this Council of Constantinople.

A disciplinary canon restrained the interference of bishops in territories outside their jurisdiction. This prudent and equitable rule would however be frequently broken, not only by ambitious schemers such as Theophilus of Alexandria or by the well meaning busybody St. Epiphanius, but even by St. John Chrysostom. Another canon directed against Rome's Egyptian ally but which found no favour with the papacy gave the See of Constantinople the second place in the Christian hierarchy after the See of Rome 'because it is the see of the new Rome'.

Not the Pope but the Emperor confirmed the council's decrees on July 30; its sessions had lasted two months and it is not surprising that it was not until the sixth century that the Western Church, in effect the Pope, recognised it as ecumenical. Nevertheless its doctrinal decrees were in fact confirmed not only by two other Roman councils held the following year 382 but also by two further councils at Constantinople (382, 383). Its doctrinal authority is assured.

These two first general councils, Nicaea I and Constantinople I, were concerned with the doctrine of the Trinity. The former (Nicaea) defined the Godhead of the Son, the latter (Constantinople) the Godhead of the Holy Ghost. The second however, by its condemnation of the Apollinarians, began a series of definitions concerned with the Incarnation, Jesus Christ the Word made Flesh, the mystery that will be the subject matter of the four succeeding ecumenical councils (Ephesus, Chalcedon, Constantinople III and Constantinople IV).

4

THE THIRD GENERAL COUNCIL: EPHESUS 430

BETWEEN the second and third General Councils almost fifty years intervened. The strong and capable government of Theo-dosius the last ruler of a united Empire was succeeded by the incompetence of his sons, Honorius in the West, Arcadius in the East. The break up of the Western Empire began. Legions largely filled and commanded by German barbarians were no sufficient defence against the invasions of their fellows. German tribes poured into France and Spain and soon overflowed into Africa. In 410 the Gothic Alaric captured and sacked Rome. The shudder produced by the disaster throughout the Empire is sensible in the contemporary letters of St. Jerome. When St. Augustine died 428, the city of Hippo, of which he was bishop, was besieged by the Vandal conquerors. Of the Teutonic invaders the Angles and Saxons, conquerors of South Britain were pagan—as were at first the Franks. The others, Visigoths and Burgundians in France, the Visigoths who conquered Spain, the Ostrogoths in Italy and the Vandal conquerors of Africa were Arian—though only the last persecuted their Catholic subjects.

The disintegration however of the temporal sovereignty left the Western Church free and strong to face the invaders. In Gaul the missionary work of St. Martin of Tours was destroying the persistent paganism of rural Gaul.[1] Reacting against the worldli-

[1] Not so successfully however but that over a millenium and a half later in the churchyard of a church dedicated to his honour men of nineteenth century Guernsey were offering flowers and incense to a prehistoric image of the Mother Goddess. See Kenrick: *Archaeology of the Channel Islands, Part Two, Guernsey.*

ness inevitable in a Church which was baptising the world, hosts of men and women were embracing the monastic life inaugurated in Egypt in the early years of the fourth century by St. Antony, whose friend and biographer was St. Athanasius. Living in solitary hermitages or in groups under an abbot who imposed a common rule of life, they peopled the deserts of Egypt and Syria. Within a few years the movement spread to the West. Human activities are inevitably marked by human limitations. Man can seek God only by ways in some respects too human. It is not surprising therefore that this primitive monasticism was disfigured by excesses and in many cases fanaticism, in particular by what we may term athletic competitions in austerity. But its life was a profound interior prayer, mystical in character, a spiritual intelligence preserved in collections of wise sayings.[1]

St. Ambrose in collaboration with the Emperor Theodosius, though at times in successful opposition to the Emperor, affirmed at Milan the independence and power of a worthy Catholic bishop. The African convert whom he baptised, St. Augustine Bishop of Hippo, by his philosophical and theological genius would dominate western philosophy and theology for the ensuing millenium. Even during life he was accepted as the doctor and champion of orthodoxy. He found the African Church a prey to the Donatists. They were schismatics who claimed that since the orthodox bishop of Carthage had been consecreted by a bishop who, they alleged untruly, had betrayed his faith in Diocletian's persecution, his consecration was therefore invalid and in consequence the orders of all in communion with him and his successors. For, according to the Donatists, the unworthiness of the minister did invalidate any sacraments he might administer. When St. Augustine became bishop the Donatists far exceeded in number the African Catholics. His eloquence and controversial writing, though *unfortunately* not without the support of an imperial decree ordering the Donatists to return to the Church, won a decisive victory. He also confuted and condemned the doctrines

---

[1] For example the collection translated by Wallace Budge as *The Wit and Wisdom of the Desert Fathers.*

taught by a British monk Pelagius and his fellows Celestius and Julian Bishop of Eclanum, a heresy called after its author's name Pelagianism. It insisted on the power of free will in the work of salvation to the detriment of divine grace. Man is of his nature free to reject sin and choose what is right though this native capacity is of course itself a Divine gift. Original sin—the doctrine that in virtue of their descent from Adam and solidarity with him all men are born in a state of sinful alienation from God incapable of any choice that can merit salvation—was rejected as a figment. Infants should indeed be baptised not however to cleanse them of sin but to make them members of Christ capable of a state of bliss, 'the kingdom of heaven,' superior to the 'eternal life' they would but for future personal sin, infallibly possess. Divine grace, it is true, is given but only to enlighten and instruct and thereby render easier good conduct possible in any case. This doctrine was unrealistic and refuted by man's actual condition of moral weakness, and it rejected fundamental Christian doctrines, the solidarity of sinful man in the total Adam, the supernatural character of the union with God to which the redeemed are called. In a succession of treatises Augustine fought the Pelagians. They were condemned by two councils of African bishops held respectively at Carthage and Milevis, 416. The bishops communicated their decisions to Pope Innocent I (401-417) who confirmed their condemnations. Pelagius however by letter and Celestius in person persuaded Innocent's successor Zosimus (417-418) to accept professions of faith couched in evasive language and keeping silence on fundamental issues. The indignant Africans assembled a third council at Carthage (417) attended by no less than 214 bishops, which renewed the condemnation of the Pelagians and when Pope Zosimus took offence at their protest a fourth council (418), attended by more than two hundred bishops, framed nine doctrinal canons against the Pelagians. Zosimus was impressed and in a Roman council condemned Pelagius and Celestius. Of the Pope's letter to the African bishops only fragments survive from which it is clear that he taught original sin and the necessity of grace to avoid sin and confirmed substantially at least the canons of this last council.

Since these councils were confined to African bishops and protested against a papal decision they have not been reckoned among the General Councils. Nevertheless their decrees in so far as they were confirmed by the Pope and the Council of Ephesus possess the authority of decrees passed by a General Council.

It was at this period that St. Jerome from his retreat in Bethlehem gave the Latin church her official translation of the Bible, the Vulgate as it came to be known. Though necessarily inadequate by the standards of modern scholarship it was a monumental achievement of erudition owing not a little to his friends and collaborators St. Paula and her daughter St. Eustochium.

The eunuch Eutropius, who from the dregs of society had risen to a temporary ascendency over the feeble Arcadius, conferred the see of Constantinople (397) on a priest of Antioch, John, already well known for the pulpit eloquence to which he owes his soubriquet Chrysostom, golden mouthed. He was courageous, austere, zealous, a friend of the poor and oppressed but wanting in tact. His diatribes against the luxury and make-up of the court ladies, his demands for what we now call social justice excited the hostility of the Empress Eudoxia, who had succeeded the fallen Eutropius as the power behind the throne. An instrument was found in the patriarch of Alexandria Theophilus, an unscrupulous man intent only on his own authority and bitterly opposed to the upstart patriarch of Constantinople, most of all when he hailed from the other rival patriarchate of Antioch. He came to Constantinople, as he said, 'to depose' John, intrigued, bribed and fanned Eudoxia's hatred of her episcopal censor. At an uncanonical council mainly composed of his Egyptian followers he condemned Chrysostom. Banished and recalled St. John's scarcely veiled denunciations of what he regarded as superstitious honours paid to the Empress' statue led to his final deposition and banishment. The rigours of a harsh climate, lack of the amenities his weak health required, and finally a forced journey he was too weak to endure, produced his death in 407.

John had appealed to Pope Innocent who, having demanded in vain his restoration, excommunicated his intruded successor and Theophilus. Even the Church of Antioch was excommunicated until its bishop restored the commemoration of St. John in the Mass. It was another of the many schisms between East and West preceding the final breach. After some years Atticus of Constantinople and Theophilus' nephew and successor Cyril were restored to communion on their liturgical recognition of John. Somewhat later Arcadius' son Theodosius II solemnly translated to Constantinople the body of his parents' victim, publicly asking God's pardon for their sin.

The issues decided in the third and fourth general councils (Ephesus 430 and Chalcedon 451) concerning the incarnation of the Word are not easy to make clear. For their statement involved subtleties and niceties of language easily misunderstood and opponents did not always attach the same meaning to the same word. It is easier perhaps to grasp what was at stake.

Two schools of theology confronted each other, the school of Antioch and the school of Alexandria. The former was primarily concerned to distinguish the divinity and the humanity of Jesus, to make sure that there should be no confusion between them, no affirmation of the former at the expense of the latter. The school of Alexandria, on the other hand, emphasised the Word as the Person of Jesus since the Word made flesh *is* Jesus Christ.

At this period the great teacher of Antiochene theology was Theodore Bishop of Mopsuestia. Though his language is somewhat ambiguous he certainly understood the union between the Word and humanity of Jesus too loosely, as a relationship or indwelling to be explained by the unique love shewn by the Father to Jesus *as to a son*. He does not indeed refuse to term our Lady the Godbearer, theotokos, Mother of God—a title employed by earlier theologians and generally current. But it must not in his opinion be taken strictly. It means only that her human son is in a peculiar sense God's dwelling place. Indeed the human Jesus is the adopted rather than the natural son of God.

The leader of the Alexandrian school was the patriarch St.

Cyril. Unlike his uncle and predecessor Theophilus whose sole interest was self interest, Cyril's supreme concern was Catholic orthodoxy. Moreover it was not for him a matter solely of correct formulas. His penetrating intelligence perceived the profound significance and comprehensive bearings of the dogmas he expounded and defended. Compared with Cyril's the Antiochene theology is superficial, clever dialectic rather than insight. On the other hand in the defence of this faith he was unscrupulous in his choice of instruments. For him the end did in fact justify the means. And a dark cloud hangs over his memory. The most brilliant don at the Alexandrian university, professor of astronomy and mathematics and the Neo-Platonic philosophy was a woman, Hypatia, a woman moreover of unimpeachable character. She was however a pagan and a friend of the pagan prefect who had vainly attempted to defend the Jewish community against Cyril's persecution. In consequence a mob of fanatic monks and other Christians attacked her, dragged her into a church, tore off her clothes and scraped her to death with potsherds. There is no proof that Cyril instigated this atrocity. In charging him with this[1] Bertrand Russell is affirming what he cannot prove. But he did not punish or even condemn it and must therefore be accounted an accessory after the fact.

Since Theodore expressed his ideas in theological treatises read chiefly in Antiochene circles, they aroused no opposition. When however in the year of his death (428) an Antiochene priest of the same school, Nestorius, was appointed patriarch of Constantinople, trouble was not slow to break out. For Nestorius was by nature violent and intolerant, not the man to confine his views to his study. His language is more careful, as Tixeront puts it, 'less Nestorian' than Theodore's. Nestorius professes indeed one Person in Christ. But this Person is not simply the person of the Word but the resultant of the Incarnation, leaving moreover in existence subordinate persons, the person of the Word and the human person. This subtlety however in Tixeront's judgment, since it is found only in a work of Nestorius' old age, may be a later ex-

[1] *Wisdom of the West*, p. 138.

cogitation. The union, that is to say, between the Word and the humanity of Jesus, is after all moral rather than real, truly personal. The human Jesus is not in the strict and proper sense by nature son of God. Nestorius denies what is called the communication of properties (qualities—characters) between the two natures. We cannot ascribe to God Jesus' human actions and sufferings. 'It is clear that the son of David was not God the Word.' 'God incarnate did not die but raised from the dead him in whom he was incarnate.' Mary was not strictly the Mother of God, though the term may be admitted in the sense that her son is the temple of God.

Theologians speak of a communicatio idiomatum between our Lord's Divinity and Humanity, that in consequence of their personal union what He does as God may be said of the Man though not *as* Man. What He did or suffered as Man may be said of God the Son though not *as* God. The substance of the somewhat elusive Nestorian heresy may perhaps be concisely stated as a denial of this communicatio idiomatum. Nestorius' language however is often ambiguous, even inconsistent, sometimes orthodox, at others 'Nestorian'. The historian Socrates to whom we owe most of our knowledge of the Council of Ephesus and its antecedents, personally acquainted with Nestorius, regarded him as muddle-headed and ill-trained in theology. A definitive, consistent or entirely certain statement of his doctrine is therefore impossible. We can be sure only of its unorthodox tendency. When Nestorius preached these views, particularly his distaste for the title theotokos, the scandal and uproar were great. The Church of Constantinople and his suffragan bishops were divided for or against him. When Cyril learned of these events he took up his pen against Nestorius' doctrine and wrote to Nestorius, who returned a disdainful reply. Thereupon he appealed to the Emperor, Theodosius II, his wife and sister. Finally about the middle of 430 he wrote to Pope St. Celestine (422-432). Celestine summoned a council at Rome which affirmed the orthodoxy of the title theotokos and condemned Nestorius. He communicated this sentence to the leading Eastern bishops and in a letter to Nestorius ordered him to retract his errors publicly within ten days on pain of excommunication. Writing to Cyril he empowered him to act in his name against Nestorius. This surely was an error of judgment. Not only the traditional hostility between Alexandria and Constantinople, but Cyril's intolerant and unscrupulous temper disqualified him for the position of papal representative. An Egyptian synod over which Cyril presided drew up twelve condemnations and despatched them to Nestorius, demanding his immediate subscription. Not only did these condemnations exceed considerably the papal demand, they employed an Alexandrian terminology differently understood elsewhere and *as understood elsewhere* unorthodox. In particular the document spoke of 'a natural union' between our Lord's Godhead and his humanity. Though St. Cyril meant only a real as opposed to a merely moral union, the phrase could and would be understood to affirm a fusion of two natures—the more so because Cyril was accustomed to speak of 'one incarnate *nature* of the divine Word', understanding by nature person. Nestorius rejoined by counter-anathemas.

Cyril's action swung over John Patriarch of Antioch to the side of Nestorius. The Antiochene bishops whose theological expert was now Theodoret, bishop of Cyrrhus denounced Cyril's anathemas to which they opposed twelve counter anathemas, some ambiguous, others definitely Nestorian, in language at least.

All parties appealed to Caesar whom the Pope had rightly but unrealistically attempted to byepass. Theodosius II in conjunction with his Western colleague Valentinian III summoned a council to meet at Ephesus the following June 8th. Nestorius would be admitted to plead his cause. Pope Celestine accepted the council, suspending meanwhile the sentence he had passed on Nestorius and appointing two bishops Arcadius and Projectus to represent his Roman council and a priest, Philip, as his personal representative. Of Cyril's council and its condemnations he knew nothing. When the bishops gathered at Ephesus on June 8th, Nestorius attended with sixteen suffragans to support him, Cyril brought fifty Egyptian bishops. Though John of Antioch and his suffragans were known to be on their way, they had not yet arrived.

Nor had the papal legates. On June 22 in the teeth of protests by the imperial representative Count Candidian, Cyril refused to wait longer and opened the Council. In a letter addressed to the Emperors he informed them that two Antiochene bishops who had arrived before their colleagues sanctioned the opening in John's name. Unfortunately these two bishops bearing the alleged communication were among the Antiochene bishops who protested against the premature opening of the Council. Nor could the Antiochenes have made this protest, if the Council had been informed by John's emissaries that he had authorised the opening before their arrival. Cyril must therefore have made a false statement in his letter to the Emperors. His motive for hastening the opening was no doubt his fear, not unjustified, that the Antiochene bishops might prevent a condemnation of Nestorius by the Council or a conciliar definition of the authentic Catholic doctrine. And Theodosius' acceptance of the Council was indispensable and in face of Antiochene opposition not easy to obtain. Cyril must therefore present his case as favourably as he could.[1]

When the session opened 159 bishops and a deacon representing the Bishop of Carthage were present. Nestorius refused to appear. He was condemned, deposed and excommunicated. Mary was pronounced theotokos, God bearer, Mother of God. During the sessions more bishops arrived and a total of 198 signatures was secured. That evening the bishops were triumphantly escorted to their lodgings.

A few days later on June 26 or 27 John and his suffragans arrived. They formed themselves into a Council apart which on the ground of this premature action, formally condemned Cyril and his supporters but kept silence about Nestorius.

A little later the legates arrived. On July 10 a second session was held. The legates read a peremptory letter from Celestine. The council must not debate Nestorius' teaching but promulgate

[1] On two occasions the minutes of the Council mention its recognition of Cyril as the Pope's representative. Since however papal legates arrived to give orders to the council in Celestine's name this is hardly credible. Presumably the Council recognised Cyril's authority as the Pope's representative until the legates' arrival.

the sentence he had already passed against him. He had however already been condemned.

At a third session on July 11 the legates who had read the minutes of the first session confirmed the Council's decrees. Speeches were made against Nestorius. One of these spoke of Peter 'continuing to live and judge in his successors'. A letter was despatched to Theodosius.

In the fourth session on July 16 fruitless attempts were made to obtain the attendance of the Antiochene bishops.

In its fifth session on July 17 the council excommunicated the recalcitrant Antiochenes and addressed further letters to the Pope and the Emperor. The African condemnations of Pelagius, Caelestius and their followers were read and approved.

In the sixth session on July 22 (the minutes are incomplete) the Nicene creed in its original form was reaffirmed, the composition of any further creed forbidden. This however will not prevent the following council from adopting the enlarged creed of 'Constantinople'.[1]

At the seventh and final session on July 31 or August 31 a limited autonomy was granted to the Church of Cyprus. Canons were promulgated condemning the Nestorians and Pelagians, also some disciplinary canons. Ephesus was the first ecumenical council whose minutes survive.

After considerable hesitation and much manoeuvring and bribery by Cyril, the Emperor, hostile at first, accepted in October the Council's decisions except its condemnation of the Antiochenes. The bishops could now return home. He banished Nestorius and replaced him by Maximian. Pope Celestine confirmed the Council's decrees. But he also excepted its condemnation of the Antiochene bishops.

The Antiochene schism lasted some two years. Through the good offices of Celestine's successor, St. Sixtus III (432-440) Cyril and the Antiochenes were reconciled by their joint subscription of a formula composed probably by Theodoret. Cyril consented to give up for this occasion his Alexandrian terminology

---

[1] See above p. 37.

for language more acceptable at Antioch, to speak of a 'union of two natures' as the Antiochenes understood 'nature' instead of one 'nature' as he understood the term. The meaning of theotokos was explained so as to exclude any suggestion that Mary was mother of the Godhead.

We cannot but ask ourselves whether if Cyril, in his original approach to Nestorius, had shewn the same conciliatory temper and made the same explanations, the conflict might not have been averted and with it the Nestorian schism. In the event, a defiant Nestorianism which later hardened into an unqualified rejection of the theotokos, spread from Edessa across the frontier into Persia, where it became the creed of the Persian Christians. In the 13th century the Nestorian Church had bishops in China.

A Nestorian monk from Pekin Mar Sauma appeared in Western Europe. Since he was willing to pay his homage to the pope he was admitted to say Mass in St. Peter's and in Guienne gave communion to our King Edward I.[1]

The Ephesian crowd who escorted the bishops triumphantly with torches to their lodgings, presumably regarded their decree as primarily an honour paid to Mary. And in fact her divine Motherhood is and has proved to be the keystone, justification and substance of the devotion to our Lady which has grown ever since. Cyril however can have seen it only as safeguarding the truth of the Incarnation. His contempt for women did not altogether spare the greatest among them. Confronted with the spectacle of the crucifixion Mary, he tells us, lost her faith in her son's Godhead and resurrection, almost her reason. We should not however be scandalised. If Peter and the other apostles failed, what can be expected of a weak woman?[2]

---

[1] See Christopher Dawson: *The Mongol Mission.* pp. XXVIII-XXIX.
[2] So Cyril's Commentary on St. John. See: *The Image of God in Man according to Cyril of Alexandria,* Walter J. Burghardt, S.J., p. 30.

5

THE FOURTH GENERAL COUNCIL: CHALCEDON 451

THE uneasy truce between Antiochene and Alexandrian theology did not last long. An abbot at Constantinople, Eutyches, launching an attack against the school of Antioch, taught that Christ, in consequence of the Incarnation, has not two natures but one alone and that, unlike his mother, he does not share our substance, is not consubstantial with us. The first of these propositions might be no more than the adoption of Cyril's terminology, nature being understood as person. But it would seem impossible to understand the second otherwise than as a denial that the human nature of Jesus is the same as our own, completely human, that Jesus is truly our fellow man, a denial therefore of a true Incarnation. He probably held, as Tixeront suggests, that our Lord's human nature was somehow transformed or absorbed into his Divinity. The patriarch of Constantinople, Flavian, summoned Eutyches before a council and on his refusal to retract, deposed, degraded and excommunicated him (448). The condemnation was subscribed by 32 bishops and 23 abbots. Eutyches appealed against the sentence to the pope, the patriarch of Alexandria. Dioscurus who had succeeded Cyril, and other bishops. And he prevailed upon the Emperor, still Theodosius II, to convoke a council to reconsider the sentence of the first. It was summoned to meet at Ephesus on March 30, 449. Meanwhile Flavian wrote to the pope. He was St. Leo I the Great (440-461). Leo was the Pope who turned away from Rome the dreaded Hun Attila, mitigated

the sack of Rome by the Vandals. He despatched three legates
to the forthcoming council: Julian, Bishop of Puteoli (Pozzuoli),
a priest, Renatus, who died on the journey, and a deacon, Hilary.
They brought with them the famous letter (Tome) in which Leo
gave his magisterial decision on the points at issue. Couched in the
sonorous rhythms of Leonine prose, it was resonant with Roman
majesty. Leo did not argue. He stated unambiguously the Catholic
doctrine of the Incarnation, Jesus Christ is one Person not two.
But in this one Person there are two natures, the divine and the
human, without confusion or intermixture. Each of these natures
possesses its distinctive faculties and mode of action. Nevertheless
the personal (hypostatic)[1] union involves a communication of properties, 'the Son of Man truly comes down from heaven when
the Son of God assumes human flesh. The Son of God is truly
said to have been crucified and buried ... when he endured these
things ... in the weakness of His humanity.'

When the legates reached Ephesus they found the council under
the conduct of Dioscurus of Alexandria, a violent and unscrupulous prelate determined to support Eutyches and defeat his
Constantinopolitan rival. The bishops who had condemned
Eutyches were excluded on the plea that their sentence was being
submitted to the Council's judgment. Eutyches' profession of
faith was approved, the doctrine of the two natures in Christ condemned. There were scenes of naked violence, bishops compelled
to sign by the threat of blows. Flavian was beaten up. He died
shortly afterwards. The papal legates must flee for their lives.
Well might this Council go down in history as the robber synod
of Ephesus. Theodosius however approved its decrees.

On September 29 Leo presided over a well attended council at
Rome, which condemned the Ephesian council and despatched
two letters of protest to the Emperor, who disregarded them. In
the following July (450) Theodosius II died childless and his
throne passed to his sister St. Pulcheria who had intermittently

[1] The Greek word *hypostasis* literally identical with the Latin word *substantia* which
the Latins used to mean substance and to translate the Greek *ousia* but had been
used by the Greeks as a synonymn for *ousia*, was now understood as person, translating
the Latin *persona* and equivalent to the Greek *prosopon*.

governed the Empire during her brother's incompetent reign. For Theodosius was more interested in his handwriting which was renowned for its beauty than in the meaning of what he wrote. Sister, wife, eunuch in turn governed his empire. Pulcheria gave her hand though not her virginity, vowed long since to God, to a general named Marcian. She favoured orthodoxy against the Egyptians as did the new patriarch Anatolius. A council at Constantinople condemned Eutyches and subscribed Leo's Tome.

Marcian however desired a general council. It met at Chalcedon[1] on October 8th, 451—the Fourth Ecumenical Council. Between 500 and 600 bishops attended, more than in any future council until the Vatican. The Antiochene teacher Theodoret was among them. All except the papal legates and two African bishops were orientals. No more than 15 to 20 Egyptian suffragans attended Dioscurus. The Emperor, and the Empress were present in person when the Council opened and again at the sixth session. The papal legates were Paschasius bishop of Lilybaeum in Sicily, a priest Boniface and another bishop Lucentius. As Leo required they presided. Leo's letter to the Council, peremptory as Celestine's to the Council of Ephesus, demanded the acceptance without further debate of the dogmatic letter, the Tome, he had addressed to Flavian. At the second session, October 10, the Tome was read together with the enlarged 'Nicene' creed and Cyril's letters to Nestorius. They were formally accepted. The Tome in particular was received with shouts of acclamation: 'Behold the faith of the Fathers, the faith of the apostles ... Through Leo Peter has spoken.'

Though the Council lasted less than a month, October 8 to November 1, only 16 sessions were held.[2] Only the first six however were concerned with doctrinal questions. The latter were occupied with discipline. Thirty disciplinary canons were finally passed. They were concerned with the clergy, their conduct, ordination and rights, with monks and nuns, episcopal authority and jurisdiction. The fifth session witnessed a vigorous protest against

---

[1] A suburb of Constantinople on the other side of the Bosphorus.

[2] Some say 21 sessions. If so the Council must have continued longer.

imperial claims to decide doctrinal issues. There was at first considerable opposition to the promulgation of a new doctrinal decree. However after an abortive attempt to issue an ambiguous formula, a decree in conformity with Leo's Tome was finally accepted and on October 22, the sixth session, it was solemnly promulgated in the presence of the Emperor and Empress: ' . . . We teach unanimously one sole and identical Son Jesus Christ our Lord of Godhead and Humanity alike complete, truly God and truly Man, composed of a rational soul and body, Consubstantial in his Godhead with the Father, in his Manhood with us, like us in all things except sin . . . consisting of two natures without mixture, transformation, division or separation. For the union has not abolished the distinction of the natures: each has preserved its proper mode of being and is conjoined with the other in one unique person (hypostasis).' Two natures in one person was the definitive formula accepted by 355 bishops. It was the formula prescribed by the papacy. Chalcedon did not explain, could not explain, did not profess to explain the hypostatic, that is the personal, union of two natures in Christ. It stated it as a fact, the fundamental fact of the Christian religion.

The Council officially promulgated the 'Nicene' creed as we know it today. Substantially it is the baptismal creed of Jerusalem as used in the fourth century. It incorporates the doctrinal affirmations of Nicaea and Constantinople.

Dioscurus was condemned, deposed and banished though his suffragans at Ephesus were pardoned. Theodoret was pronounced orthodox and restored to his see though only after a reluctant condemnation of Nestorius. A letter from Ibas of Edessa to Mari was pronounced orthodox—though the next ecumenical Council would condemn it.

The acclamation of the bishops at Chalcedon, 'Peter has spoken by Leo,' was a testimony by the oriental churches to papal supremacy and the doctrinal authority of the Holy See. As such it is of no little importance. On the other hand their acknowledgment depended on imperial assent. Only thirty-two years later the eastern bishops as a body to comply with the command of the Emperor Zeno, would defy without a qualm a papal excommunication and in consequence remain for the next thirty-six years in schism severed from the Catholic church.

Indeed this very Council passed disciplinary canons contrary to the known wishes of the Holy See. Usurpations by the patriarchate of Constantinople on the jurisdiction of other metropolitans were sanctioned and once more it was granted the second rank in the ecclesiastical hierarchy because Constantinople was the seat of empire. It should even share the privileges of the Roman See. When this canon was passed at the sixteenth session (November 1) the legates protested. Not only did the Pope protest. His confirmation of the Council was confined to its doctrinal decisions. From his distant exile the aged Nestorius who probably died on the eve of Chalcedon, welcomed Leo's Tome. It expressed, he said, the truth he had always championed. But it seems clear from his own statement that he did not understand it as Leo meant it.

6

THE FIFTH GENERAL COUNCIL:
CONSTANTINOPLE II 553

NICAEA had not put an end to Arianism. Chalcedon did not put an end to Monophysitism. Less indeed. For whereas Arianism as an organised heresy is extinct, Monophysitism is still the creed of Christian churches. As in the case of the Arians and in more recent times the Protestants, those who agreed in opposing the Catholic church disagreed among themselves. The majority of the Monophysites were orthodox in their beliefs, condemning Eutyches' denial of Christ's humanity. But they were obstinately attached to St. Cyril's terminology: 'one nature incarnate of the divine Word,' also expressed as 'one nature of God incarnate'. They rejected as Nestorian the two natures formula adopted at Chalcedon. Their heresy, that is to say, was not false doctrine, but persistent refusal to accept the terminology defined by the Church. On their left wing however more radical groups sprang up, who, like Eutyches, taught that somehow or other the humanity of Jesus was not truly human like our own, but had been absorbed by his Godhead or alternatively was a transformation of his Godhead into flesh. These extreme groups however were comparatively few. The solid and dangerous opposition to Chalcedon came from those who combined an orthodox meaning with heretical language. The Roman-Greek Empire had not destroyed the nationalist sentiments of Coptic Egypt or Aramaic Syria. Deprived of a political they found an ecclesiastical expression. As the Irish clung the more passionately to their Catholic

faith and their priests, because they found in them a bulwark
and champions against their English rulers, the Egyptians and
Syrians supported passionately their native bishops against dic-
tation from Constantinople or the equally alien Rome. Unfortunately in this instance they attached themselves in consequence
not to Catholicism but to Monophysitism.

Whenever the hand of the central government weakened,
Monophysite councils installed with violence and bloodshed
Monophysite patriarchs at Alexandria—Timothy (Aeluros) (the
Weasel) and Peter Mongos (the Stutterer). Nevertheless imperial
authority was prevailing over the rebels when in 482 the Emperor
Zeno supported, if not instigated, by his patriarch Acacius, in
the hope of conciliating the disaffected provincials, issued a formula of doctrinal ambiguity, from its purpose named the Henotikon, formula of union. Peter Mongos signed it and in return was
permitted to oust from the see of Alexandria the orthodox
patriarch. The Henotikon was possibly composed by Acacius.
It did not reject Chalcedon. It byepassed it with an underhand
thrust at any who 'at Chalcedon or elsewhere' had dissented from
the faith now promulgated. The 'Nicene' creed was reaffirmed,
and the decrees of Ephesus, also St. Cyril's twelve condemnations.
Nestorius and Eutyches were condemned. Jesus was declared
in His divinity consubstantial with the Father, in His humanity
with us. Divinity and humanity must neither be separated nor
confused. But of the offending formula 'two natures' nothing was
said. In its positive statement the formula was orthodox. But
Chalcedon was abandoned.

Pope St. Felix III (483-492) in a Roman council deposed and
excommunicated not only Peter Mongos but Acacius himself
(484). Acacius refused to submit and excised the Pope's name
from the liturgical commemorations (diptychs). Once more the
Eastern Church had preferred the Emperor to the Pope and was
schismatic. Felix's decision was courageous, for all the new
Western monarchies were Arian and it was now the Pope against
the world. For no less than thirty-five years the schism continued.
Negotiations for peace by the patriarchs of Constantinople foun-

dered on the papal insistence upon a posthumous condemnation
of Acacius, and a more conciliatory attitude on the part of Pope
St. Anastasius II (496-498) cost him unfounded suspicions of
heresy still believed in the Middle Ages.[1] The accession of a
Monophysite emperor, Anastasius, resulted in the open triumph
of Monophysitism, not only in Egypt where all the recent patriarchs had been Monophysite, but in Antioch where Severus, the
Monophysite leader, became patriarch. When the situation was
at its worst, the Emperor's death restored the Catholic faith. His
successor Justin (518) guided by his nephew and future successor
Justinian, determined to restore Catholic orthodoxy and union,
opened negotiations with Pope St. Hormisdas (514-523).[2] The
Pope's terms were uncompromising, no less than complete surrender (519). The oriental bishops must sign the formula to
which Hormisdas' name is attached. The primacy of the Roman
see is affirmed and its indefectible constancy in the profession
of the true faith. This in substance is the papal infallibility to be
defined by the Vatican Council. Nestorius, Eutyches, leading
Monophysite bishops and Acacius are anathematised, Chalcedon
and Pope Leo's doctrinal letter accepted. Obedience is pledged
to the apostolic see in which religion is preserved in its solidity
and integrity, and the name of any bishop out of communion with
the papacy was to be expunged from the diptychs. The patriarch
of Constantinople swallowed the bitter pill, his suffragans signed
on the dotted line. Severus was deposed and Egypt alone remained openly defiant. The papacy had won a brilliant victory.
The Formula of Hormisdas would remain on record as a formal
and official acknowledgment of papal authority by the eastern
bishops. Unfortunately as always it depended on imperial assent.
In a few years a council convoked by an emperor would excommunicate a pope. In fact the rhythm is constant: when the emperor obeys the pope or agrees with him the oriental hierarchy
obeys the pope, when he defies the pope, the oriental hierarchy
defies the pope. The papal victory was therefore insecure and

[1] See *Dante Inferno, Canto XI.*
[2] Surely a Persian by origin. His name, identical with that of a Persian martyr,
means servant of Ormusd, Ahura-Mazda.

more apparent than real. For it had been made possible only by the Emperor and throughout the East Caesar would in fact remain as before head of the Church.

When the Emperor persisted in his Catholicism, the Syrian Monophysites went underground—in Egypt they bore sway on the surface—and a Monophysite Bishop of Edessa, James Baradai, by numerous consecrations and ordinations, organised behind the scenes the Monophysite Church which, bearing his name, is called Jacobite.

Even before St. Augustine's death his teaching on grace had been attacked in southern Gaul by many who were far from defending the doctrines of Pelagius. They were led by Cassian, a master of monastic spirituality. They have received the name of semi-Pelagian. Tixeront (III, 252) sums up their opinions in three propositions: (1) Apart from grace man can desire a supernatural union with God though he cannot attain to it, can move towards faith though he cannot truly believe. (2) God wills the salvation of all men not only of the elect and offers all the necessary grace. It is in their power to accept it and persevere. (3) Divine predestination is determined by God's foreknowledge of the subject's merits or demerits. Of these three propositions the first and in part the second are heretical. The others are still debated by Catholic theologians. In any case these men were not heretics. For they did not reject the Church's decision. Cassian indeed is reckoned among the saints. The struggle between the semi-Pelagians and the Augustinians persisted intermittently. A papal declaration almost certainly drawn up by the future pope Leo formally condemned the semi-Pelagian teaching as regards man's natural desire of a supernatural union with God, his natural power to accept it when offered. On the other issues the Pope refused to pronounce. After a long truce the conflict was renewed. Finally a Council which opened at Orange, 3 July 529, issued a profession of faith mainly the work of Pope St. Felix IV (526-530). The semi-Pelagian teaching about grace was condemned, the Augustinian affirmed. Grace was pronounced in-

dispensable for every step on the road to salvation and for the
effective reception of every grace offered. A positive divine predestination to evil was emphatically repudiated. This was the
sole mention of the subject otherwise passed over in silence.
Though no more than 14 bishops were present, all from Gaul,
the papal confirmation has given the decisions of the Council
a doctrinal authority equivalent to that of an ecumenical
council.

A thousand years later the Protestants, and in their train Baius
and Jansenius, dotting the i's and crossing the t's of Augustinian-
ism, will oblige the Church at the Council of Trent and by a series
of papal utterances, to state the converse of the seemingly exclusive insistence upon the efficacy of grace, to defend the efficacy of
the human will and man's ability without *supernatural* grace to
make choices naturally good. The Pelagians in effect opposed free
choice to grace, as if the operation of one must exclude the other.
Even the semi-Pelagians were attempting to demarcate a province
for free will without grace. As Père Bouyer has shown, this pre-
supposition, that the operation of grace excludes the operation
of human free will, the action of God the action of man and vice
versa, would prove one of the principal causes of the Protestant
rejection of Catholic doctrine. In fact the cooperation of grace
and free will throughout the entire process of salvation is so
intimate that neither excludes the other. This cooperation however is a mystery incapable of clear conceptual statement and
visible only to a profound intuition; it has necessarily been expressed by a succession of complementary doctrinal formulas
superficially irreconcilable and in conjunction alone a satisfactory
statement of what is perceived by spiritual insight but cannot be
thought.

As regards the kindred mystery of predestination, whether or
not it is determined by God's foreknowledge of our merits, the
Church has consistently refused to pronounce.

Finally it is worth remarking that even free choices that are
merely naturally good, are like all else that is naturally good, a
natural grace of God. For there is nothing good anywhere or in

any respect, of any kind or at any level which is not God's free gift.

In 476 the Rutulian chieftain, Odoacer deposed the last Western Emperor, Romulus Augustulus. He was succeeded by the Ostrogoth Theodoric and his successors tolerant Arians. In the fifth century Ireland was converted by Palladius and Patrick and in 496 the first Teutonic Catholic kingdom was established by the conversion from paganism of the Frankish King Clovis.

Justinian, already the power behind his uncle's throne, succeeded him in 527 to reign thirty-eight years. A man of irreproachable private morals, of monastic austerity in diet and sleeplessness, he is renowned for his consolidation of Roman law. He reconquered Italy, Africa, even a part of Spain, though at the cost of a crippling expenditure and the wholesale devastation of large areas of Italy in particular of Rome and its environment. But he was possessed by an itch for interference in theological questions combined with ruthless intolerance for all beliefs but his own. Until her death in 547 he was under the influence of his wife Theodora. The truth about her early years is beyond recovery. For we cannot trust the salacious scandalmongering of Procopius.[1] But she would seem to have been what we should now call a striptease artiste in a Constantinopolitan cabaret. Visiting Egypt with a lover she was converted, no doubt by the example of the Egyptian ascetics, to a moral and devout life. Unfortunately her conversion was to the Monophysite Christianity dominant in Egypt. Returning to Constantinople she earned her livelihood by spinning. The young heir Justinian met and married her, prized her assistance indeed so highly that on his accession he made her his imperial colleague. Though she could not declare herself a Monophysite, her Monophysite sympathies induced her to do all in her power to further the Monophysite cause. She had secured a patriarch of Monophysite views and the invitation of Severus the Monophysite doctor to Constantinople. Pope St. Agapitus (535-536) however who had

---

[1] Though a contemporary, indeed, our primary source for the history of Justinian's reign, Procopius, was an inveterate scandalmonger and violently prejudiced.

visited Constantinople on a political errand, intervened and obtained from Justinian a Catholic patriarch and the expulsion of Severus. He died however before his return and Theodora decided to give the papacy to his deacon Vigilius who had accompanied him to Constantinople, on a promise, it is said, of papal approval for her Monophysite protegees. On Vigilius' return he found a Pope, the choice of the Gothic king, already elected and installed; St. Silverius (536-537), son of Pope Hormisdas.[1] Rome however was now in imperial hands and the Roman general Belisarius arrested Silverius on a charge of treason, deposed and banished him. Though his appeal to Justinian was successful, Theodora contrived a second trial and condemnation. This time Silverius was banished to an island near Naples where he died[2] leaving Vigilius pope (537-555) by the grace of Theodora. Vigilius, there is reason to believe, played a double game. In accord with the Emperor he officially professed the creed of Chalcedon. It was his public teaching as Pope. In a private letter however addressed to three eastern patriarchs, among them Severus and the Monophysite patriarch of Alexandria, he professed the same faith as theirs, and affirmed in Christ a composition of two natures no longer distinct.[3]

A few years later Justinian was persuaded that the Monophysites might be reconciled, if the writings of three Nestorianising theologians Theodore of Mopsuestia, Theodoret of Cyrrhus and Ibas of Edessa were officially condemned. The condemnation would not be a condemnation of Chalcedon. Theodoret, however, and Ibas had been admitted at Chalcedon to communion and moreover Ibas' doctrinal letter had been pronounced orthodox. The condemnation therefore would seem to

[1] For many centuries it was the custom in the church of Rome for secular priests to be married men pledged on reception of major orders to live in continence with their wives who by way of compensation received their husbands' title—deaconess priestess, bishopess as the case might be.

[2] According to one account he was murdered, according to another died of under nourishment. He is venerated as a martyr (June 20).

[3] See E. Amann: *Vigile*, in the Dict. de Theologie Catholique. The authenticity of the letter is disputed. Amann is disposed to accept it. He believes moreover that Vigilius' successor Pelagius I (556-561) refers to this letter when he says that his predecessor condemned the teaching of Pope Leo. It would be difficult otherwise to account for Theodora's continued goodwill towards Vigilius.

discredit Chalcedon and on that account be likely to please the Monophysites. Justinian therefore issued an edict (544) condemning writings of Theodore, Theodoret and Ibas' letter, writings known as the Three Chapters. Vigilius, taking account of Western opposition to the condemnation, persistently refused to confirm it. The Emperor compelled Vigilius, now his subject, to come to Constantinople where he arrived in January 547. Theodora's death did nothing to ease his position. Alternately bullied and cajoled the Pope vacillated. Opposition to the imperial demand was followed by a private condemnation of the Chapters and finally on April 11 548 Vigilius issued his Judicatum addressed to the patriarch Mennas. He condemned Theodore and his writings, Ibas' letter and any writings by Theodoret against St. Cyril's theology. When the news reached the West it unleashed a storm of protest directed not against a solemn papal definition of doctrine but against what seemed an unworthy submission to imperial violence. The African bishops formally excommunicated Vigilius. 'The bishops of Africa assembled in synod exclude from Catholic communion Vigilius, bishop of Rome, unless he repent.'[1] Their opposition was broken not removed by Justinian. He brought their leaders to Constantinople and bullied or bribed them into submission. Vigilius took fright and to gain time agreed with the Emperor to refer the matter to a council. He secured the return of his Judicatum but by a secret promise to condemn the three chapters.

Justinian however would not wait for its assembly. He issued (551) a profession of faith fortified by thirteen anathemas and doctrinal explanations. He returned to the Cyrillian formula 'one incarnate nature of God the Word'—though explaining that nature (physis) must be understood in the sense of person (hypostasis). The Three Chapters were condemned. Vigilius, assaulted in church by imperial troops, escaped over the city roofs,[2] and by boat and thence to Chalcedon where he excommunicated the

---

[1] See Victor of Cartenna Chronicle quoted by Amann ' Trois Chapitres '. It will be widely held by canonists and theologians that a general council may depose a Pope for heresy—hardly however a provincial council.

[2] He was over 80 years old.

prelates concerned in the Emperor's edict. Justinian in turn yielded. Mennas and his fellow bishops repudiated the imperial edict—and apologised though disclaiming it for the violence done to the Pope. Vigilius returned to the city. A new patriarch Eutychius (Mennas had died) accepted the four councils and St. Leo's dogmatic writings and referred the Chapters to the future council.

After long delays the Council destined to be the Fifth Ecumenical Council met in Sancta Sophia on May 5, 553. The number of bishops ranged from 150 to 164. The overwhelming majority were Greeks. But there were eight African bishops. Eutychius presided. Dissatisfied at its composition, Vigilius stood aloof reserving his decision. At the fourth, fifth and sixth sessions, May 12-May 19, the chapters were read and condemned. On May 14 the Pope communicated to Justinian his own judgment of the Chapters, the Constitutum. He refused to condemn Theodore after death a man never condemned during his life. He also refused to condemn Theodoret. He did however condemn 60 extracts more or less faithful from Theodore's writings and five propositions ascribed though wrongly to Theodoret. Ibas' letter, he pointed out, had been pronounced orthodox by the papal legates at Chalcedon and therefore he would not condemn it now. This considered and free judgment should, Amann thinks, be regarded as the genuine judgment of the Holy See.

Three days later (May 26) at its 7th session the Council took up Vigilius' challenge. At Justinian's demand it condemned and excommunicated the Pope. At its 8th and final session (June 2) it condemned the Three Chapters and the person of Theodore, condemnations embraced in the 14 anathemas it pronounced. Though it employed Cyril's 'Monophysite' terminology 'one incarnate nature of God the Word', it formally accepted the four previous councils including therefore Chalcedon. Nevertheless it condemned Ibas' letter which Chalcedon had pronounced orthodox. Thus it closed, defiant of the Pope, a schismatic and antipapal council. Justinian proceeded to enforce signature upon any bishop in his power. Vigilius may have been banished. We do not know. Pressure was certainly brought to bear upon him broken, as he was, in health. For on December 8 (553) he wrote to Eutychius a letter of surrender. He retracted his recent Constitutum ascribing to the devil his previous opposition to the condemnation of the Chapters. The following Spring, February 23, 554, he renewed his surrender in a second Judicatum. Once more he retracted his opposition to the Council's condemnation of the Chapters and endorsed it. He even declared against his better knowledge that Ibas' letter was not genuine and cannot therefore have been approved at Chalcedon. Anyone maintaining its authenticity is an 'impudent and deceitful heretic'. He did not however confirm the Council as such, nor therefore its other doctrinal statements. How indeed could he have confirmed his own excommunication? At last he was permitted to return home. But he died in Sicily on his way (555). For the wrong done to Silverius and his complaisance to Theodora Vigilius had paid a bitter reckoning.

In 543 a local synod had endorsed Justinian's condemnation of errors taught by Origen or attributed to him—notably the final salvation of all men and angels. At this fifth Council Origen's name was included in a list of condemned heretics. Fifteen Origenist doctrines, some taught by Origen himself, others by Palestinian monks who claimed to be his disciples, were specifically condemned. These condemned propositions which however do not include the final salvation of all men affirm inter alia the pre-existence of human spirits, the fall of spirits angelic and human into material bodies created by a spirit inferior to God, a demiurge, the final annihilation of matter and the amalgamation of all spirits into one personal Christ, the Christ-Spirit being their head, united to the divine Word. These propositions were probably condemned before the Council was formally opened and therefore are not the decision of an Ecumenical council.[1]

At Constantinople in spite of imprisonment, Pelagius Vigilius' archdeacon had campaigned vigorously against the Council not sparing the Pope's weakness. Now however he retracted his opposition, confirmed the Council and returned to Rome as Justinian's

[1] For all this I follow G. Fritz in the article *Origenisme* in the Dictionnaire de Theologie catholique.

nominee for the papacy. It is not surprising that he was confronted by universal indignation. The public with no justification charged him with his predecessor's murder. The clergy denounced his condemnation of the Three Chapters.

Only two bishops could be found to consecrate him. Though he defended his change of front in condemning the Chapters he affirmed the personal orthodoxy of Theodoret and Ibas and did not mention the Council. His success was far from complete. Many bishops refused his communion and the provinces of Milan and Aquileia held out for many years, the latter even until the close of the following century. Pope Gregory the Great (590-604) once more confirmed the condemnation of the Chapters though not the Fifth Council as such.

The Fifth Council had little justification for its existence. Born of an imperial whim, assembled in spite of the Pope's opposition, its decisions forced upon his weakness and his successor's ambition, it did nothing to conciliate the Monophysites, in the West produced widespread hostility even schism, dealt a serious blow to the prestige of the Holy See. Fortunately Gregory the Great would shortly revive it. On the other hand the Council taught no false doctrine, did not repudiate Chalcedon. The entire issue, as Amann points out, was not a matter of doctrine which was not disputed but of what are called dogmatic facts, whether particular writings were or were not orthodox, a question which, so far as the Three Chapters are concerned, possesses no importance or relevance today. Even at the time the controversy was much ado about very little.

Meanwhile about 555 St. Benedict founder in succession of the monasteries of Subiaco and Monte Cassino promulgated the rule which adapting monasticism to the Latin temper and background provided an unfailing current of prayer and enabled Benedictine monks to play a leading part in constructing the religion-culture of Latin Christendom.

7

THE SIXTH GENERAL COUNCIL:
CONSTANTINOPLE III 680-1

THE Sixth Council was an aftermath of Chalcedon, a final repudiation of the persistent Monophysite opposition to its formula. Unlike its predecessor it enriched the dogmatic teaching of the Church, completed as well as confirmed her condemnation of Monophysitism. As in the fifth century it was supported by imperial patronage and depended upon imperial favour. Once more, as after Chalcedon, emperors attempted a compromise which would reconcile the Monophysites with the Church.

Before telling the story we must cast a glimpse at the condition of Christendom in the seventh century. Hardly had Justinian reconquered Italy when it was invaded 568 by another Teutonic tribe, the Lombards. They ravaged a large part of the peninsula expelling the Benedictines from Monte Cassino—they did not return until 717—and established a powerful kingdom in Northern Italy which for two centuries would threaten what remained of imperial Italy. They also were Arian. As a result of conquest or conversion all the Arian states except the Lombard had become Catholic, and the Lombard rulers also became Catholic before the seventh century closed. England was being converted by a mission from Rome—it landed in Kent 597—and a mission from Irish Iona. The decision of the synod at Whitby (664) to adopt the Roman rather than the Celtic determination of Easter—for, as King Oswy observed, the keys of heaven were given not to St.

Columba but to St. Peter—effecting the triumph of the Roman
missionaries, forged a particularly close bond between the Anglo-
Saxons and the Holy See. All this strengthened the papal power in
the Latin West. On the other hand Rome and a considerable part
of Italy were now under the rule of the Eastern Emperor whose
representative, the Exarch, ruled at Ravenna. The Exarch was
an inefficient ruler and in practice the Pope had become the temporal governor of Rome and the neighbouring territory. But he
was more or less the Emperor's subject and the Emperor might
and on one occasion did lay hold of a pope who defied his ecclesiastical decrees. In the East the Emperor Heraclius expelled the
Persians from a brief conquest of the Eastern provinces Syria,
Asia Minor, even Egypt (629). But he had hardly restored
Byzantine rule when a Moslem conquest permanently wrested
the East from Christian government. The Caliph Omar conquered Damascus in 633, Jerusalem in 637, Alexandria in 641.
Whoever originated the heresy to be known as Monothelitism,
its first ecclesiastical champion was Sergius patriarch of Constantinople. In agreement with the Monophysite leader Severus
Sergius taught that there is in Christ only one 'energeia', activity,
operation, mode of operation.[1] Consequently Sergius and his
followers affirmed, though the phrase emerged somewhat later,
that he has only one will, volition, 'thelema'. Whence the name
Monothelite, one who affirms only one will in Christ. To speak
of one operation or will in Christ is an approach to the language
of the Monophysites who spoke of one nature. Monothelitism
was in fact an offshoot of Monophysitism, and a compromise
with it. As such it found favour with the Emperor Heraclius confronted, as he was, with the hostility of his Monophysite
subjects. He appointed one of its champions, Cyrus, patriarch
of Alexandria. Cyrus was successful in effecting a temporary
reunion with the more moderate Egyptian Monophysites on the
basis of an agreed formula. It consisted of nine condemnations. Once more Chalcedon was shelved. Cyril's formula 'one

---

[1] The term is extremly difficult to translate, ambiguous in itself. Pope Vigilius
writing to Justinian (June 547) had spoken of 'one sole operation' in Christ.

incarnate nature of God the Word' was adopted, the doctrine of one operation affirmed. Anathema to those who denied 'that there is but one Christ the Son, performing his actions whether divine or human by one sole operation at once divine and human, theandric'. Further reunions followed with the Armenian Monophysites and the Antiochene whose patriarch was recognised.

A monk however named Sophronius, shortly afterwards elected patriarch of Jerusalem, vigorously opposed the Monothelite formulas. Sergius first, then Sophronius appealed to the pope, Honorius I (625-638). Whatever many Catholic writers have said, Sergius stated his own teaching fairly enough though silent as to Cyrus' compromise with the Monophysites at the expense of Chalcedon. His letter was calculated to win the approval of a pope averse to controversy. He had modified his original position. He now advocated silence on the question of one or two operations and argued that to affirm more than one operation or will would suggest two divergent wills. Honorius, in his reply (634), agreed that we should not speak of one or two operations, a subtlety best left to the discussion of grammarians and philosophers, as we might say to linguistic analysis, and certainly no article of faith. Let it suffice to say that Jesus Christ acted in his two natures divinely and humanly. There is nothing here of Cyrus' attempt to byepass Chalcedon. Certainly, Honorius continued, He had only one will. For since he experienced no rebellious desire, his will could not differ from his Father's. Evidently Honorius understood by one will, a will identical in its choices not one principle or faculty of volition. His mistake was nothing more than failure to insist on accurate statement. His terminology alone was faulty. And it would soon be rejected decisively by his successors[1] (see below p. 68). Nevertheless Honorius' toleration and in part acceptance of Monothelite language encouraged the Monothelites, weakened Sophronius' defence of more accurate language. A second letter from Honorius once more forbade the expressions one or two operations. En-

[1] For a detailed and admirably objective statement of Honorius' letters and the theological problem involved, see the article *Honorius* by E. Amann in the *Dictionaire de Theologie Catholique*.

couraged by his success at Rome, Sergius drew up the doctrinal statement which Heraclius adopted and imposed in 638, the Ecthesis, Profession of Faith. Its language closely resembled that of Honorius' letters. It was forbidden to speak of one or of two operations in Christ for the latter might be taken to imply wills possibly conflicting. There is however but one will. 'For never did his flesh, quickened by a reasonable soul, exercise its natural activity in separation, on its own initiative, and against the assent of the Word to which it was hypostatically (personally) united but when, in the manner and to the extent, the Divine Word willed'. It would be difficult surely to find heresy in this explanation. For what is true of the union with God of a mystic on earth or the blessed in heaven, must *a fortiori* be true of the union between Christ's human soul and the Godhead. The mystics however speak of this union in the terms used by Sergius about Our Lord. St. John of the Cross, speaking of the soul in the supreme degree of mystical union, says that 'she cannot make acts. For the Holy Spirit makes them all, moving the soul to make them, for which reason all her acts are divine since she is actuated and moved by God.'[1] And of the blessed soul in heaven, when the work of deification will be complete, he says 'her will will be God's will, her love God's love. For, although even then "in heaven" the soul does not lose her will ... the two wills are united in one single will and one single love of God. Wherefore the soul loves God with his own will and energy (fuerza)'.[2] Unlike St. John however the Monothelites refused to say that the human will is not lost. When therefore Tixeront blames the Monothelites for teaching that Our Lord's human will was moved to its choices by the Divine, that 'Christ's will acts solely at the command and under the impulse of the divine will ... by which his human will' is moved[3] he condemns the Catholic mystics and we cannot

---

[1] *The Living Flame of Love*, 1.5.

[2] *Spiritual Canticle*. xxxviii. 3. Pere Poulain, S.J., (*Des Graces d'Oraison*, Ch. XXIX, note 29) argues that St. John is speaking the language of appearances. He gives no reason for his opinion. When St. John is in fact using the language of appearances, *apparent* but not real identity between the deified soul and God, he says so.

[3] *Histoire des Dogmes*. III. p. 174-5.

follow him. Père Jugie[1] is justified when he terms this condemnation of the Monothelites Nestorian in tendency. Never did
the defenders of Catholic orthodoxy against the Monothelites,
Sophronius or Maximus of Tyre, combat their adversaries on this
score. In fact Jugie concludes: 'when we study attentively those
Monothelite writings which have come down to us, for example
the Ecthesis, it would be difficult to discover any opinion (pensée)
truly heretical. What is heretical in their formulas, taken by
themselves, is their silence as to the natural operations and wills
of the two natures'. That is to say an orthodox meaning is expressed in an ambiguous language which if admitted could be
understood to imply the absence in Christ of these human faculties, will and operation. There is a refusal to use the correct terminology. 'Terminological inexactitude,' on one occasion the
parliamentary euphemism for lie describes exactly the Monothelite heresy. In this it resembles its Monophysite parent, a heresy
of terminology not meaning.

By the close of 642, all the protagonists were dead, Heraclius,
Sergius, Cyrus, Pope Honorius. But the Ecthesis had not been
withdrawn and Sergius' successor was another Monothelite,
Pyrrhus. In this year 642, Pope John IV (640-642) wrote to the
new Emperors, Constantine III and Heracleon demanding the
revocation of the Ecthesis and unwarrantably explaining Honorius' meaning away as referring only to Our Lord's human will in
its complete mastery of desire. The expulsion of Pyrrhus to make
room for Paul II and the accession to the Empire of Constans II
(641) did not alter the situation. Another protest by Pope Theodore (642-649) was in vain. Finally in 648, the Emperor Constans replaced the Ecthesis by a new edict, the Type. It was not
a doctrinal statement but a prohibition to speak of one or two
wills or operations thus imposing silence on both parties. Disobedience would be punished with the utmost severity.

The new pope St. Martin I (649-655) made a vigorous reply.
In a council at Lateran attended by 105 bishops, the entire question was discussed in sessions lasting a month. Finally a series of

---

[1] Article *Monothelisme*, Dictionaire de Theologie Catholique.

canons condemned the Type and its supporters, affirmed that in Jesus Christ there are 'two natural wills and two natural operations, the divine and the human'. Constans took his revenge. After one unsuccessful attempt, he effected the Pope's arrest (653). Subject to brutal ill usage, Martin was taken to Constantinople where in December 652 he was tried and condemned for treason. He was degraded, dragged through the streets in chains and half naked. Only the intercession of the dying patriarch saved him from execution. He was exiled to the Crimea where he soon died of the sufferings he had undergone in defence of the faith, September 16 655. His Feast is on November 12. Another Catholic champion, St. Maximus, was mutilated and died in consequence.

The Roman clergy were far from imitating St. Martin's courage. They elected Eugenius (654(5)-657) who however became lawful pope on Martin's death.[1] His legates at Constantinople even accepted a novel and unorthodox formula that Christ possessed three wills, two natural, one hypostatic. The succeeding popes, regarding discretion as the better part of valour, maintained a peace of silence with Constantinople and in 663 the emperor responsible for Martin's murder visited Rome in person and was received by the servile acclamations of pope, clergy and people.

In 668 Constans was succeeded by Constantine IV. To end the estrangement between the eastern and western churches, he invited Pope Agatho (678-681) to send delegates to a conference at Constantinople to examine the doctrinal question. The pope agreed. To prepare the ground he held a council at Rome attended by 125 bishops, and local synods elsewhere. Once more Monothelism was solemnly condemned. He despatched to Constantinople three bishops, three priests, a deacon and a sub-deacon. They bore a text with them, Agatho's Dogmatic Letter. It affirms two wills and activities in Christ and once again, anticipating in substance the Vatican definition of papal infallibility, insists on 'the faith of this Apostolic Church of Peter which has never

[1] Strangely Eugenius has found a place among the Popes venerated as Saints.

diverged from the truth and whose authority has always been followed by the Catholic Church'.

When the legates reached Constantinople, September 680, Constantine summoned the bishops of the patriarchates of Constantinople and Antioch. Unexpectedly, the patriarchs of Alexandria and Jerusalem, though under Moslem rule, sent plenipotentiaries. The intended conference thus became the Sixth Ecumenical Council (Constantinople iii).

The Council was held in the domed hall (Trullus) of the imperial palace. The legates presided, though Constantine was the honorary president. Its eighteen sessions were protracted from the opening on November 7 (680) to the close on the following September 16 (681). The membership, no more than 50 bishops, orientals, at the opening session, had risen to 174 at the close. The Monothelite leader and stalwart was Macarius of Antioch who attempted to prove from the Fathers the formulas he professed. The legates produced from the Fathers a catena of passages to the contrary. Agatho's dogmatic letter teaching two operations and wills in Christ was read and accepted with acclamation: 'Peter has spoken by Agatho'. (Fourth Session November 16.) Many sessions were occupied with reading doctrinal evidence. Macarius who refused to yield was deposed (Ninth Session March 8 681).

Thirteenth Session, March 28 681

The leading Monothelites, all dead, were condemned and among them Sergius, Cyrus and Honorius: 'We have decided to expel from the Church of God and anathematise Honorius Pope of the old Rome because we find from his writings to Sergius that in all things he held the latter's view and confirmed his impious doctrines'. Certainly Honorius had agreed with Sergius.

Thirteenth Session, April 26 681

A Monothelite priest failed to fulfil his undertaking to prove his position by raising a dead man to life!

Sixteenth Session. 9th August, 681

A doctrinal statement put forward by a Syrian priest that Christ had three wills, a divine-human, a divine and a human, was put forward and rejected.

Seventeenth Session. 11th September, 681

The Catholic doctrine on the Monothelite issue was promulgated: 'We profess in our Lord Jesus Christ, the Word, God's only Son . . . two natural wills and two natural operations without separation, division, separation or mixture. . . . They are not however opposed . . . but His human will without resistance or rebellion obeys and is subject to His Omnipotent Divine Will'.

At the final session (September 16 681) held in the Emperor's presence—he signed its decrees—the Monothelite leaders were once more anathematised by name.

Thus Monothelitism was condemned. The affirmation that our Lord's human will was wholly moved by his Divine Will, his operation by the Divine Action, as Sergius had insisted, was not condemned. What was condemned was language which could be understood—though the Monothelites did not so understand it— to deny the existence of a distinct and complete human will and operation.

The following January Agatho died and was succeeded by St. Leo II (682-683). He confirmed the council's decrees. Honorius in particular he condemned 'because he did not illuminate this apostolic see by teaching the apostolic tradition but by an act of profound treachery attempted to subvert her immaculate faith'.[1] The condemnation was unjust. As is evident from his letters, Honorius' *meaning,* as indeed Sergius' meaning in the Ecthesis, was orthodox. The terminology alone was faulty. It had been

---

[1] So runs the Latin original. The Greek translation is somewhat different: 'He permitted her immaculate faith to be defiled.' Not only is the original preferable to a translation. The latter is less likely. For 'attempted' implies failure whereas 'permitted to be defiled' implies an actual defilement which Leo would hardly have admitted.

corrected by subsequent popes, finally by an ecumenical council confirmed by the Pope.[1]

The earlier Monothelites, Sergius, Cyrus, the unfortunate Honorius, were not and could not have been formal heretics. For the terminology they rejected had not yet been defined by the Church. Their condemnation therefore was as unjustified as would be, for example, a condemnation of St. Bonaventure or St. Thomas Aquinas for denying the Immaculate Conception.

In another respect these anathemas and a similar anathema at the Fifth Council are unacceptable. 'We have decided to expel from God's Church' persons already deceased. Death had finally excluded them from the Church Militant and, as Savonarola will remind his judge, the Church Militant has no power to exclude any soul from the Church Suffering or Triumphant. Her writ does not run beyond the grave. To define an acceptable terminology should have sufficed without unwarranted personal condemnation.

Eleven years later, 692, the Emperor Justinian II summoned another council in the same domed hall where the Ecumenical Council had assembled. It was concerned solely with questions of discipline and as it provided in the Emperor's intentions a disciplinary supplement to the doctrinal decrees of the Fifth and Sixth Ecumenical Councils, has received the appellation the Quini-Sext Council in Trullo, 'the Fifth-Sixth Council in the Dome'. 24 bishops attended, all Byzantine, and the two permanent papal envoys. Its canons reaffirmed the second place accorded by Chalcedon to the see of Constantinople and sought to extend to the entire church the distinctive discipline of the Byzantines. Although the two legates signed—probably they dared not protest —the anti-Latin animus was evident. The decrees notwithstand-

[1] Throughout the Middle Ages Honorius' name stood in the Roman Breviary, in a lesson for the feast of St. Leo II among the condemned Monothelites his identity unrecognised. When the Protestants triumphantly paraded a pope thus officially condemned his name was removed from the list. Baronius, moreover, the Catholic historian of the Church, asserted that the patriarch Paul, condemned by the council, expunged his own name from its minutes and substituted the name of Honorius. Not only is there no evidence to support Baronius but, as Amman observes, even if Paul could have effected this substitution in the archives of Constantinople, he could not conceivably have made the corresponding alteration in the Roman archives. Baronius' explanation is a disconcerting example of 'edification' preferred to historical truth.

ing were transmitted to the Pope St. Sergius (687-701) and when he withheld his signature, the Emperor made an unsuccessful attempt to take him captive. Further attempts were made in vain to secure a papal confirmation and finally the Canons were literally shelved, 'enrolled in the archives of the Roman Church'.

8

THE SEVENTH GENERAL COUNCIL:
NICAEA II 787

As the seventh turned to the eighth century, a powerful surge of
Moslem conquest threatened to overwhelm the Christian world.
In Africa the Moslems conquered Carthage in 698, and by 708
their rule had reached the Atlantic. In 711 they crossed into
Spain which they speedily overran. Only a small territory in the
north west remained in Christian hands to be, however, the
nucleus in the centuries to come of a re-conquest. In 730 the
invaders crossed the Pyrenees and for some years ruled south
western France. It was the victory at Poitiers in 732 of the
Frankish ruler Charles Martel which turned back the Moslem
tide. Sicily would later fall under Moslem rule (829-1060), and
the Arabs obtain a foothold in Italy itself. In the East, an assault
on Constantinople had met with a crushing defeat (673-678), but
a series of short lived and incompetent Emperors made possible
not only the Arabs' African conquests but a second siege of the
Capital. The Moslem conquest of the Byzantine Empire to be
effected seven centuries later, was imminent. The military genius,
however, of Leo the Isaurian who reigned from 717 to 740, re-
pelled the invaders. His son, Constantine V, drove them out of
Asia Minor and recaptured Cyprus. The new dynasty had saved
the Eastern Empire and placed its power on a firm military basis.
At the same time the Isaurian Emperors by legislative and economic reforms consolidated the empire internally.

Unfortunately, they interfered in the theological domain and launched an attack upon the use and veneration of images. The heresy thus initiated is known as iconoclasm, image-breaking. The primitive church had not been iconoclastic. Images—largely scriptural scenes with symbolic meaning—decorated the Christian cemeteries and no doubt, when it was safe, their places of worship. Indeed, contemporary Judaism, as excavated synagogues have proved, also tolerated such religious paintings. These images, however, were pictures not statues, as in fact is the rule in the Eastern Church to this day. A sculptured image would have been too reminiscent of the pagan idol. Nor was there as yet any veneration of images. Development had not yet taken the path that would lead to miraculous images, crowned images, images as objects of pilgrimage, visiting images. The beginnings of such veneration, paid first to the cross, appear, not without opposition, in the fourth century. It may well have been assisted by the traditional homage paid to the images of the emperor— flowers, lights and incense. In the East, from at least the sixth century, it was universally accepted. In the West, veneration took root more slowly. It is doubtful whether Gregory the Great saw in images more than a means of teaching the illiterate. The 'veneratio' he requires for a cross and image of our Lady to be removed when a stolen synagogue was returned to the Jews may mean no more than reverent treatment. Veneration of images was, however, well established by the eighth century in the Church of Rome in close touch with Constantinople. Leo the Isaurian rejected alike the employment and veneration of images. The source of his iconoclasm is unknown. It may have represented an oriental reaction—Leo was a Syrian—against the Hellenic regard for the human form. A faction of bishops supported him from the first. It was in 726 that he launched his first edict against images, ordering their destruction. It produced a widespread revolt in Italy and no iconoclast emperor was able to enforce his edicts beyond the Adriatic. Even in the East there was violent opposition. It was defeated and the patriarch Germanus who refused to condemn images was deposed and strangled.

Rome now took action once again to defend the Catholic faith.

Though Pope St. Gregory II (715-731) had supported the Emperor against political rebels, he condemned the new patriarch and addressed a letter of protest to Leo. His successor St. Gregory III (731-741), not content with despatching further protests, gathered a council of 93 members at St. Paul's (November 731) at which he excommunicated any who instead of venerating images in accordance with 'the ancient customs of the Apostolic Church', destroyed, profaned or blasphemed them. Leo's reprisal was a naval expedition which deprived the Pope of his patrimonial estates in Sicily and southern Italy and intruded Byzantine bishops into sees of southern Italy. More he could not do. For the Pope had entrenched himself as the de facto ruler of Rome and other Italian territories—the Papal States.

Faced by Byzantine hostility and the pressure of Lombard invasions, Pope Stephen II[1] (752-757) following the policy of his predecessor Zacharias (741-752) turned for help to the Carolingian rulers of France. Only with their aid could the papacy retain its government of a considerable portion of central Italy and transform it into a government de jure. The Pope's claim to this territory and Frankish assistance to hold it was supported by the opportune forgery of the Donation of Constantine whereby the Emperor transferred to the Pope temporal sovereignty over the Western Empire. Visiting France Stephen obtained a promise of assistance from its ruler Pepin whom in return he crowned as the first Carolingian monarch. His judgment that the de facto ruler was entitled to depose a roi fainéant, the last Merovingian, was understood by subsequent canonists,[2] probably by Stephen himself, not as merely a moral judgment but as the exercise of a supreme temporal jurisdiction. Pepin first, later his son and successor Charlemagne, defeated the Lombard aggressors finally annexing their kingdom. The result of their interventions was a papal state which 'had reached very approximately the boundaries which it was to retain until 1860'[3] roughly 1100 years.

[1] Strictly Stephen III. For his predecessor, pope for two days and never consecrated was in fact Pope Stephen II.

[2] Writers on the law of the Church, Canon law.

[3] Peter Partner 'The Papal State under Martin V'.

Charlemagne however, if not his father, regarded these papal territories as his gift and subject to his supreme authority. Already in the West the struggle for temporal supremacy between Church and Empire had begun though as yet more or less latent.

In the East, St. John Damascene, a monk and renowned theologian whose Summa of Christian doctrine is still authoritative in the East, in three vigorous treatises defended the use and veneration of images. He was credulous in his use of doctrinal sources and accepted too readily legends of miracle-working images. But his theological defence and explanations would be permanently endorsed by Catholic theology. The West, however, unlike the East has not followed him in ascribing a quasi-sacramental character to images, the effect of a sanctifying power bestowed on them by the subject they depict. Safe moreover under Moslem rule[1] St. John denied the Emperor's competence to determine questions of faith: 'It is not for kings to legislate for the Church.' It was the Catholic reply to Leo's claim 'I am priest as well as emperor.'

Leo's son, Constantine V, Copronymus (740-775), proved a more virulent and determined iconoclast than even his father had been. For political reasons he held his hand at first. But in 753 he inaugurated a new and more savagely intolerant attack upon images. He gathered in his palace of Hieria a council of 338 bishops exclusively, however, from the patriarchate of Constantinople. It forbade the manufacture or veneration of images. Theological arguments were put forward, supported by texts from Scripture or the Fathers. Penalties were enacted against anyone who in public or private should make, display or venerate an image. Sacred vessels, however, or ornaments must not be destroyed because an image has been depicted upon them. St. John Damascene and other defenders of images were anathematised.

The concluding canons, however, are in a different strain. They affirm the lawfulness and value of invoking the interces-

[1] The story which has found its way into the Roman liturgy, that Constantine in revenge accused John to the Caliph of treason, his hand was cut off but by our Lady's ntercession miraculously restored, is legendary.

sion of our Lady and the Saints. For the Emperor was disposed to deny these doctrines and even the servile prelates of Hieria would not yield so far. For the time Constantine was content to launch a ruthless destruction of images and persecution of those who venerated them. When he found the monks more stalwart than the secular clergy, he turned his fury against them. There were many martyrs. Finally he declared against the veneration of relics and saints.

A council held at Jerusalem (767) and representing the patriarchates of Antioch, Jerusalem and Alexandria (768-772) pronounced in favour of images and their veneration as did a council held at the Lateran by Stephen III (IV) (769). Constantine was powerless to coerce subjects of the Caliph or a Pope now strengthened by alliance with the Carolingian kings of France. The short reign of the Emperor Leo IV relaxed the persecution and when in 780 his widow Irene, whose beauty had raised her from the populace to the imperial throne, became regent for her son, Constantine VI, her secret orthodoxy became a determination to restore the orthodox faith. Her first step was to appoint as patriarch an upholder of images, Tarasius.

The Empress called a Council to re-establish images and their veneration. It met at Constantinople on August 17, 786. A mutiny of iconoclastic troops broke it up on the same day. Irene, however, suppressed the revolt and effected a purge in the army. The Council, therefore, reassembled a year later on September 24, 787, but for greater safety at Nicaea, the scene of the first ecumenical council. Pope Hadrian I (772-795) was represented by two legates, an arch priest and an abbot, both named Peter. They had been empowered only 'to enquire into the necessity for ... an ecumenical council'. Eventually, however, they decided to participate as the papal representatives in Irene's council. Two monks represented the three patriarchates under Moslem rule. There were in all about 300 members of the Council. Tarasius presided. Its sessions lasted almost a month.

A number of iconoclast bishops abjured their heresy and were re-admitted to communion. The legates read letters from the

Pope to Irene and Tarasius and asked the assembled bishops whether they accepted the veneration of images as taught in the synodical letters of 'the most blessed Hadrian, Pope of the older Rome'. To which the bishops replied: 'We follow, we receive, we admit'. Texts from Scripture and the Fathers favourable or regarded as favourable to images were read. The iconoclastic decrees passed at Hieria were condemned, the six previous ecumenical Councils were accepted. There followed (7th Session, October 13) a formal definition that images not only of the Cross but of our Lord, 'our inviolate Lady the Holy Mother of God', of angels and saints should be set up and receive 'salutation and reverent obeisance' not, however, adoration, *latreia*, which 'according to our faith is due to the Godhead alone'.[1] Images should be venerated with lights and incense. 'For honour paid to an image is paid to him it represents.' The iconoclastic leaders were condemned. At the same session, the Council enacted twenty-two disciplinary decrees which have won the admiration of the Protestant historian Harnack. Many are concerned with the monastic life. Pluralism was condemned. All the bishops subscribed the Council's decrees.

At the Empress' request the final session, October 23, 787, the eighth, was held in her palace at Constantinople. She presided, addressed the Council, and with her son signed its profession of faith.

Her presence, it seems, gave such scandal that the Latin versions mutilate their account of this session. The scandal, however, was not only her sex but her character. Unscrupulous and ruthless in her ambition, she had her brothers-in-law mutilated, her own son blinded.[2]

Since outstanding papal claims to estates and ecclesiastical jurisdiction usurped by the Byzantine emperor were not recognised, Hadrian did not confirm the Council. But he accepted its

---

[1] St. Thomas Aquinas, however, would later teach that a relative *'latreia'* is due to the Cross. Theology would also distinguish between *latreia*, adoration due to God, *dulia*, service due to the saints and *hyperdulia*, the eminent service due to our Lady.

[2] Notwithstanding, her zeal for orthodoxy won her in earlier days the honour of sanctity among the Greeks.

decrees and at his command its acts were translated into Latin.[1] Moreover, his letter to Charlemagne (see below p. 82) amounted to a doctrinal confirmation, This Council is the last accepted as ecumenical alike by the Roman Catholic Church and the Churches in communion with Constantinople.

The Emperor Leo V (813-820) was an iconoclast. He chose his patriarch, assembled a Council which condemned Nicaea and restored Hieria, destroyed images and persecuted their defenders, though he refrained from making martyrs. His successor, Michael the Stammerer (820-829), was more moderate, accepting the employment though not the veneration of images. Theophilus (829-842) was a more violent iconoclast and renewed the persecution. His widow Theodora, however, as regent for her son, acted as Irene had done before her. A Byzantine council confirmed the decrees of Nicaea (843). It was the final defeat of iconoclasm, which the Greek Church commemorates to this day by a feast of orthodoxy.

In the West the triumph of Nicaea was not so rapid. The Frankish protector of the Church had become, in the person of Charlemagne (768-814), her patron and ruler. Charlemagne was devoted to the Catholic faith. He reorganised the hierarchy and employed his authority to impose upon the clergy decent standards of liturgical observance and pastoral duty. In the larger churches he established a regular common observance among the clergy. Securing the services of the best available scholarship, he fostered education and he endeavoured to build up an edifice of Catholic culture. It was the first Renaissance of Western Culture inspired by the Catholic religion. He conquered the pagan Avars and Saxons and finally succeeded in making them subjects and Catholics. The Saxon leader, Widukind, who had fought pertinaciously against him, finally submitted, was baptised and is even honoured as a minor saint, Blessed Widukind.[2] With the exception of Britain and the remnant of Christian Spain,

---

[1] The first translation was faulty in the extreme and misrepresented the Council's teaching. In the following century Anastasius, the Papal Librarian, made a more accurate translation.

[2] Strangely the Nazis set him up as a hero of Teutonic paganism.

Western and Catholic Europe was united under his rule. So great indeed were his services to the Church that despite the laxity and irregularity of his sexual life, he has received liturgical honours as Beatus. Nevertheless, he claimed and exercised not only a temporal sovereignty over the papal states, but the ecclesiastical sovereignty exercised so disastrously by the Byzantine Caesars.

It was perhaps as a counterpoise to this imperial surveillance that on Christmas Day, 800, Pope St. Leo III (795-816) placed on Charlemagne's head an imperial crown as Roman Emperor crowned by God.[1] No doubt he would have it appear, as in fact it did appear to posterity, that far from the Pope depending upon the emperor, emperors and kings owed their sovereign rights to the Vicar of God. Indeed, if we can trust Eginhard's report Charlemagne was taken by surprise and was displeased with the ceremony. It produced a series of intermittent conflicts between Emperor and Pope in which each by turns usurped upon the jurisdiction of the other and sought supremacy over him. For secular and sacred were so closely interwoven in the fabric of mediaeval society that disengagement, however desirable, was impossible. The sole possible independence of the Church from the State was supremacy over the State. And for the moment, the State was decidedly in the ascendent.

This ascendency had already appeared in the indecisive conflict between Charles and Pope Hadrian in respect of the Council of Nicaea. In due course, Pope Hadrian communicated to Charles the Latin translation of the decrees of Nicaea. Charles read them with disfavour. And it was not solely because the translator had mistranslated the veneration due to images by *adoratio*, adoration, the correct translation of the *latreia* reserved to God alone. For Charles and his Frankish clergy rejected any veneration of images though admitting their employment. Charles ordered the composition, possibly by Alcuin, his favourite scholar and theologian, of a lengthy and bitterly hostile criticism of the Seventh Council. Images should not receive even the marks of respect due

[1] Leo certainly secured by this coronation Charlemagne's support against a powerful faction of hostile nobles who had attempted to mutilate him and charged him with crimes from which he had just purged himself on oath.

to living persons. Jesus and the Saints reject worship so wrong headed, and the simple people are unable to see beyond the image to its subject. Candles should not be lit or incense burned before images. Even their lawful use for decoration and instruction is of indifferent value. It is known as the Caroline Books. From this compilation 85 texts, chapters, were extracted and sent to the Pope. Hadrian replied point by point correcting the mistranslation and defending the decrees of Nicaea. 'Wherefore we accept that synod'. It is uncertain whether this passage between Pope and King preceded or followed the Council assembled by the latter at Frankfort in 794, at which the Council of Nicaea and the cult of images were condemned, though in more moderate terms. Papal legates were present and subscribed the condemnation. Nor did the Pope condemn the legates for repudiating Nicaea. It would be imprudent to launch a frontal attack upon Charles. So matters rested.

In 824 the Eastern emperor Michael, who as we have seen, accepted the employment of images but rejected their veneration, precisely the position of the Frankish church, wrote in that sense to Charlemagne's son and successor Louis I. Louis took his ambassadors to Rome and obtained the consent of Pope Eugenius II (824-827) to hold an assembly of bishops to discuss the question. It met in Paris (825), pronounced strongly against the veneration of images, once again rejected the decrees of Nicaea, even condemned in strong terms Pope Hadrian's defence of the Council. 'He said what he wanted to say, not what he ought to have said'—made 'statements opposed to truth and the authoritative teaching of the Church'. No sequel is recorded. We must therefore conclude that the Pope, to avoid open conflict, kept silence. Rome seemed to be taking the road to Byzantium. There is later evidence of Frankish opposition to the veneration of images. In spite of Hadrian's endorsement of Nicaea, which indeed had after all but accepted his own doctrinal statement, it was not until after 880—when the Carolingian Empire had disintegrated—that the Seventh Council was added in the papal profession of faith to the six acknowledged as ecumenical.

Until the eleventh century, the Frankish Church admitted only six ecumenical councils. For example, the celebrated humanist Gerbert, Archbishop of Rheims, finally Pope Silvester II (999-1003), did not acknowledge Nicaea. So stubborn and persistent was the Frankish refusal to venerate images.

9

THE EIGHTH GENERAL COUNCIL:
CONSTANTINOPLE IV 869-870

THE speedy disintegration of Charlemagne's imposing empire was due to three causes: (1) The power of local princes and nobles too strong for the control of a central government lacking sufficient machinery and resources. (2) Barbarian invasions from the north and east. (3) The traditional Frankish custom of treating a kingdom like a private estate and dividing it between the sons of the late king.

This is a half world, a world of limited being—intermediate, so to speak, between the Fullness of divine being and nonentity, being therefore that both is and is not. In consequence, everything created[1] has two aspects, positive and negative. Gain in one direction involves loss in another, what is good in one aspect is in another aspect bad or at least unsatisfactory. Every good quality has its defects. No climate, for example, no race, or social group, no human achievement or personality, is *wholly* good or *in all respects* better than another.

So was it with the fall of the Carolingian Empire. From the point of view of civilisation, culture, man's earthly happiness, it was a disaster. It involved internal anarchy, feudal oppression, successful barbarian invasion. The first Renaissance was checked, the development of mediaeval culture retarded, indeed set back, the seed sewn of wars between independent European nations, particularly the millenial feud between France and the German

---

[1] Unless supernaturally elevated into the plenitude of God.

85

rulers beyond the Rhine among whose effects have been two World Wars. On the other hand, humanly speaking, the disintegration of the Carolingian Empire alone made possible the spiritual independence of the Papacy, threw off the Byzantine yoke Charlemagne had imposed. Those who believe that man's supreme good is not earthly peace or culture, valuable though they are, but the eternal union with God the Church exists to promote, a purpose best promoted when she is free from State control, a control moreover condemned implicitly by our Lord's commission to St. Peter, will regard the downfall of the Carolingian Empire as on balance a gain.

Imperial weakness was the more necessary because the Papacy would itself be weak. Though there were one or two Popes of outstanding character and achievement, for example St. Leo IV (847-855) and St. Nicholas the Great (858-867) the Papacy was entering a tunnel where Popes would for the most part be insignificant and some even positively immoral. It was well that no powerful secular state, certainly no stable empire, confronted their weakness.

In the East, the final condemnation of iconoclasm was followed by a series of conflicts between the Emperors and their local patriarchs on the one hand, popes on the other. Periods of schism would alternate with periods of reconciliation though even during the latter with little intercourse between the estranged Churches.

In 858 the patriarch of Constantinople, Ignatius, offended the court by refusing communion to the Emperor's uncle, Bardas.[1] Under pressure and for the sake of peace, he resigned. His successor was Photius, a distinguished civil servant, the most learned man of his age, devout and of irreproachable morals. He was, however, a layman and his consecration at Christmas 858 was hurried on without observance of the periods canonically required between each step in his ordination. A noisy faction of bishops declared for Ignatius. He and they were formally deposed by a Council

---

[1] His justification is uncertain. Dvornik considers him the innocent tool of a political faction.

convened by Photius (859). Emperor and patriarch appealed to Rome and Nicholas I despatched two legates to Constantinople to conduct an enquiry. Exceeding their powers, they presided at a further Council (861) which renewed the deposition of Ignatius though acknowledging the papal right to try a patriarch. Nicholas, however, refused to recognise Photius unless better evidence were produced to justify Ignatius' deposition. No reply came from Constantinople. In the late summer of 865, Nicholas held a Council in Rome. Photius and his supporters were condemned, Ignatius pronounced the lawful patriarch. The Pope's hostility to Photius had been whetted by partisans of Ignatius who had reached Rome. The Emperor Michael III wrote to Nicholas a letter of expostulation in which he denied the right of the Papacy to interfere in a purely disciplinary affair. Nicholas' answer (865) was a letter in which he insists on papal supremacy. Without papal assent, no council's decrees are valid. He offers, however, a re-trial of the issue between Ignatius and Photius. A further quarrel between Pope and patriarch arose in respect of Bulgaria, recently converted. Photius claimed it for his patriarchate, Nicholas for his. Photius addressed a letter (867) to the other patriarchs condemning the Pope, a condemnation confirmed by a Council held in the same year. For the first time an Eastern patriarch formally passed judgment on a Pope.

The same year, however, a palace revolution brought to the throne a new Emperor, Basil I (867-886). For political reasons he restored Ignatius, compelled Photius to resign. He committed judgment upon Photius to the Pope, now Hadrian II (867-872).[1] He held a synod which condemned Photius, his supporters and his Councils. Three papal legates, Donatus, Stephen and Marianus were despatched to a Council to be held at Constantinople. It opened in the imperial palace, October 5, 869. It was the Council which would finally be recognised by the Catholic Church as the Eighth Ecumenical Council. No more than 12

---

[1] Hadrian had his personal troubles to face. On his accession his wife was still living and he had a daughter. A powerful nobleman sought the hand of the latter and when it was refused by her father, he kidnapped mother and daughter. When the Pope appealed to the Emperor for aid both were murdered.

bishops attended the opening session—only 103, the highest number, were present at the closing session. That is to say, the bishops
hostile to Ignatius boycotted the Council. Moreover the severe
sentences demanded by the Pope against Photius' adherents
alienated Byzantine sympathies. The Emperor insisted upon presiding instead of the legates. The attitude of the latter was dom-
ineering. They required the subscription of a profession of faith
expressing unqualified submission to papal authority. It was the
formula of Hormisdas (see p. 56) adapted to condemn the
Photians. About that condemnation their language was peremptory: 'A truce to words . . . submit or you will be condemned to
everlasting fire and flames.' The Greek bishops were hostile and
there was a movement in favour of declaring the five patriarchates equal. The sessions were suspended for three months (November 5, 869 to February 12, 870)—presumably until the legates
and the Emperor had reached an agreement. Finally, however, their
demands were accepted in substance. The Libellus, the profession of faith, was signed, Photius and his supporters condemned.

At the final, the tenth session, February 27, 870, twenty-seven
disciplinary canons were enacted. They condemned interference
by the state in episcopal elections, an affirmation of what should
rather than of what would be the observance, even in the West.
Papal supremacy was reaffirmed and no one can be permitted, as
Photius had done, to condemn the Pope.

The legates, however, had not left Constantinople before
Ignatius and a conference containing representatives from the
other eastern patriarchates, in reply to an embassy from the Khan,
decided that Bulgaria should be attached to the patriarchate of
Constantinople. For this reason Hadrian did not confirm the
Council's decrees, but protested to the Emperor against the Bulgarian usurpation. He had, it would appear, made his recognition
of Ignatius conditional upon his abstaining from interference in
Bulgaria. Secure in his office, Ignatius paid no attention to Hadrian's protests, renewed by his successor.

In the course of the following years, Basil became reconciled
with Photius and recalled him from exile. Finally, even the two

rival patriarchs were reconciled. When, in 877, Ignatius died, the Emperor restored Photius to the patriarchate.

Basil and Photius asked the Pope, now John VIII (872-882) to recognise the appointment. John needed imperial assistance against the Saracens who threatened Italy. In 846 they had raided Rome and occupied St. Peter's. He decided to grant Basil's request and at a Roman synod, cancelled the sentences passed against Photius and his supporters by the Council of 869-870. The following winter, 879-880, a Council at Constantinople, with the sanction of the papal legates, recognised Photius as patriarch. Photius, however, refused the apology required of him by the Pope for his former attacks on the papacy and his uncanonical procedure. Nevertheless, the three legates subscribed a formula which not only recognised Photius as 'legitimate and duly elected patriarch' but condemned the Council which had condemned him, the Council of 869-870, the Eighth Ecumenical Council. 'I repudiate and anathematise the synod that was summoned against him in this Holy Church of Constantinople.' The condemnation was subscribed by the 383 bishops present and by the delegates from the other patriarchates.

A compromise was reached about Bulgaria. It would be recognised as belonging to the Roman patriarchate, but the clergy would be Greek.[1]

Pope John confirmed the Council's reinstatement of Photius, was even prepared reluctantly to dispense with his apology. But his language was qualified and studiously vague. His formal approbation was confined to the reinstatement of Photius and his supporters, and of this he spoke as a merciful concession *not* as the annulment of an unjust or uncanonical decree. Moreover, he complained that his communications to the Council had been tampered with and he disassociated himself from anything his legates might have done in excess of their commission. 'We approve' he wrote to the Emperor Basil 'whatever has been mercifully done in Constantinople by the synodal decree reinstating the Very Reverend Patriarch Photius and if perchance at the same synod our

[1] A few years later a national Bulgarian patriarchate was established.

legates have acted against our apostolic instructions, we neither approve their action, nor attribute any validity to it.'

From the Pope's letter, as Dr. Dvornik has put it before us,[1] it is evident that he did not, as Dr. Dvornik maintains, confirm his legates' condemnation of the Council of 869, which on the contrary he implicitly repudiates. On the other hand he certainly did not regard it as ecumenical. For a time the schism had been healed.

Since the decrees passed against Photius by the Council of 869-870 had thus been reversed by the Holy See, it is not surprising that as late as the eleventh century it was not recognised as ecumenical. Pope St. Leo IX writing in 1055 to Peter of Antioch acknowledged only seven ecumenical Councils, all the Councils then recognised at Rome. Around the close of the eleventh century, however, canonists struggling in the dispute about investitures (see below p. 94-p. 99) to maintain the rights of the Church against the State, found its decrees forbidding lay interference with episcopal elections a valuable weapon. Accordingly they embodied these decrees in their collections of Canon Law and ascribed these to an Eighth Ecumenical Council which, as Dvornik puts it, 'they discovered' for the first time. It soon acquired ecumenical status. That is to say, in Dvornik's words, the 'Eighth Council was listed among the ecumenical councils in virtue of an extraordinary error committed by the Canonists at the end of the eleventh century.'

What can we say? How can a Council which for two centuries the papacy did not regard as ecumenical be in fact ecumenical as the same papal authority has pronounced it to be? The Council of 869-870 had not confined its work to the condemnation and deposition of Photius, the restoration of Ignatius. It had reaffirmed papal supremacy. It had passed the valuable and opportune disciplinary decrees which led to its final recognition as ecumenical. At the time of its recognition its condemnation of Photius—which, as we have seen, was reversed not quashed by John VIII—had lost all significance. What alone could possess

[1] *The Photian Schism*, p. 209.

validity and value was the recognition of papal supremacy, the disciplinary decrees. The former did but repeat, and in the words of Hormisdas' formula, what had already been declared and accepted at Ephesus, Chalcedon, the Second Council of Constantinople, the Second Council of Nicaea. The Council added nothing to its meaning or authority. The disciplinary decrees therefore were the sole distinctive utterance of the Council which the Church might approve or reject. And it was precisely these decrees which she did finally stamp with her approval. This approbation surely, and no more, was intended when the Fourth Council of Constantinople was recognised as ecumenical.

10

THE NINTH GENERAL COUNCIL:
LATERAN I 1123

AT the time of the Eighth Council, the Church was entering the darkness from which she would emerge only after a century and a half, some seventy years before the Ninth Council.

There was indeed light in the darkness. These dark centuries witnessed the foundation by St. Romuald of the Camaldolese hermits, of wider effect the reform of Benedictine monasticism under the authority of Cluny ruled by a succession of saints in close touch with the papacy. In England there was the religious revival and reform associated with Alfred the Great and St. Dunstan. The Scandinavian countries having poured out hosts of pagan pirates and invaders, were converted to Christianity. Bohemia under St. Wenceslaus (d.929) and Hungary under St. Stephen (d.1038) received the Catholic faith. Slavonic kingdoms in the Balkans became Christian. In 988 Vladimir, Grand Duke of Kiev and Muscovy, exchanged paganism for Christianity, a harem for holiness. He inaugurated the conversion of Russia. However since Vladimir derived his Christianity from Constantinople the Russian Church would shortly drift into the final schism between the Orthodox and the Catholic Church. In fact, during this dark age there was a missionary effort more extensive and successful than anything achieved later until the sixteenth century. Nor was there any dearth of saints. Catholic holiness never has been, never can be, extinct. Nevertheless, by and large, these were the Dark Ages of Church history.

This period of darkness has been aptly denominated by Fliche et Martin's title to the volume of their history which relates it: the Church in the Power of the Laity.

From the papacy downwards, sees and other ecclesiastical benefits were filled by the appointment of the lay ruler, the emperor, the king, prince, nobleman or other landowner. These lay patrons too often abused their patronage by giving the bishopric, abbey, or other benefice in their gift to unworthy kinsmen or followers, commonly a layman who pocketed the revenues, or by selling it. Moreover, the law of celibacy was no longer enforced. Popes were chosen either by the most powerful member of the Roman nobility or, when in the tenth century the imperial power revived —German henceforward—, under the three Ottos, by the Emperor. We should not credit too readily the slanderous gossip of contemporaries about the popes' private lives. Only a small minority of the large number who in rapid succession occupied the see of Peter lived scandalous lives. Nevertheless, if we must not denigrate, we should not whitewash. Though, for example, there is no convincing evidence that John XII (955-964) was the monster of debauchery depicted from hostile sources by Duchesne, he was certainly not a chaste young man. Far more scandalous, surely, was the number of Popes and antipopes—it is not always easy to distinguish between them—who were mutilated or murdered themselves or mutilated or murdered others. The savagery of these Dark Ages did not stop short of the papacy. The radical evil was this lay appointment. Theophylact, his wife Theodora, their daughter Marozia, her son Alberic during the earlier years of the tenth century held the papacy in their pocket. Marozia could even appoint as pope John XI (931-936), her illegitimate son by pope Sergius III (904-911).[1] The emperor made better appointments as indeed did Alberic. But the bondage of the Church to the powerful laity remained. Divine Providence, however, ordained that these unworthy or insignificant popes should not be mouthpieces of dogmatic teaching. They were content to

[1] Mgr. Mann denies this relationship, Fr. Philip Hughes is doubtful. The writer, however, of this chapter in *Fliche et Martin's* History accepts it as established, so he tells us, by the testimony of the official Liber Pontificalis.

4

carry on, on the whole competently the normal administration of the Church.

This lay appointment was in fact rooted in the feudal system which took shape during this period of transition. According to this system, the sovereign, in the Empire, the Emperor, was the sole landlord. Princes or nobles held their domains (fiefs) from him as his tenants—tenants-in-chief, for which they did homage to him. Lesser landlords in turn held their estates from these tenants and so forth down to the peasants. The rent consisted in an obligation of military service and the payment of certain dues to the overlord. Bishoprics and abbeys, in fact all benefices whose rights and revenues derived from the land they held, were integrated into this system. They also were fiefs of a landlord, emperor, king, nobleman downwards, owing feudal services and appointed by the overlord. Not unnaturally the overlord wished to choose his tenant. In token of this, the imperial or royal over-lord *invested* bishops with these fiefs by placing a ring on their finger, a crozier in their hands, the homage due for their fief. The ceremony however inevitably suggested that the bishop derived his ecclesiastical jurisdiction from the lay ruler. It is referred to by historians as lay investiture.

In the eleventh century a reaction set it. Led by popes and supported by earnest churchmen, a movement arose to restore freedom to the Holy See and the clergy in general, reimpose celibacy, stamp out the widespread simony, sale of benefices. Such a reform, however, inevitably involved conflict with lay rulers, above all the Emperors. Even the canonised Henry II (1002-1024) kept a firm hold on the Church and, though a laudable desire to provide a worthy pastor was Henry III's motive, when at the Council of Sutri (1046) he deposed one if not two popes, it was none the less uncanonical. The first great reforming pope, St. Leo IX (1049-1054) was also Henry's choice. He launched a powerful attack on lay appointment, clerical marriage and simony. Unfortunately, against the Norman invaders of Italy he employed a less Christian method of warfare, leading an army against them, to his own well deserved defeat and imprisonment.

For this abuse the great reformer St. Peter Damian rightly denounced Leo. The year of Leo's death (1054) marked the final rupture with the Byzantine Church. It was the result of faults committed on both sides, the arrogance of the Greek patriarch Michael Cerularius and his hatred of Roman interference, but also the behaviour of the legates sent by Leo to Constantinople. Not content with charging Cerularius with heresies he did not hold, they took upon themselves to excommunicate the patriarch by a document laid on the altar of St. Sophia during Mass. Later attempts to repair the breach failed (see chs. 15, 18). Nevertheless, it was long before acts of inter-communion ceased entirely, if indeed they ever have.

Leo's successor Victor II (1055-1057) was the last imperial nominee. Henceforward the many nominees appointed by an emperor would be anti-popes. Though Nicholas II (1058-1061) owed his see to an acceptance by the Empress Regent[1] of the Roman candidate, he decreed that henceforward the pope must be elected by the Roman cardinals, bishops, priests, deacons of the Roman Church.

The protagonist of the Roman reform and papal freedom was Hildebrand who, for many years the power behind the papal throne, was elected pope in 1073 as Pope Gregory VII (1073-1085). His pontificate was an unremitting struggle for the reform against the emperor Henry IV and his German bishops. His motive was not, as it has been widely represented, ambition. He aimed at freeing and reforming the Church.

When for a moment in the famous episode of Canossa, Henry IV made a show of humble submission, it was but a successful manoeuvre to deprive his enemies of papal support. As the conflict proceeded between the reformers who employed and supported papal authority and the imperialists, many of the latter, bishops and archbishops, pushed to an extreme the imperial claim to rule the Church. The Emperor was declared the source of ecclesiastical jurisdiction—lord of the pope.

---

[1] Agnes, widow of Henry III. She was throughout a zealous supporter of the papal reform.

Gregory's means were not always as admirable as his ends. When Henry's usurpation upon the rights of the Church was met by Gregory's deposition of the Emperor, it was a counter usurpation upon the rights of the secular sovereign though a papal deposing power had in theory been affirmed as early as Gregory the Great. And the Pope's final decision to invoke the military aid of the Normans resulted in their sack of Rome and his own virtual imprisonment by his allies. Nevertheless, his struggle had not been in vain. Whatever the conflicts and revolts, the Church would uphold her freedom and persist in the work of reform.

Since the ceremony of investiture gave a visible and symbolic form to lay rule over the Church, it became the centre of the struggle. Urban II (1088-1098) waged brilliantly the contest against the Emperor, King Philip I of France, and the imperial anti-pope 'Clement III'. On the other hand, his success in launching the first of seven crusades to recover the Holy Places of Palestine from Moslem rule was more truly defeat, a spiritual defeat of Christianity by Islam. For the crusade employed in the service of Christendom the Mohammedan weapon of the Jihad, the Holy War. This first crusade, most successful of the seven, conquered Jerusalem, massacred its Moslem population and established a Latin kingdom in Palestine.

When Henry IV's son, Henry V, renewed his father's anti-papal policy and refused to abandon investiture, the new Pope Pascal II (1099-1118) offered in return for its abandonment to surrender the territorial possessions and jurisdiction of Catholic prelates. It was a noble gesture in the right direction. Unfortunately, it was utterly unrealistic. The Church was too firmly embedded in the structure of mediaeval society to be wrenched apart. Bishops and abbots would not, indeed they hardly could, give up their lands and temporal lordship. For without them they could hardly have maintained even their spiritual jurisdiction against encroachments of the lay ruler. An indignant protest followed, whereupon the Emperor arrested Pascal and sixteen cardinals. To such pressure Pascal capitulated. He crowned Henry and yielded the right of investiture. On all sides the supporters of clerical independence rose in revolt against the papal surrender. The Archbishop of Lyons broke into gross personal abuse of Pascal, calling the Pope bully and coward. The Archbishop of Vienne, Pascal's legate in France, called a Council on his own authority, which declared investiture heretical and excommunicated the Emperor. He even wrote in threatening terms to Pope Pascal: 'If you break with King Henry we shall be your faithful and devoted sons. *If you remain in union ... we shall withdraw from your obedience.*' He justified his threat no doubt by the consideration that simony was generally accounted heresy. Lay investiture was simoniacal, therefore heretical, and a pope who favoured heresy forfeited ipso facto his papal authority. The Pope bowed to a storm blowing, after all, in the direction he desired and revoked his concession. Eight years later, the stalwart Archbishop was himself elected Pope Callixtus II (1119-1124).

Callixtus effected a satisfactory settlement of the 'investiture' dispute. At a Council held at Worms (1122) an agreement, the Concordat of Worms was reached with the Emperor. Henry V renounced his claim to invest bishops by ring and crozier. Henceforward he would bestow the temporalities of the see by a touch of his sceptre. No one could any longer suppose the monarch the source of spiritual jurisdiction. On the other hand, a pledge that bishops should be freely elected was seldom observed. Overlords were determined to choose their tenants. Finally, the Church would formally grant the French and Spanish monarchs the right to nominate all bishops and abbots. Popes, however, would be freely elected by the cardinals.

This narrative must at this point be interrupted to recall events of greater importance. In 1108 St. Bruno, an eminent teacher and ecclesiastic of Cologne, with six companions established in an Alpine valley near Grenoble the first Carthusian monastery La Grande Chartreuse. The Order combines the life of the solitary with the community life of the monk.

Towards the turn of the eleventh and twelfth centuries there was established at Citeaux a community of monks living in accordance with the primitive austerity and simplicity, as they under-

stood it, of St. Benedict's rule. They had exchanged for white
the black Benedictine habit. Despite the successive rule of three
saints, Robert, Alberic and Stephen Harding, the community
flourished only in holiness. Lack of recruits threatened extinction
when in 1113 St. Bernard led to Citeaux a body of thirty novices
drawn from the Burgandian nobility. Henceforward the order
grew with amazing rapidity. Two years later Bernard was despatched to found the daughter-house of Clairvaux. In 1119 St.
Stephen issued his Carta Caritatis a constitution which bound
together all Cistercian houses by ties with an immediate mother
house and Citeaux. Its admirable combination of centralisation
and liberty rendered it a model for future organisations of the
religious life. A system of lay brothers cultivating the monastic
estates opened the religious life to the illiterate. Meanwhile St.
Bernard by his holiness, zeal, ability and attractive personality
became the prophet and mentor of the contemporary church.
When he died in 1153 there were more than 300 Cistercian monasteries containing hundreds of monks, by the end of the century
530.[1]

In 1123 Callixtus summoned at St. John Lateran, the Cathedral
of Rome, the Ninth Ecumenical Council. It inaugurated a series
of Councils widely different from the eight hitherto studied.
Their composition was Latin not Greek. Indeed in Italy
the majority of members were Italian. The number of
abbots, moreover, present at some of these early Latin councils,
greatly exceeded the number of bishops. The councils were
summoned not by a lay ruler but by the Pope. They were chiefly
concerned not with doctrine but discipline, moreover largely with
the same subjects, the decree of one council repeating or reinforc-
ing a decree of its predecessor. Some decrees re-enacted decrees
passed at local councils. Even exerpts from the writings of Church
lawyers, the canonists, were enacted as decrees. For this is the age
when the great collections of Canon Law, pre-eminently Gratian's
Decretum, were compiled. Many decrees dealt with particular
moral or social abuses—even individual examples of encroach-

[1] For all this see Dom David Knowles.

ment on the territory of the Church. The importance and interest of these Councils, therefore consists not so much in their achievement, mainly local and temporary, as in the expression they gave to the Church's action in a particular historical environment.

The First Lateran and Ninth Ecumenical Council met on 19th March, 1123. No minutes survive. There were certainly two, probably three sessions. As was the case in subsequent councils of few sessions, the business must have been prepared beforehand. Abbot Suger who was present, speaks of three hundred bishops attending, Pandulph of 997 members of the Council, certainly a gross exaggeration. Besides the 300 bishops there was no doubt a considerable body of abbots.

The Concordat of Worms was read and approved. The purport of the decrees, as in succeeding councils, was to reinforce the movement of practical reform. Decrees were passed against simoniacal elections of bishops and other clergy, against clerical wives and concubines—only women who are near relatives may live in priests' houses—against marriage in the forbidden degrees, against coiners. Once more concubinage and marriage in major orders were forbidden. Other decrees encouraged and protected Crusaders. They are granted 'remission of sins'. This is the grant of a plenary, a complete, indulgence. Some of the earliest indulgences known to Church history were granted to Crusaders.

Indulgences are confined to the debt of temporal punishment which may be due to him whose guilt has been remitted, a debt which at an earlier period had been paid by severe penances. They are, in fact, a systematised application of the solidarity of Christians as members of Christ's mystical body. When the guilt has been removed which cuts off an individual member from the life of this spiritual organism, he can benefit by a communication of its life of holiness. As the brain controls and directs the life of the body, the government of the Church controls and directs this movement of the spiritual life of the Church to the benefit of her members. Since the Church has no jurisdiction beyond the grave, indulgences for the dead, first granted by Sixtus IV (1471-

1484) must be understood as particular applications of the Church's prayer, as, it has been said, a particularly solemn form of prayer for the dead. Unfortunately, abuses long attended and defiled the practice of indulgences.

(1) From the outset they were employed to promote holy wars against the Moslems, heretics, schismatics, sometimes even rulers politically opposed to a pope. (2) Since alms giving might be among the good deeds for which an indulgence was granted, indulgences might in fact be purchased, an abuse not removed until the Council of Trent (see below, p. 198).[1] (3) Preachers led the people to believe erroneously that the operation of an indulgence was infallible even for the dead, without regard to the recipient's dispositions, provided he was not in mortal sin.

Another decree passed by the Council protected Crusaders' property during their absence. Those who have taken the Cross are to be compelled to keep their pledge. Pilgrims also are made the subject of special protection. Monks must not leave their monasteries to visit the sick or celebrate public Masses. Those who break the truce of God, that is to say, make war on their neighbours during the close season the Church had established, would be excommunicated. This enactment, like the truce itself, was an attempt, not wholly unsuccessful, to mitigate at least the persistent private warfare between bellicose barons. Ordinations by the anti-pope Gregory VIII were declared null.[2] Bishop Conrad of Constance was canonised.

---

[1] Not completely even then. Regard for the Spanish crown led to the survival to the present day of Cruzada indulgences purchasable in all places once subject to the Spanish monarch.

[2] Discussion of this decree is reserved till we treat of a similar decree passed by the next ecumenical council.

11

THE TENTH GENERAL COUNCIL:
LATERAN II 1139

ON the death of Pope Honorius II (1130) two opposing factions among the cardinals elected two claimants to the papacy: Innocent II (1130-1143) and 'Anacletus II'. As yet, no law prescribed the proportion necessary for a valid election. Though Innocent was elected first, a greater number of cardinals elected Anacletus. It would seem that neither candidate was canonically elected. Another election should have been held. No one, however, appears even to have suggested this course. The prophet and teacher of the Church at this time was St. Bernard. He came forward as Innocent's energetic champion, deciding, however, in his favour not on any canonical grounds but simply because he regarded Innocent as the better man. His preference was 'the intuition of his own conscience'. 'He had never made a fetish of Canon Law.'[1] Bernard won over the French crown and Church, his friend St. Norbert, the German. Innocent triumphed and must be regarded as legitimated by the election of the Church.

His victory assured, Innocent determined to ratify it by the voice of a General Council. The Tenth Ecumenical Council Lateran II, met in April 1139, on April 4th at latest. Its canons survive, but its history is little known. Three sessions were probably held. Contemporary estimates of the attendance range from 500 to 1000. Some five hundred to six hundred bishops and

[1] See *Dictionnaire de Théologie Catholique.*

101

abbots were probably present. The final session was certainly held before April 17th.

The anti-pope and his supporters were solemnly condemned. Innocent's vengeance degraded even cardinals who had later submitted to him, in particular Cardinal Peter of Pisa, who when his support was still valuable, had been welcomed and confirmed in his cardinalate. This vindictiveness, in some cases amounting to perfidy, the more inexcusable, because the papal election had been so dubious, evoked St. Bernard's fruitless protest. Unnamed heretics were condemned who rejected the Eucharist, Baptism, the priesthood and marriage. They were to be excommunicated and punished by the secular rulers. The heretics envisaged were no doubt the earliest Cathari to make their appearance in Western Europe. In the Balkans they were known as Bogumils, probably from their founder's name. For these Cathari, later to be widely known from their strong foothold in Provence, Albigenses, rejected all the Catholic sacraments, above all marriage. They regarded matter and therefore the human body and its procreation as the work of an evil being, either as some taught, a bad god, co-eternal with the good God or, as others taught, a rebel angel. They were divided into two classes, the Believers who accepted the teaching of the sect and supported it, and the Perfect who ruled it. The latter, having received the only sacramental rite they practised, an imposition of hands, the Consolamentum, were henceforth bound to strict continence and rigid dietary rules. No flesh might be eaten or the product of any animal. Thus, it was believed, they escaped to the utmost measure possible the bondage of evil matter and after death would be free from it everlastingly.

Of the thirty Canons passed by the Council, no less than twenty-three repeated previous legislation. A majority in fact were contained in Gratian's Decretum. Laymen were forbidden even to hear Mass said by priests who keep a concubine. It was a prohibition incapable of enforcement and its enforcement does not seem to have been seriously attempted. Laymen were forbidden to possess benefices or tithes. The right of cathedral chapters to elect bishops was confirmed. Safety was guaranteed to clerics, monks, pilgrims, merchants and tillers of the soil. The truce of God was again enforced. A canon (7) pronounced the marriage of clergy in major orders (from the subdiaconate upwards) not only as hitherto unlawful but invalid.[1] Marriage within prohibited degrees and usury, taking interest[2] were forbidden. Special penalties were enacted against arson, a crime particularly easy and destructive when most houses were built of wood, also for violence against the clergy. This was the first solemn declaration of the sanctity attaching to their persons in virtue of their orders. Churches and cemeteries must not be violated. Tournaments were forbidden. 'The art, deadly and most hateful to God, of those who use catapults and shoot arrows in warfare against Christians and Catholics we forbid on pain of anathema' (excommunication). These canons, in particular the prohibition of archery as too lethal a weapon, deserve particular attention today. There are many who would wish the pope in this secularised world where, moreover, vast numbers are more or less nominal Catholics, to forbid 'under pain of anathema' all concerned in the preparation of nuclear weapons or serving in the armies of States which make them. Certainly the moral law and in particular the conditions of a justifiable war as laid down by canonists and moral theologians sufficiently condemn such weapons as immoral. But what prospect of success would there be for such a papal prohibition? Its sole result would be widespread disobedience and probably persecution by the State. In this wholly Catholic Europe of the twelfth century, a pope in an ecumenical council condemns forms of warfare adopted universally by mediaeval rulers. Not one even troubles to object. No notice whatsoever is taken of the prohibition. Archery indeed will win many a battle. Later, Innocent III renewed this condemnation. Once again it is ignored. The mightiest mediaeval pope, a pope sufficiently powerful to defeat kings, for example, our King John, was impotent to make any Catholic ruler abandon

[1] Nevertheless clerical marriage long persisted in some countries, particularly in Scandinavia and Iceland.

[2] See below, p. 104.

the weapons it was advantageous to employ. The prohibition of tournaments was equally ignored. The tournament, in fact, seems to us one of the most characteristic mediaeval institutions.

The canon against usury, interest, was the second of a series of such conciliar condemnations which will culminate when the Council of Vienna (q.v.) will brand usury as heretical. The condemnation was based on the conviction that money cannot breed and the lender therefore is entitled only to the return of his loan. Money however does breed indirectly by its use e.g. in the purchase of livestock or fruit trees. In fact even mediaeval moralists permitted interest on several counts, e.g. undue delay in repayment of the loan whereby the creditor incurred loss, partnership in a commercial enterprise. Reaction against Calvin's permission of interest stiffened the Church's opposition to it. In practice however the prohibition could no longer be enforced. In a mercantile, industrial and capitalist society individuals and groups, if they were to survive economically must charge interest on a loan. Finally in the nineteenth century the Church recognised the inevitable, somewhat tardily it is true, and permitted interest. Whether an economic system which she resisted to the bounds of possibility and beyond is from the Christian standpoint ideal may be questioned. In any case the moral principle underlying the condemnation of usury that a loan *in itself* is no title to interest is unaffected by the economic question whether in fact a loan does not normally involve the surrender of a profitable use of the money lent and on that account, *though not in itself* is a just claim to interest.

The final canon (30) runs: 'Moreover, we make void ordinations conferred by Peter Leone (the anti-pope, Anacletus) and by other schismatics and pronounce them null'. This canon, like a similar canon passed by the first Lateran Council against ordinations by the anti-pope Gregory VIII, raises the difficult question of reordinations. During the earlier centuries and once more since the great theologians of the thirteenth century, the Church has taught and practised the doctrine that ordinations conferred in due form and with due intent even by schismatical bishops are valid. From the eighth century, however, the papacy lost sight of this truth and contravened it in practice. A Roman Council of 769 declared null all ordinations conferred by the anti-pope 'Constantine II' (767-769), admittedly a duly consecrated bishop. John VIII (872-882) commanded the reconsecration of the Bishop of Vercelli because he had been consecrated by an excommunicated bishop; Sergius III (904-991) the reordination of all ordained by Pope Formosus (891-896) falsely supposed an anti-pope but admittedly a bishop. Another Roman Council held in 864 ordered the reordination of all ordained by Leo VIII, possibly an anti-pope. The reforming popes of the eleventh century not only declared null ordinations by anti-popes and their adherents but assimilated simonists to schismatics. Leo IX (1049-1054) reordained many who had purchased their orders. It is indeed probable that at the period of these Lateran Councils, in accordance with an influential theological opinion, ordinations and consecrations by bishops themselves consecrated in Catholic unity were not repeated on reconciliation, the sacramental powers thus conferred being regarded as tied up and therefore ineffective until reconciliation with the lawful pope, and that we must understand in this sense the nullity intended by the Councils. For this was the doctrine taught in Gratian's authoritative text book of Canon Law. Even so, the doctrine invalidated ordinations conferred by a bishop consecrated in schism. In any case at an earlier period, the eighth and ninth centuries, schismatic ordinations, or those held to be such, were regarded and treated as null.[1] Saltet in the Dictionnaire de Theologie Catholique[2] concludes: 'the politico-religious conflicts of the ninth and tenth centuries combined with the growth of theological ignorance, produced in Catholic teaching nothing less than a misconception of the theology of orders ... not a doctrinal development but a theological regression of long duration and serious import'.

At the Vatican Council those who opposed the definition of papal infallibility brought up these papally commanded re-

---

[1] Two contemporaries, Auxilius and Vulgarius, protested against these reordinations and defended the true doctrine.

[2] *Art Réordinations.*

ordinations. 'The reply' comments Saltet 'was sometimes loss of temper. The facts must be admitted and the theologians must take them into account when demarcating the scope of infallibility.' A simpler and, it might seem, more satisfactory solution of this problem suggests itself, that as head of the Church and guardian of the sacraments, the pope has power to alter the conditions required for a valid ordination, as he has in fact altered the conditions required for a valid marriage. Theologians, however, do not favour this conclusion.

12

THE ELEVENTH GENERAL COUNCIL:
LATERAN III 1179

SETTLEMENT of the dispute about investitures did not, could not, bring to an end the struggle between the temporal and spiritual ruler in a society in which secular and sacred were knit so intimately. Barely thirty years had elapsed since the Concordat of Worms when the Emperor Frederick I Barbarossa began his reign (1152). Fired with ambition to restore the absolute supremacy of the Roman and Byzantine emperors, he was soon at war with the papacy. As Roman Emperor he claimed suzerainty over the Pope. Having established his rule in Lombardy, he summoned a council of bishops to decide a papal election disputed between Alexander III (1159-1181) and 'Victor IV' elected by only three cardinals. When Alexander refused to recognise his competence as judge, Frederick called a Council of his supporters which declared Victor pope (1160). Victor would be succeeded in turn by other imperial nominees, 'Pascal III' and 'Callixtus III'. In 1167, Barbarossa captured and sacked Rome where his anti-pope recrowned him. Alexander's final victory was, however, secured some years later when a league of revolting Lombard cities inflicted a decisive defeat on the Emperor at Legnano (1176). He found himself obliged to recognise Alexander, made his submission at Venice and was absolved by the Pope (1177).

Alexander took advantage of his victory and peace with the Emperor to summon another General Council, the Third Lateran

Council and Eleventh Ecumenical Council. He was well equipped
for the task. For he was the most eminent canon lawyer of his
age. The Council opened at the Lateran on March 5th; 291
bishops are listed but more than 300 attended, 124 of them
Italian, and even more abbots. There were bishops from France,
Spain, England, Ireland, Scotland, Germany, Denmark and
Hungary, and from the Crusaders' Latin kingdom in Palestine.
Three sessions were held on March 5th, 7th or 14th, 19th or 22nd.
Twenty-seven disciplinary decrees were passed. Ordinations by
the anti-popes and their supporters were annulled. In this instance, however, it is fairly clear that in the case of those consecrated or ordained outside the schism and those ordained by
bishops so consecrated, their orders were regarded as valid but
their exercise suspended. And this may well have been, as we
have seen, most probably the meaning of the earlier conciliar
decrees (Lateran I and II). Henceforward a majority of two-
thirds would be required for a valid papal election. No one under
fifty years of age might be consecrated bishop. Money payment
for sacraments was forbidden. Benefices might not be promised
during the life of the present occupant. Monks must be admitted
free of charge and must not own private property. Pluralism was
forbidden, the prohibition of clerical concubinage renewed.
Clerics may not act as advocates or executors of a will. Laymen
may not appoint to a benefice without the bishop's consent, deprive
the holder of his benefice, plunder or tax Church property,
Churches or clergy.[1] Every cathedral must support a schoolmaster
to give free instruction not only to clerics but to other poor youths.
This was at least a gesture on behalf of free education for the poor.
Laymen may not interfere with the exercise of episcopal jurisdiction. Once again, usury and tournaments are ineffectively condemned, the truce of God enforced on pain of excommunication
for repeated breach. Security is once more pledged to priests,
monks, strangers, merchants, cultivators of the soil, on pain of
excommunication. Lepers must be provided with special churches

---

[1] It was customary, however, for the clergy to tax themselves *voluntarily*, it was
professed, to support the king.

and cemeteries and are freed from tithes. Excommunication is denounced against all who provide Saracens with munitions of war or materials for shipbuilding, assist them in warfare against Christians or serve on their pirate vessels, also on all who enslave or rob Christian seafarers or ship-wrecked Christians. Saracens, it would seem, have no rights. Neither Jews nor Moslems may possess Christian slaves, nor may Christians take service with them. Since the property of Jews was legally held to be the property of the monarch, Christian rulers were disposed to confiscate the possessions of Jewish converts, which they could no longer claim as their own. The practice was forbidden.

The canons of these councils are for the most part directed to two purposes, freedom for the Church and her ministers, the promotion of decent standards of behaviour among Christians. Neither object, however, was in practice fully achieved, in some cases not at all.

A severe condemnation was pronounced against the Cathars now strongly established in South Western France. The followers of Peter Waldo who demanded from all Christians a life of apostolic poverty were mildly rebuked. The Pope still hoped for their return to orthodoxy. In fact, they developed into a sect of Protestant character, the Waldenses. A Crusade was launched against gangsters, bandits and murderers—perhaps disbanded soldiers.

This twelfth century witnessed another renaissance of culture, the codification of Canon Law hand in hand with a revival of Roman Civil Law, the beginnings of scholastic philosophy with the speculation of Abelard and the controversies it aroused, the theological summary compiled by Peter Lombard, the contemporary birth of the University of Paris and Gothic architecture, the foundation of the military orders of the Templars and Hospitallers, monks and soldiers in one, to assist in the Crusades and the defence of Christian Palestine, of the Cistercians and the White Canons. Crude and harsh in certain of its manifestations, fresh and vigorous life was rising in the veins of Western Christendom.

Of particular importance was the cultural renaissance more

humanist and literary and in this akin to the renaissance of the fifteenth century than thirteenth-century scholasticism. Bishop Henry of Blois, King Stephen's brother, brings back to England from Rome an antique statue. Monastic libraries are rich in classical texts. Over the birth of Gothic architecture presides an aesthetic philosophy of light and mathematical harmony, of Neo-platonic origin and identical with the aesthetic professed by artist and architect of the later Renaissance. We should in fact regard Carolingian culture as the first renaissance, twelfth century culture as the second, the Renaissance so-called as the third. All alike are characterised by a return to classical antiquity and a Christian humanism.

13

THE TWELFTH GENERAL COUNCIL:
LATERAN IV 1215

IT was not long before the inevitable struggle between Pope and
Emperor for supremacy over a society in which secular and
sacred, politics and religion, were so intimately interwoven broke
out anew. When Frederick married his son and heir Henry to the
heiress of the King of Sicily, the papal territory was exposed on
both flanks to the power of the Hohenstaufen Emperors. Papal
protests were unavailing. It is indeed difficult to discover any
religious or moral justification for them. In consequence war
was waged in Italy between Henry, now joint emperor with his
father, and the Pope. Meanwhile, in 1187, Saladin reconquered
Jerusalem from the Christians. The Crusade organised to recover
the city failed. It cost the life of the aged Emperor Frederick,
drowned as he was marching through Asia Minor. Henry himself
died in 1197 when he had succeeded in establishing his power in
Italy.

The following year the greatest mediaeval pope, Innocent III
(1198-1216) began his pontificate. Like Alexander III he was
an eminent canonist. His achievements were many. He formally
established what would be the intellectual centre of mediaeval
Europe, the University of Paris (1205). He blessed the birth of
the two great orders of preaching friars—the Franciscans or the
Friars Minor, followers of St. Francis of Assisi, and the Dominicans, the Friars Preachers. The former were founded to revive
the evangelical life led by Jesus and his Apostles, though unlike

the Waldenses, in obedience to ecclesiastical authority; the latter, though accepting the Franciscan way of life, to combat heresy. Dominic and his followers were employed against the heresy of the Cathars (see above p. 102) who, supported by local rulers, dominated extensive territories in South Western France. Unfortunately, when preaching proved insufficient to vanquish the heresy, Innocent invoked the aid of barons from Northern France and proclaimed a Crusade against the Albigenses. The Crusaders were led by Simon de Montfort, father of the Simon who summoned the first English Parliament. After some years of arduous fighting they were victorious. The strongholds of heresy were won for de Montfort, ultimately for the French king. Venetian interests diverted a Fourth Crusade against Constantinople and the city fell to the Crusaders. They set up a Latin emperor and a Latin church (1204) not without sacriligious insults to the sanctities of Greek religion and wholesale plunder of relics. Though the conquest had been made in defiance of his prohibition, Innocent accepted the *fait accompli*, a decision which not surprisingly inspired the Greeks with a hatred of the Latins so intense that two attempts at reunion, at the Second Council of Lyons and later at the Council of Florence, would be rendered abortive. With monarchs, Innocent took a high hand. He compelled the Kings of Portugal and Leon and the more powerful King Philip Augustus of France to dismiss women they had married in defiance of ecclesiastical law. An interdict compelled John of England to surrender to the Pope when he had refused to accept the papal choice of an Archbishop of Canterbury. John even accepted the Pope as his feudal overlord and, although his motive was to secure papal support against recalcitrant barons, the effect was to enhance papal power in the political field. In Germany when the imperial election was disputed, Innocent claimed a papal right of decision. He imposed his will on the Emperor Otto as the price of recognition. When Otto turned against him, he replaced him by his 'own ward', Henry VI's son Frederick. Four kingdoms, Sicily, Portugal, Aragon, and England were now papal fiefs. Innocent built up to its height the antithesis of the imperial claim to rule the Church. It is the Pope, not the Emperor, who is head of the intertwined secular-religious society, the Emperor, and this is true a fortiori of every monarch, derives from the Pope his imperial authority, to be used in the service of the Church and obedience to her earthly head. 'If he refuses obedience, he forfeits his authority and the Pope may depose him.' Constantine's donation (see above p. 26-7, 77) is now regarded as the recognition of a supreme temporal authority already possessed by the Pope as the Vicar of Christ to whom "all power in heaven and on earth" has been given by His Father. "The plenitude of Papal power embraced every conceivable aspect of human life." "The Sovereign Pontiff holds God's place on earth." It embraces mankind, infidels as well as Christians. Innocent IV will declare: "It is our faith that Christ's Vicar the Pope possesses authority not only over Christians but also over all unbelievers since Christ possesses authority over all." He may therefore punish infidels for their sinful worship of idols or refusal to admit Christian missionaries. He governs the Emperor as the soul governs the body. Imperial and all other secular jurisdiction derive from him. For the Church and in the divine intention humanity is one body and one body cannot possess two heads.[1]

From the same principle of unity the imperialists drew their opposite conclusion. The anonymous eleventh-century writer of the York Tracts, probably an Archbishop of York or Rouen, had pressed to the utmost the claims of the secular monarch. The Pope has no authority superior to that of other bishops. The King on the other hand is superior to the priest, for he has received the royal power which stems from Christ's Godhead, the priest the sacerdotal power derived from His humanity. The King is 'the figure and image of Christ as God', is indeed 'Christ', invested with the authority of Christ as God. Such was the extremity of monarchical claims.

At the other extreme, Innocent speaks of the Pope as 'set in the midst between God and man, on this side of God, on the

---

[1] For all this see Ullmann: *Mediaeval Papalism passim.* Quotations and conclusions have been taken from this study.

other side of man, less than God but more than man'. His words will be echoed a century later by the canonist Joannes Andreae: 'The Pope is the marvel of the world . . . he is neither God nor man but . . . intermediate between both'.[1]

We may deplore these conflicting usurpations, both alien to the teaching of the Gospel. Once, however, the integration of Church and State is admitted, and it was taken almost universally for granted,[2] religion must prefer papal to imperial or regal supremacy of the Church-State society. For religion not secular politics is the supreme human value and though ideally it should not be defiled with politics, when the union is inevitable, religion must rule politics not vice versa.

The practical weakness of the imperial claim to supremacy over Catholic Christendom as contrasted with the papal was the fact that whereas the supreme ecclesiastical authority of the Pope was accepted everywhere, imperial authority was confined to a portion of the area. Elsewhere supreme temporal jurisdiction devolved upon a national monarch. Under such circumstances belief in one head of the Christian society must operate in favour of the papacy against the empire. On the other hand the national monarch because he confines his claim to jurisdiction to the area where it is effectively exercised will succeed, when the Emperor had failed, and not only assert his independence of the papacy in the temporal sphere but restrict in many ways the pope's ecclesiastical government.

In such a situation and to promote his aim, a papal government and organisation of Christendom, Innocent summoned an Ecumenical Council which should confirm and assist his endeavour, the Fourth Council of the Lateran and the Twelfth Ecumenical Council.

It was a far more important and imposing assembly than the previous papal councils. And it was marked by two innovations.

[1] Quoted from a papal sermon by Dr. W. Ullman: *The Growth of Papal Government in the Middle Ages*, p. 429, note 3. The quotation from the York Tracts was taken from the same book, p. 200.

[2] Dante will deny it and point to a better and more genuinely Christian relationship between Church and State. But he was a voice crying in the wilderness and if the Emperor to whom he appealed had been successful, he would have enslaved not emancipated the Church.

The Council was prepared for two years before it met. Preliminary invitations were despatched. And the membership was no longer confined to the clergy. In addition to 19 cardinals (the mediaeval college was very small) and some 400 archbishops and bishops[1] and 800 religious superiors, there were representatives of the laity in large numbers. 'All the secular governments from empires and kingdoms down to municipalities and feudal rulers were represented.' It was not that the layman would have a share in framing or discussing the Council's decrees—that was very far from the Pope's intention. What he desired was a body representing not the clergy alone but the laity also, that is to say, the Church as a whole, which as such would accept his rulings, more particularly perhaps because so many of the decrees concerned the laity.

The bishops came from Italy, a majority of course, France, the British Isles, Germany (a few), and Latin prelates from the East. The Maronite patriarch, ruler of the Syrian community in the Lebanon (to this day united to the Holy See) attended, also two bishops from Livonia and Estonia.

The Council opened on 11th November, 1215. Before this first session and between the others private meetings were held.

Innocent inaugurated the Council by an address in which he spoke of the dangerous position of the Holy Land and of the Albigenses. He was supported by reports made to the Council by the Patriarch of Jerusalem and the Bishop of Agde (South Western France).

At the second session (20th November) the Pope as suzerain of England excommunicated the barons who had risen against John and Archbishop Langton who had supported them, nullified, as extorted by force, John's oath to observe Magna Charta. Innocent no doubt saw the Charter, not without reason, as an attempt by the barons to weaken the royal authority established by Henry II and return to the baronial anarchy of Stephen's reign. The session, however, was principally occupied with the rival claims to the empire, of Otto of Brunswick and Frederick II

---

[1] Jedin gives an exact number 404.

still a minor and Innocent's ward. When the discussion led to a brawl between the representatives of Milan and the Court of Montferrat, Innocent dissolved the session.

The third and final session was held on the 30th November. Innocent peremptorily declared Frederick Emperor, conferred part of the possessions of Count Raymond of Toulouse on the Catholic leader Simon de Montfort. The doctrine of the Trinity propounded by Abbot Joachim of Flora in which he would seem to have distinguished insufficiently between the Godhead and the Persons, was condemned but, in welcome contrast to the anathemas of some earlier councils, his orthodoxy of intention and holy life were recognised. No less than 70 decrees were passed.

Were the prelates but a sounding board for the proclamation of Papal decrees? Not entirely. The Council rejected a scheme put forward by the Pope to finance the curia by a system of regular contributions levied universally. At least when their purse was affected the bishops could display independence.

Two canons are Professions of Faith directed respectively against the Cathars and Joachim's Trinitarian error. In the former, which affirms the sacraments against Catharist denial, the term 'transubstantiation' was officially used for the first time to denote the change at consecration of bread and wine into Our Lord's Body and Blood. This, however, was not a doctrinal development. It was purely a matter of terminology.

Decrees were passed on the rights of patriarchal sees, on provincial councils, on the procedure of Church courts trying criminal charges. Since, for the time being, the See of Constantinople was in Latin hands, the decree of Chalcedon which accorded it second place before the other Eastern patriarchates, was at last accepted by the papacy. Every Church sufficiently wealthy must provide a teacher for poor clerics, every metropolitan church in addition a teacher of theology. No new religious order might be founded. Anyone wishing to embrace the religious life must join one of the orders already approved. Innocent, however, had already given his informal approbation to St. Francis and his followers, and St. Dominic when his order of preaching friars was approved the following year, would avoid or evade the prohibition by adopting the Augustinian rule adding merely special constitutions. Nevertheless, the prohibition would render the position of other nascent orders of friars precarious because formally illegal. It would finally fall into abeyance.

Canons were passed against clerical incontinence, drunkenness, gambling, hunting and the wearing of secular dress. Green and red are particularly forbidden. No cleric may take part in trials involving a capital sentence, participate in executions, fight or even, since it involved bloodshed, act as surgeon. Nor may he bless an ordeal.[1] The clergy must attend the divine office, say or hear Mass regularly. For 'there are priests, even bishops who say Mass hardly four times a year, neglect even to hear it and when they do, chatter with lay folk and pay no attention to the Mass'. Every Catholic of either sex must confess at least once a year to his/her Parish priest and receive Holy Communion. Nothing is said of the qualification taught by Catholic theology that the obligation of confession binds only those conscious of grave (mortal) sin. Either the Council took it for granted, or assumed that everyone would commit at least one mortal sin a year, or more probably the principle had not yet been worked out in the theological schools. Bl. Benedict XI (1303-4) would declare that although not strictly necessary, yearly confession even of sins already absolved was valuable and should be preached as such.[2]

Once more pluralism was condemned. Its prohibition by the Third Lateran Council had produced little effect. Neither would this or any other mediaeval condemnation. Other canons regulated legal procedure, condemning abuses. Patrons must respect the rights of the clergy they appoint to a benefice. For good cause and with papal sanction, the clergy may offer voluntary contributions to their rulers. The matrimonial impediment of consanguinity, relationship by blood, and affinity, relationship by marriage, was restricted to the fourth degree, third cousins. It was a reform long overdue. For in a population comparatively small

[1] The decision of guilt or innocence by subjecting the accused to a physical test of endurance.
[2] Denzinger: Enchiridion, 470.

and composed of communities mainly stationary, the impediments of consanguinity and affinity, hitherto imposed to the seventh degree, sixth cousins, the latter moreover contracted by any sexual relationship however casual, must have made marriage extremely difficult and extremely uncertain.[1] The canon, moreover, pointed out that the *fourth* degree is recommended by the fact that the body is composed of four humours, the world composed of four elements![2] Clandestine marriages, that is marriages not solemnised publicly in Church, were forbidden. They were not, however, declared invalid until the Council of Trent. Tithes were to have a priority over any other tax. During an interdict[3] bishops might say an occasional Mass in private. Itinerant preachers in quest of alms must be authorised by the Pope or diocesan bishop. Pilgrims must not be deceived by lies or forgeries. Several canons were passed against simony. Though voluntary offerings at marriages and funerals were to be encouraged, they must not be demanded. A canon was passed against Jewish userers from whom Christians were to be protected by the State.[4] Jews and Moslems must wear a distinctive badge—a canon discreditable to the Council and savouring of Hitler rather than Christ.

Another canon introduced a system of visitation between houses for Benedictine monks now grouped for the first time into provinces. The Council closed with the papal proclamation of a Crusade to save the Holy Land, the Fifth Crusade. It would leave two years later and prove a failure.

In all these early Latin councils of the twelfth and thirteenth centuries we notice a preponderance of legal decisions concerned, for example, with the procedure of Church courts, elections, property rights. For they belong to the centuries which elaborated and codified the structure of canon, that is of Church Law, the

[1] See article by Egerton Beek in the *Dublin Review*, 1921.

[2] Canon Law today restricts the impediment further to the third degree, second cousins.

[3] An interdict is the prohibition of the Office Mass and most sacraments. It was employed as a weapon against contumacious rulers with the hope that their subjects thus deprived of the consolations of their religion might rise in revolt. It had just failed against King John who had yielded only to the threat of a French invasion papally blessed.

[4] Jews could and did lend at interest to Christians. Without grave sin Christians could not charge interest from fellow Christians.

age of the great Canon lawyers among whom were three Popes, Alexander III, Innocent III. Innocent IV who summoned ecumenical councils. In the mediaeval Church indeed proficiency in Canon Law was the quickest and surest way to ecclesiastical advancement. This preponderance of Canon Law will excite Dante's Indignation (Paradiso IX 133-135). The pressing task, however, of all mediaeval government was to establish the reign of law against the constant threat of lawlessness, of relapse into anarchy and private warfare. It was a situation which necessitated and therefore justified this ecclesiastical legalism.

14

THE THIRTEENTH GENERAL COUNCIL:
LYONS I 1245

As we might have expected in a world but half real, the Catholic Church in the thirteenth century displays an obverse and a reverse, the former brilliant, the latter dark.

The new orders of friars, Franciscans and Dominicans, were reviving a truly evangelical way of life and, determined to use learning in the service of Christ, took command of the intellectual movements of the century. In many places, in England at Oxford and Cambridge, Universities where all branches of study were taught were springing up and the friars would soon be preeminent in the philosophical and theological schools. The philosophy of Aristotle, re-discovered about this time, took possession of the schools. At first it was found difficult to reconcile it with the faith and in consequence papal prohibitions forbade it to be taught. Both however would soon be harmonised in a comprehensive and subtle integration of philosophic knowledge and revealed theology. The great architect of this synthesis was the Dominican St. Thomas Aquinas (1225-1274). His master, the Dominican St. Albert the Great (c.1200-1280) had begun it. But by temperament and interest he was more of a scientist than a philosopher. St. Thomas was the greatest philosopher the Church has produced and though one must not credit him with an infallibility to which he made no claim himself, no sound philosophy can neglect his monumental achievement. For it is a philosophy, heir of Aristotelianism and Neoplatonism, a philosophy of being in all its forms and degrees, a philosophy firmly based on the certainties of human experience and common-sense rising to the summit where Divine revelation and grace meet, fulfil and crown the utmost reach of natural wisdom, a philosophy in which the rights and insights of mind and spirit[1] are recognised and reconciled.

Another outstanding philosopher of the older Platonic-Augustinian school was the Franciscan St. Bonaventure. Both St. Bonaventure and St. Thomas taught at the University of Paris. Since they taught in the philosophical and theological schools, these philosopher-theologians are known as the schoolmen, their philosophy as scholasticism. With St. Albert, Grosseteste and Roger Bacon, who foretold motor vehicles, aeronautics and under water exploration, science, defunct since the Greeks, was re-born.

The turn of the century would be distinguished by yet another great philosopher Duns Scotus, the subtle doctor, and the greatest Christian poet Dante. A truly catholic vision of reality at once profound in its religious depth and comprehensive of all that was known, was open to the Christian intelligence. It was mirrored by the splendour of Gothic architecture and art, the cathedral and the abbey, and by the beautiful liturgical worship offered in these sanctuaries to the Creator of beauty. Nor was there a lack of saints. Moreover, the Christian society was envisaged as an integral structure, a living organism at whose summit presided Christ's earthly Vicar.

Such in the barest outline was the obverse of thirteenth century Catholicism. Unfortunately the reverse is as evident.

Despite the intellectual achievement of the schoolmen, the mass of the clergy were grossly ignorant, very many ill-living. The average bishop was at best a competent official, often employed in the service of the monarch or a feudal lord, living in luxury and state amid a populace ignorant of their religion, superstitious, condemned to squalor and poverty. Bitterly indeed would Pope Gregory X complain of his bishops (see below p. 132).

---

[1] To use Bertrand Russell's useful designation and distinction *'Principles of Socia Reconstruction.'*

The papal claim to supreme temporal authority led to the adoption of Caesar's weapons. The Crusade, the Holy War, now extended to heretics first, then to Catholic rulers condemned by the Church, the establishment of military orders, departed far from Christ's methods of extending God's kingdom. Heresy was fought not only by prayer and preaching but by the atrocities of the Albigensian Crusade and the establishment of the Inquisition. Gregory IX—ironically, as cardinal, St. Francis' friend and protector[1]—definitely sanctioned the death penalty, and death by fire for the convicted heretic. It was the first time that the papacy had ever formally sanctioned the death penalty for heresy[2]. A few years later in 1252 Innocent IV, the Pope who summoned the Thirteenth Council, not only approved but commanded in inquisitorial procedure the use of judicial torture which Pope St. Nicholas I, followed more recently by the canonist Gratian, had condemned as opposed to human and divine law.[3] A particularly unpleasant feature of the Inquisition was the invitation, indeed exhortation, of Catholic children to denounce an heretical parent.[4] Torture chamber and stake—these have no place in the service of Christ's 'kingdom of truth and life . . . of justice, love and peace.' So long, however, as the Church was bound up so intimately with the political kingdom of force, power and greed, that divine kingdom could not appear in its purity. The papacy had thus entered upon the downward path which in the following century would lead to the massacres of Cesena in 1377 and Faenza in 1376, to a band of mercenaries looting, murdering and raping, to the war cry 'the Church, the Church'.[5]

A desperate struggle was soon engaged between the papacy and Innocent III's erstwhile ward, the Emperor Frederick II. Brilliant, cultured, patron of art and learning but cruel, unscru-

[1] Even St. Francis, however, could ordain in his Testament that an obstinately heretical friar should be handed over to the Inquisition.

[2] It had been condemned by Pope Siricius when employed for the first time by the Emperor Maximus in the teeth of St. Martin's protests.

[3] For the contradiction see Philip Hughes, *A History of The Church* (ed. 2), Vol. 2, p. 411, also Canon Vacandard, French historian of the mediaeval Inquisition Article '*Inquisition*' in Hasting's *Encyclopaedia of Religion and Ethics*, Vol. 7.

[4] See Alfonso de Castro: *De Justa Punitione Haereticorum*, Lib. II.CH.VI.ed. 1568, pp. 281.

[5] See Alice Curtayne: *Life of St. Catherine of Siena*, pp. 95, 120-1.

pulous, probably sceptical at bottom of revealed religion, Frederick, entrenched firmly to the north and south of the papal states was determined to restore the majesty and unbridled autocracy of the Roman Empire, to achieve an imperial supremacy over Church and State alike. The Popes, hard pressed, refused no weapon spiritual or unspiritual: excommunication certainly but deposition also and the organisation of a Crusade, and, to pay the troops, heavy papal taxation of all countries and Churches where the papal writ was acknowledged. Zeal, resources, energies, which should and might have been employed in evangelising the masses and in missions to the Tartars, then ripe for conversion, were diverted to this war, political as well as religious and largely fought by weapons not religious at all.

It was at the height of this struggle with Frederick and to promote its success that Innocent IV (1243-1254) decided to summon an ecumenical council. Like Innocent III an eminent canon lawyer, Innocent IV carried the claims of papal prerogative even higher than his predecessors. As God's earthly representative he could dispense with the letter (*verba*) of the gospel though not the spirit (*mentem*), could dissolve, though he never attempted to do so, a consummated Christian marriage.[1] Nevertheless, in his war against the Emperor he needed the moral and material support of his spiritual subjects—and a council afforded the best means of obtaining it. The Pope also sought, as in the case of the Twelfth Council, support for another Crusade in the East. Preparatory letters were despatched, representatives of lay rulers invited. The Council's principal objective was announced; Frederick's deposition. Since Frederick's power in Italy rendered Rome unsafe, the Council was summoned to meet in Lyons. There the Pope would enjoy the protection of the royal Saint Louis IX of France, but in a city subject to the temporal government of its archbishop. Meanwhile, he raised the College of Cardinals from nine to twenty-two.

[1] See Brian Tierney: *Foundations of Consiliar Theory,* p. 89. This brochure published by the Catholic University of Washington, in England by the Cambridge University Press, is indispensible together with the writings of his master Ullmann we would understand the canonist background of mediaeval Catholicism.

After a preparatory meeting on 26th June to fix the agenda, the opening session was held in St. John's Cathedral on 28th June, 1245. The numbers attending are unknown. The English monk and historian Matthew Paris not a reliable authority, reckons 140 archbishops and bishops. 100 names are known: 13 cardinals, 3 patriarchs, 34 archbishops, 29 bishops, 5 abbots, the Franciscan and Dominican Generals, Archdeacons, canons and laymen. Of these there were 38 members from France, 30 from Italy, 11 from Germany and the northern countries—fear of Frederick prevented many attendances from his dominions though the archbishops of Mainz and Cologne attended—8 from England among them Bishop Grosseteste of Lincoln, philosopher, scientist and practical reformer, four from Spain, five from the Latin East. Baldwin II, the Latin Emperor of Constantinople was present.[1] To state his case against the Pope, Frederick sent 6 ambassadors.

At the first session, Innocent sang Mass and preached. His soul, he said, was afflicted by five sorrows: the misconduct of prelates and people, the progress of the Saracens, the Greek schism—large portions of the Byzantine territory were under Greek and schismatic rulers—Tartar invasion—at one moment the Tartar hordes had threatened to overrun the whole of Europe—the persecution of the Church by the Emperor Frederick. An imperial envoy duly entered his protest. A delay of ten days was granted for the receipt of Frederick's reply, or his personal attendance.

The second session was held on 5th July. Despite indignant protests by the Pope's more ardent supporters, a further delay of 12 days was granted.

The third session was held on 17th July. Frederick was solemnly excommunicated and deposed. 'We forbid anyone henceforth to obey him as Emperor of Germany or King of Sicily.' A new election of an Emperor must be held, the Pope with his cardinals' advice would provide a king of Sicily. At the close of the sentence, lighted candles were extinguished by the bishops and thrown to the ground. At this session English noblemen en

---

[1] A royal mendicant, his reign was indeed mainly devoted to begging for help against the Greeks who were rapidly reconquering the territories lost in 1204 to the Crusaders.

tered an ineffective protest against bestowing English benefices on foreigners.

A final session on 25th August closed the Council.

The feast of our Lady's birthday, September 8, was provided with an Octave finally abolished only in 1955. But Edmund of Canterbury, recently dead, was not, as had been said, canonised by the Council.

22 canons were certainly passed of which eight confirm earlier legislation. No alternative vote would be admitted at elections— as now in British Parliamentary elections. Several canons regulate judicial procedure.

When a new bishop or abbot takes office, inventories of the property of the diocese or monastery must be made. This property must not be alienated and debts must be paid off. Regulations were laid down in regard to the incurring of future debts. One half of the income of benefices whose incumbents are non-resident shall be attached by papal collectors and used to assist the Latin Empire of Constantinople and the Christian kingdom in Palestine. Greek armies threatened Constantinople. The Saracens had recently recaptured Jerusalem, this time a final conquest. Crusaders are granted privileges and a plenary indulgence, misleadingly termed 'the pardon of their sins'. Strong measures are urged against the Tartars whose savagery is described in revolting terms. Finally, a Crusade is proclaimed, to which the clergy must contribute a twentieth of their revenues. It would be the Sixth Crusade, yet another failure during which St. Louis would be captured.

The Council was followed by the organisation of a Crusade against Frederick. All who took part in it were granted the privileges and indulgences accorded to Crusaders against Islam. A rival emperor was elected in Germany and in 1248 the papal troops in Italy won an important victory. It was, however, Frederick's sudden death in December 1250 which assured final success to the papacy. His son Manfred, it is true, was able to establish himself in Naples and Sicily. But the papal candidate for his throne St. Louis' brother, Charles of Anjou, ambitious

5

and capable, at the battle of Benevento in 1266 inflicted a crushing defeat on Manfred who was himself slain. It was the end of Hohenstaufen power, indeed of imperial rule in Italy. Not until the sixteenth century would an Emperor prove a serious threat to papal independence. After his death Innocent IV had conquered. But it was at the cost of debasing and secularising the methods employed by the papacy and arousing bitter resentments, as for instance in England, against papal demands for the necessary funds, demands which made the papal government appear a burdensome and extortionate moneymaking machine. Moreover, the costly effort left the papacy weakened before the rising power of the national monarchies as they overcome feudal anarchy and consolidate their government, extending its authority over their entire domains.

15

THE FOURTEENTH GENERAL COUNCIL:
LYONS II 1274

WHEN in 1274 Pope Gregory X (1271-1276) whose personal holiness has earned him the title of Blessed, *Beatus*, summoned another ecumenical council, it was no longer to combat an empire decisively defeated. Its purpose was one particularly relevant to-day, a purpose which will also be the purpose of the Seventeenth Ecumenical Council, the Council of Florence, an aim which undoubtedly Pope John XXIII's Council will have particularly in view, namely reunion with the separated 'Orthodox' Churches. In 1261 the Greek Emperor Michael (VIII) Palaeologus had reconquered Constantinople from the Latin Emperor Baldwin II. But although Baldwin, who died in 1273, was himself of little menace to his conqueror, when his son Philip married the daughter of Charles of Anjou, Michael was confronted by a dangerous and daring foe. To his rear, rival Greek principalities threatened his insecure throne. Under these circumstances, he determined to detach the Pope from his Latin enemies by effecting a reunion with the papacy, and in company with his patriarch Veccos, approached Pope Gregory. If Michael's motive was political, the fact that Veccos will remain a champion of reunion till his final defeat and death, argues on his part at least sincerity. Gregory at any rate was not the man to reject overtures in which he saw the hand of God. He therefore convoked a Council to effect a formal reunion of the Latin and Greek Churches. No doubt to avoid the dangerous proximity of Charles who, when triumphant, had proved himself a dubious ally of the papacy, he summoned the Council to meet at Lyons. Once more, preliminary invitations were issued. The Greek Emperor Michael was invited to send plenipotentiaries. Other monarchs were invited among them Philip III of France. Particularly urgent was the invitation to Edward I of England, a crusading champion. James I of Aragon also received a pressing particular invitation. Despite the notorious laxity of his private morals, James was a zealous Catholic champion who won Valencia and Majorca for Christendom, devout, patron of saints and religious orders.[1] The two leaders of Christian thought, St. Bonaventure and St. Thomas Aquinas, were summoned to a Council to be concerned mostly with doctrinal issues. St. Thomas, however, died en route at the Monastery of Fossa Nova. St. Bonaventure became the luminary of the Council.

The attendance was large, Chroniclers speak of more than 1,000. The official minutes mention 125 names. There were certainly more than 200 bishops. They included all the six German archbishops, 31 French bishops, 25 from the Spanish peninsula, 25 English. There were prelates from Italy, France, Germany, England, Spain, and the Latin East. St. Thomas' teacher St. Albert the Great and the Servite[2] Master-General St. Philip Benizi, the Dominican Peter of Tarentaise, later to be Innocent V, were present. The German Emperor, the Kings of France, England, Sicily and Cyprus sent representatives, also the Tartar Khan. King James of Aragon attended in person. The Council opened at Lyons on 7th May, 1274. In his inaugural address, the Pope defined the objects of the Council: recovery of the Holy Land, reunion with the Greeks, moral reform. The Greek envoys had not yet arrived.

At the second session on the 18th May, news was received

[1] The story that on the same night Our Lady appeared to St. Peter Nolasco, St. Raymond of Penafort and King James to command the foundation of the Mercedarian order for the redemption of Christian captives is derived from a forgery of the seventeenth century. Indeed she would not have found it easy to choose a night on which she could have appeared appropriately to the king.

[2] The Servites (Servants of Mary) were an order of friars particularly devoted to the contemplaton of Our Lady's sufferings. They were struggling for the recognition they finally secured.

that the Greeks were definitely on the way. On receipt of the news, a solemn Mass of thanksgiving was sung at which St. Bonaventure preached.

At the third session on 7th June, after a sermon by Peter of Tarentaise, the Council passed 12 canons. It was presumably at this session, certainly before the arrival of the Greeks, that the Council promulgated a confession of faith in respect of the principal doctrinal issue between the Latins and Greeks, the procession of the Holy Spirit from the Father and the Son, 'Filioque'.

The majority of grievances brought by the Greeks against the Latins concerned trivial matters of discipline or liturgical usage. The Greeks objected to the Latin use of unleavened bread in the Eucharist, some even denied that it was valid matter for consecration, the Latin fast on Saturdays, the Latin use of milk foods between Septuagesima and the beginning of Lent, that the Latins confined confirmation to bishops[1] and despised a married clergy.[2] Their most serious gravamen, however, was their objection to the Latin addition to the 'Nicene' Creed that the Holy Ghost proceeds from the Father and the Son. Increasingly the Greeks will deny the doctrinal truth of the statement. The Holy Ghost, they say, proceeds from the Father through the Son. To speak otherwise, they argue, is by implication to deny the Divine Unity which can admit but one source of the Divine Processions. To meet this objection, the Council now defined that the Holy Ghost proceeds indeed eternally from the Father and the Son *but* as one source not two distinct sources and by one not two distinct outbreathings (spirations). The Greek view seemed to subordinate the Son to the Father. The Greeks were, however, unanimous and had been from the outset, in objecting to the addition 'and the Son', 'Filioque' to the Creed as unauthorised. Here, certainly, they were on firmer ground. The addition had been first made by the Spaniards in 589 when King Reccared was converted from

---

[1] This is no longer strictly the case. Parish priests not only may but *must* confirm anyone who is dying unconfirmed, even little children.

[2] An objection to Latin baptism because it is administered by sprinkling not immersion—it has even been declared invalid—was not raised so early. Throughout the Middle Ages babies were still baptised in the Latin Church by nude immersion in the font.

Arianism with its subordination of the Word. It spread very slowly, to the Gallican Church first of all. Charlamagne, however, convinced that the clause was a genuine part of the Creed, had pressed it upon Pope Hadrian I (796) and, it would seem, introduced it into the Mass when he adopted the Roman rite. Hadrian's successor St. Leo III, though he sent some Palestinian monks a profession of faith affirming the Filioque, refused Charlamagne's request to add the words to the Nicene Creed. Indeed, he asked the Emperor in vain to abandon the addition which continued to spread in the West. It was not until 1014 when Benedict VIII (1012-1024) acceded to the request of the Emperor St. Henry II and introduced into the Mass at Rome the recitation of the Creed that the Filioque was accepted as part of the liturgical text.

The Council, though defining the doctrine of the double procession, made no decision as to the liturgical use of the Filioque.[1]

On 24th June, the Greek envoys arrived. They represented the Emperor and the Greek episcopate. One had been patriarch of Constantinople. They presented letters accepting the confession of faith which the papal nuncios had prescribed. They had come, they declared, to profess 'entire obedience to the Holy Roman Church, to acknowledge her faith and her primacy'.

For the moment the Greek and Latin Churches were officially reunited, the schism healed. On 29th June, Pope Gregory celebrated a solemn Mass of thanksgiving for the union at which St. Bonaventure preached. When the Creed was sung, the Greeks repeated three times in Greek 'Who proceedeth from the Father and the Son' and they intoned the solemn liturgical acclamations of the Pope.

On the 4th July, ambassadors arrived from the Tartar Khan.

At the fourth session on 6th July, Peter of Tarentaise and the Pope preached. As representative of the Emperor, Michael George Acropolita professed the faith of the Roman Church and did obeisance to the Pope. 14 canons were enacted.

On 15th July, St. Bonaventure died and was buried.

[1] At the present day, though the Eastern uniates are obliged to profess the doctrine of the Filioque, they are not required to use the clause liturgically.

At the fifth session, 16th July[1] a Tartar envoy was baptised. The Pope commanded all bishops and priests to say a Mass for St. Bonaventure's soul. 14 canons were enacted.

At the sixth and final session, on 17th July, a further canon was passed and the Council was concluded. At this Council Rudolf of Habsburg was declared Emperor in preference to his competitor Alfonso of Castile. He was the first Habsburg Emperor. King James of Aragon was compelled to do homage to the Pope as his feudal vassal. King Philip of France surrendered the Venaissin to the Pope. The papacy thus acquired an enclave in France. The Tartar embassy attempted in vain to conclude an alliance with the Christian rulers against Moslem Egypt. The alliance, of which Edward I was a persistent advocate, might have won Palestine and Egypt for Christendom.[2]

On 1st November, Gregory published 31 canons. All except three had been passed by the Council. The first is the doctrinal definition of the double procession.

A canon first enacted on 16th July laid down detailed regulations for the conduct of the Conclave of Cardinals electing a Pope. If no Pope is elected within eight days the cardinals must fast on bread and water. The many lengthy conclaves of later date prove the penalty a dead letter.

Several canons regulate episcopal and other ecclesiastical elections. Anyone who, to take revenge because his candidate has not been elected, plunders the possessions of the Church or molests the electors, incurs excommunication. A bishop who ordains in another bishop's diocese is forbidden to ordain for a year, during which time his own clergy may seek ordination from neighbouring bishops. Bigamists, that is to say men who have been twice married, are debarred from the clerical state. Divine service must not be suspended in virtue of an alleged custom, still less holy images thrown out on to waste ground. This canon was no doubt directed against the irreverent, even blasphemous, orgies celebrated yearly in many, especially French, cathedrals by canons

---

[1] Some of these dates seem uncertain. The detail of these mediaeval councils cannot always be ascertained with certainty.

[2] See Christopher Dawson: *The Mongol Mission.* Introduction XXVII-XXXI.

and choristers—the so called Feast of Fools. Grosseteste, in fact, had lately suppressed this abuse in his cathedral of Lincoln. Law suits must be speeded up, advocates' fees fixed. Absolutions from excommunication or other censures, extorted by fear of violence are invalid. Prelates must not alienate church property to laymen without the Pope's consent. To obtain his protection, the clergy had sometimes transferred property to a powerful lord retaining the yearly revenues it produced. The prohibition by the Fourth Lateran Council (Q.V.) to found new orders is renewed. Reverence must be observed in liturgical worship. Everyone must bow the head at the name of Jesus. 'Nothing must disturb the peace, there must be no brawls, loud cries, debates, meetings municipal or otherwise, no frivolous and worldly conversation.' Neither markets nor courts of law may be held in churches or cemeteries. Excommunication is decreed against anyone be he nobleman or king who kills or offers violence to the bearer of an ecclesiastical censure. Further enactments are passed against usury.

An attempt made at this Council to launch a new Crusade and tithes granted in its support came to nothing. The age of Crusades had passed and in 1291 the last Christian foothold in Palestine, Acre, would fall.

At the Council, Gregory confessed and lamented his inability to carry out the moral reforms he desired. 'Prelates,' he complained, 'were bringing the entire world to ruin.'

In the Byzantine Empire the union provoked violent resistance from large sections of the clergy and laity, bitterly hostile, as they were, to the Latin Church. The brutality with which the Emperor suppressed these revolts further embittered the opposition. A Council held at Constantinople (1277) though accepting papal supremacy, refused to take an oath to that effect as being opposed to Greek custom, or to add the Filioque clause to the Creed.

When Nicholas III (1277-1280) in arrogant tones demanded the oath and the clause, he played into the hands of the opposition and rekindled revolt against the union. His successor Martin IV (1281-1285), a personal friend of Michael's enemy Charles of

Anjou, rebuffed the Emperor's embassy sent to congratulate him on his accession. Provoked by this rudeness, Michael, though he did not formally renounce the union, removed the Pope's name from the liturgy. Martin allied himself with a league formed by Charles, Venice, and other Latin rulers for the reconquest of Constantinople 'to exalt the orthodox faith, re-establish apostolic jurisdiction and restore the Latin empire.' The attempt was frustrated only by the revolt which cost Charles Sicily. In support of the league, Martin excommunicated Michael. The same year (1281) Michael died, hated by his subjects, and his son and successor Andronicus broke off relations with the papacy. Successive Greek synods rejected the Filioque. In 1297 Veccos died in prison, the one man who could have saved the union had it been possible to save it. So short lived was the reunion of Lyons. Though the stupidity and pride of Pope Nicholas and Pope Martin hastened its demise, in any case it was unlikely to be permanent. Byzantine hatred of the Latins had been fed by the sack of Constantinople, the forcible latinisation of the Church, outrages committed against its worship and the establishment of a Latin kingdom. As a writer in the *Dictionnaire de Theologie Catholique* observes, the union was both too late and premature, too late for it followed the conquest of 1204, premature because that conquest was so recent. It was therefore artificial, rejected from the outset by Greek public opinion.

16

THE FIFTEENTH GENERAL COUNCIL:
VIENNE 1311-1312

POPE BONIFACE VIII, Benedetto Gaetani (1294-1303), has had
the worst possible press, to be pilloried down the ages in the
Divina Comedia by Dante. Dante's attack, like those of Boniface's many other enemies, is grossly unfair. Boniface was a well
intentioned man, zealous for the good of the Church and the
prerogatives of the Holy See. But he was tactless, when he thought
his cause was winning, arrogant, when he thought it losing, weak.
He could address his cardinals in the language of a bully. When
Cardinal Jean le Moine ventured a criticism, Boniface burst out:
'Pighead from Picardy, I want no advice from asses like you.'[1]
He was faced by an able and unscrupulous foe, King Philip IV
of France, supported by the new enemy of a universal Church,
the national sovereign state. At first, Philip's friend, Boniface,
protested strongly against royal taxation of the clergy without
his approval. It had indeed been more than once condemned by
ecumenical councils (see p. 108 and p. 117). He retreated, however, from his position and finally permitted the King to tax his
clergy in the case of a national emergency to be determined by
himself. The enthusiastic devotion shown by pilgrims from all
countries who gathered at Rome for the first papal jubilee[2] in
1300, encouraged, however, a stronger line of action and he de-

---

[1] Bernard Tierney: *Foundations of Conciliar Theory*, p. 181-2.

[2] A jubilee is a year when extraordinary indulgences are granted to pilgrims to
Rome. Originally confined to a centenary year they soon became more frequent.
This was the first.

nounced Philip's claim to try the Bishop of Pamiers in his own courts. He cited the King to a Council he intended to summon. Philip's reply was to assemble in Notre Dame representatives of the Clergy, nobility and municipalities. Papal usurpations on the rights of the French Church were denounced, the King was proclaimed the defender of the Church, subject to no one in the exercise of his temporal authority. Boniface himself was pronounced a usurper of the Holy See. The assertion, echoed, though not consistently, by Dante, was made on the ground that a Pope cannot resign and therefore that the resignation of Boniface's predecessor, St. Celestine (1294) and consequently Boniface's election were invalid. A crushing defeat in Flanders involving the death of three of his agents against whom the Pope had prophesied disaster, made Philip for the moment more amenable. He sent representatives to the Pope's Roman Synod, who acknowledged him as true Pope.

At this synod, 1302, Boniface issued the famous bull 'Unam Sanctam' in which he affirmed the Pope's supreme authority, even in the temporal sphere. We can however interpret this authority as a divine right to supreme temporal sovereignty or as an exercise of the papal authority to denounce and punish the moral delinquency of all Christians including monarchs. The language of the bull favours the former interpretation particularly in the light of canonist doctrine (see above p. 113). On the other hand when he was faced by Philip's indignation Boniface fell back upon the latter interpretation.[1] The famous pronouncement that 'it is indispensable for salvation that every human creature be subject to the Roman pontiff' is ambiguous. It can and no doubt should be understood solely of spiritual and ecclesiastical subjection: Boniface however undoubtedly intended it also of temporal and political subjection.

Philip in reply sent his councillor William de Nogaret to Italy to arrest Boniface, falsely claiming to be Pope. Meanwhile, at the Louvre, he convoked a second assembly. The Pope was denounced as a heretic, idolator, worshipper of the devil. A council

[1] See note to excerpts from the Bull in Denzinger's Enchiridion.

must judge him and Philip must summon it. Of 26 bishops present, all but one subscribed this protest. When the news of the French Council leaked out, Boniface prepared to excommunicate and depose Philip. To prevent this, Nogaret and the Pope's bitter enemy Sciarra Colonna, at the head of an Italian troop made a raid upon Anagni where the Pope was staying. Boniface was insulted, even struck. Nogaret, however, dared not kill him and the populace expelled the invaders. The shock was too much for the Pope's strength. A broken man he was brought back to Rome to die.

Boniface's successor was a saintly Dominican Bl. Benedict XI (1303-1304). Faced with general reprobation, Philip sent an embassy to the new Pope who accepted this show of repentance and forgave him. Philip, however, persisted in his demand for a Council to try the conduct of the late Pope. All Philip's supporters were pardoned except Nogaret and his fellows in the outrage of Anagni. But as the Pope was preparing to proceed against them, he died.

After a conclave of 11 months, certainly not passed on bread and water, a Frenchman, the Archbishop of Bordeaux was elected and took the name of Clement V (1305-1314). Crowned at Lyons he never left France. Of ten cardinals he created, nine were French. Finally, he settled in the papal enclave of Avignon, in the heart of Philip's territory, which for the following 70 years will be the seat of the papacy. Clement's private life was certainly all that could be desired. Nevertheless, he stands guilty of one of the worst crimes committed by a Pope. He was Philip's tool against the Templars.[1] The Templars were a wealthy order and had in fact become international bankers. Their house at Paris was 'the centre of Europe's money market'. Philip, casting greedy eyes on their wealth, launched a campaign of calumny against them. They were charged with hideous immoralities, blasphemy and idolatry. After initial resistance, Clement, bullied and threatened by Philip, allowed himself to become his accomplice.

[1] Dante symbolised the relation between Clement and Philip as a prostitute seated on the chariot which represents the Church and embracing a giant.

The unfortunate Templars were tortured into a confession of these preposterous charges. Anyone who on release from torture recanted his extorted confession was burned as a relapsed heretic. Torture was also employed outside France at the Pope's command. In England where its use was forbidden by the common law, Clement insisted upon it. Only in France, however, were the charges 'proved'.

Meanwhile, Philip had compelled Clement to open a trial of his predecessor Boniface against whose memory charges were brought as abominable and as absurd as those made against the Templars. Fortunately for Clement, a change in the international situation made Philip consent to abandon the trial. The Pope, however, quashed all the acts against the King passed by his predecessor, absolved Nogaret and the other culprits of Anagni. Philip was praised for his zeal and good intentions in his anti-papal campaign. The fate of the Templars would be referred to a Council on which the Pope had decided for some years past— the Fifteenth Ecumenical Council. In its long struggle with the papacy, the national state had won the first round.

The preliminary invitations to this Council to be held at Vienna had gone out as early as August 12th 1308. From the first, Philip's shadow lay over the Council. Though all bishops were invited, only those were ordered to attend whose names were mentioned in the letter of invitation, names believed to be agreeable to the French King. It was a hint to the others to stay at home. Two lists of these invited bishops are extant. One contains 231 names, the other in Paris 165. Leclerq[1] considers the latter list Philip's final reduction of the Papal list of 231, Jedin considers the longer list a papal amplification of Philip's list of 165. Certainty is impossible. Many of the invited bishops declined the invitation on the ground of expense.

The Council opened on 16th October, 1311. Twenty cardinals were present, 4 patriarchs, 29 archbishops, 79 bishops, 38 abbots, the Franciscan and Dominican Generals, procurators of absent prelates. The majority of bishops were French and Italian. But

[1] Article on the Council of Vienna. Dictionnaire de Theologie Catholique.

the Archbishops of Taragona, Braga, Compostella, York,
Armagh, Dublin, Cologne, Magdeburg and Bremen attended.
The Kings of Aragon and England sent ambassadors. But there
was no general representation of the lay rulers. From the first
one representative of King Philip attended, a second from 17th
February of the following year. On 20th March, Philip himself
arrived.

Until his arrival no decisions were taken. Between December
and April the question of a Crusade was discussed and the means
of financing it, a waste of time when the Crusade was an ana-
chronism. To the Pope's embarrassment a committee of bishops
urged that the Templars should be heard in their own defence.
Philip's envoys prevented any decision being taken in their
master's absence, 'without whom nothing has been done' as they
parodied the Gospel.

Two days after Philip's arrival on 22nd March 1312, the first
public session was held. The servile committee reversed its just
decision and by a majority of four to one, recommended the suppression of the Templars.

At the second session on 3rd April, Clement V by a personal
act suppressed the Templars. Some scruple of conscience, however, made him allege as his motive not the Templars' immorality
but the better administration of the Church. Much could be
said for the suppression of a religious order of soldiers and
bankers, but not in these hideous circumstances of calumny, torture and stake. Moreover, the Council was not permitted to
debate the matter. Silence was imposed under pain of excommunication. The Templars' property was transferred to the
Hospitallers. In fact the greater part of their French property
was seized by Philip, partly on the plea of expenses incurred in
the investigation and torture. Tithes were imposed for the pro-
jected Crusade.

At the third and final session on 6th May, doctrinal decrees
were passed. They were probably aimed at opinions held by the
deceased Franciscan theologian Peter John Olivi or attributed
to him. No name is mentioned. The wound in Christ's side, it is

taught, was inflicted after not before his death. This indeed is definitely stated by St. John. The teaching 'that the rational soul is not of itself and essentially the form of the body' is condemned as heretical. In the philosophical terminology then generally accepted, the decree affirms that there are not many souls in man. One soul rational and immortal not only gives the body its animal life but makes the living body what it is. The decree does not however commit Catholics to this Aristotelian terminology. In the case of inorganic matter, the form is the shape, quality, character imposed upon the material. For example, Napoleon's likeness is the form of the marble out of which his statue is sculptured. In *this meaning* of the term, however, the soul of a living organism is obviously not its form. My soul is not the shape, quality, character of my body. It would surely be more accurate to call the soul the formative principle of the body, that which gives it its form. If therefore we term man's rational soul not the form but the formative principle of the body, we are true to the meaning of the definition.

That baptism not only remits original sin in us but also confers grace and virtues was not indeed defined as an article of faith, but affirmed as the more probable opinion.

In the twelfth century, communities of women living a 'religious' life without vows had sprung up—known as beguines, and together with them bodies of mendicants known as beghards. Many, probably most, of these were orthodox and their way of life would be finally sanctioned by the Church, the beguine indeed surviving in Belgium to the present day. Some, however, had fallen victim to a perfectionist illusion. Perfection is possible in this life. The perfect man or woman need no longer fast, pray, or practise virtue, is no longer subject to the Commandments of the Church, because he is already as perfect as the souls in heavenly bliss. No one should descend from the height of contemplation to worship the Host at the Elevation. Sexual intercourse when it satisfies a natural urge is not sinful. These errors were condemned. From the start, the Franciscan Order had been a prey to dissension between those who desired to observe the extreme poverty of St. Francis and his earliest disciples, the lax, and the majority who held a middle course. The zealots who called themselves Spirituals claimed to be not only the sole genuine Franciscans but the sole genuine Christians. The Council without espousing the cause of the Spirituals decided in favour of the stricter understanding of Franciscan poverty—only a scanty use of the necessities of life. The next pontiff John XXII (1316-1334) would condemn the Spirituals and their doctrine of Christ's absolute poverty, not without the hideous accompaniment of the stake for the pertinacious.

To defend usury, interest, as lawful was pronounced heretical.

The following year the agony of the Templars came to its tragic end. The Grand Master, Jacques de Molay, because he publicly retracted the confessions extorted by torture, was burned by Philip's order in Paris with two companions. The story arose that the dying man had summoned King and Pope to answer for their crimes at the divine judgment seat. If he did so, his appeal was heard. Within a year both were dead.

17

THE SIXTEENTH GENERAL COUNCIL:
CONSTANCE
1 NOVEMBER 1414-22 APRIL 1418

THE seventy years of papal residence in Avignon have been called the 'captivity' of the Holy See to the French monarchy. This is very far from the truth. Of all the Avignonese popes only the first, Clement V, was a captive of the French king. His successor, John XXII (1316-1334) was too strong minded to be the servant of any monarch. After his death the Hundred Years War between England and France weakened the French monarchy so that it was in no position to dictate to the popes. Nor do these popes deserve the odium attached to them by the invective of an ungrateful Petrarch—Clement VI (1342-1352) legitimised his children—or a censorious St. Bridget. Friendly at first to Innocent VI (1352-1362) she finally denounced him as 'worse traitor than Judas, more cruel than Pilate ... for the sum of his misdeeds "Christ" has flung him into the abyss ... condemned his cardinals to be burned by the same fire which consumed Sodom'.[1] At worst these popes were too weak or too indulgent to restrain effectively the immorality of their relatives and entourage, too accommodating to evil in high places. Even Urban V (1362-1370) whose personal holiness has won him the title of Blessed could send the Golden Rose to Joanna of Naples, notorious for her amours and suspect of her husband's murder. Clement VI (1342-1352), whose Court for its luxury and display vied with the

[1] Revelations IV, CXXXVI, quoted by G. Mollat: *Les Papes d'Avignon*, pp. 100-101, also by Philip Hughes: *A History of the Church*, Vol. 3, p. 187.

Court of any secular prince should rather be remembered for his protection of the Jews. When the masses, terror stricken by the Black Death, launched a wide spread pogrom against the Jews charged with poisoning the water supply, Clement not only gave hospitality to Jewish refugees but excommunicated their persecutors.

What in fact rendered the Avignon papacy widely unpopular was its constant financial demands, due mainly to its position in a country devastated by war and armed marauders, and the expense of defending the papal territory in Italy. It is extremely difficult in fact to decide how far we can believe the constant and well nigh universal complaints that the papal curia had been degraded into a money-making machine and in consequence had become the fountain head of ecclesiastical corruption. Not only was gross exaggeration conventional mediaeval rhetoric. We must also bear in mind the widespread pulpit denunciations of the extortion and wickedness of the pope and the Roman curia. Whereas Catholics today are taught to revere and love the Holy Father *as a man*— 'our Pope, the great, the good'—in the later Middle Ages they heard very different teaching. In short, to point a truth by exaggerated statement, we may say that, as regards popular Catholic estimation of the Pope, as distinct from his office, the pendulum has swung from 'the Pope can do no right' to 'the Pope can do no wrong'.

Professor Barraclough has studied the system of papal provision, appointment, to benefices denounced so vehemently by mediaeval critics of the Curia. He concludes: 'One fact is certain. The system of provisions operated with all the safeguards and impartiality of a system of law. . . . Legitimate rights were not over-ridden, legitimate exceptions were not excluded. . . . There was a rigid, balanced, self-operative system of judicial procedure in which no room was left for arbitrariness and caprice and every safeguard was provided against corruption and abuse'.[1]

We can however hardly dismiss as without foundation com-

[1] G. Barraclough: *The Exercise of Papal Provisions in the Canonical Theory of the Thirteenth and Fourteenth Centuries,* quoted by Joseph Gill, S.J.: *The Council of Florence,* p. 62.

plaints so universal. Professor Barraclough's verdict may well be an exaggerated reaction to a condemnation far too indiscriminate. Boniface IX (1389-1404) did undoubtedly pursue a shameless policy of money-making, selling and re-selling benefices and privileges to the highest bidder; under him the offices of the curia began to become venal.[1] Gregory XII, though the truth about his conduct is difficult to ascertain exactly 'seems to have behaved with appalling cupidity and weakness'.[2]

Nevertheless curial corruption was certainly not the radical cause of the evils afflicting the Church. Such as it was, and it has been exaggerated, it was itself an effect of the amalgamation of secular and sacred, temporal and spiritual. National monarchs, moreover, were increasingly averse to the taxation of their subjects by a foreign ruler, even a pope. The English statutes of Provisors and Premunire forbidding papal appointment to English benefices and appeals to Rome, would indeed for almost two centuries be nothing more than unemployed weapons in the royal arsenal, a support for royal bargaining with the Pope. The latter statute, however, would finally provide Henry VIII with a lever to overthrow papal supremacy.

In the fourteenth century the philosophical synthesis constructed by the great schoolmen of the thirteenth century notably St. Thomas disintegrated. Philosophers of the Nominalist school tended to a scepticism and positivism which undermined the validity of metaphysics. Reason, they maintained, could not establish with certainty universal principles, truths exceeding the particular facts of sense perception. Religious truth, the existence of God, could therefore be certainly known only by faith in a revelation suspended in an intellectual vacuum.

At the same time national self-consciousness, even in the ecclesiastical sphere was gaining strength at the cost of supernational Catholic allegiance. A publicist in the service of the Emperor Lewis of Bavaria (1314-1347) whose disputed election Pope John XXII had refused to recognise, Marsilius of Padua defended,

---

[1] See E. I. Jacob: *Essays on the Consiliar Epoch*, p. 35-6.
[2] Peter Partner, *The Papal States under Martin V.*

particularly in his Defensor Pacis 1327, not only the complete independence of the state from control or interference by the Church but its ecclesiastical supremacy. The Erastianism of the York Tracts (see above p. 113) is reaffirmed. Marsilius' imperialism was supported by the English philosopher William of Ockham. The Emperor derives his authority not from the Pope but the electors. Ockham however did not like Marsilius deny the Pope's ecclesiastical authority though he subordinated it to the superior authority of a General Council.[1]

On the other hand, this period was the age of the great mystics, men and women in whom the spirit of the Catholic religion burned with its purest and hottest flame. It was the age of Eckhardt, Suso, Tauler, and Ruysbroeck—in England of Richard Rolle, Walter Hilton, the anonymous writer of the Cloud of Unknowing and its continuation, The Epistle of Privy Council, Dame Julian of Norwich, the two latter, authors of, what are in my opinion, two of the greatest religious classics. Contemplatives were many. In Germany there were the Friends of God. In England, we are told, Denys' Mystical Theology ran though the country like wildfire, was, that is to say, a best seller.

Two great women combined in an eminent degree contemplation and action, were in fact prophetesses. St. Bridget of Sweden addressed her exhortation and rebuke to popes, prelates and princes, wrote her book of Revelations and founded the double order of St. Saviour, called henceforward by her name, where the nuns and the monks who ministered to their spiritual needs were alike subject to the rule of the Abbess. St. Catherine of Siena, a Dominican tertiary, gathered around herself a group of devoted friends, men and women, climbed the summits of mystical union, dictated letters of spiritual guidance, of warning or entreaty, wrote her Dialogues, addressed, like her Swedish sister, popes and rulers, encouraged the vacillating Gregory XI in his resolve to return to Rome.

Urban V (1362-1370) returned to Rome but left it once more

---

[1] For all this see Frederick Copleston, S.J.,: *A History of Philosophy*, Vol. 3, Introduction, Chapters 2, 9 and 11.

and retreated to the security of Avignon and, although his successor Gregory XI (1370-1378) also returned to Rome, only his death prevented the return to Avignon on which he had decided. The exhortations of St. Catherine of Siena had lost their influence.

The Conclave elected on 8th April, 1378, the Archbishop of Bari, Bartolomeo Prignano, who took the name Urban VI (1378-1389). It was undoubtedly a free election. Urban was duly crowned. For three months the cardinals acknowledged him as Pope, seeking favours and privileges from his gift. Urban, however, a conscientious administrator of humble origin—to the end he displayed the mentality of a hardworking civil servant—and not a cardinal, had as little expectation of the papacy, as a permanent civil servant has of becoming Prime Minister. The unexpected elevation turned his head. Though he had only too good reason to denounce simony and corruption among the cardinals his outbreaks of ungovernable fury, the insults he heaped upon them—on one occasion he was held back from assaulting a cardinal in consistory, not to speak of his insolent behaviour towards princes and nobles, soon rendered his rule intolerable. Moreover, as Dr. Ullmann points out[1] the cardinals whatever their faults of character, were aristocrats whose behaviour was conventional. Urban, a man of the people, took pleasure in snubbing those of better birth than his own, princes of the world or the Church. In short, his behaviour was unconventional. The cardinals had expected in vain that the Pope they had raised up would know his social place and do their bidding. Dismayed and indignant, they withdrew to Anagni, declared Urban's election null, because it had not, they said, been free (2nd August) and a little later, assured of the support of Charles V of France, elected (18th September) Cardinal Robert of Geneva Pope Clement VII (1378-1394).

This began a schism which for more than thirty years divided the Church and seriously reduced the prestige and authority of the Holy See.

[1] *The Great Schism.*

So far as personalities are concerned, the choice in these first years was between a madman and a bad man.

For the schism destroyed Pope Urban's sanity. He quarrelled wantonly with valuable supporters and, when cardinals of his own creation alarmed by his irrational behaviour, considered putting him under arrest, Urban who discovered or guessed their intent, had them tortured by a former Corsair notoriously anti-clerical in his sympathies, and privately put to death. While the aged Cardinal of Venice was being tortured, Urban walked up and down outside the building reciting his office. Nevertheless, to the end he retained the incorruptible honesty and the conscientious and careful administration which had long since become a habit with him.

His rival's wickedness appears from the fact that only a year before claiming the place of Christ's Vicar, he had been responsible for the massacre of Cesena. Modern historical research has proved Urban VI was the lawful pope. He had been freely and canonically elected.[1]

Nevertheless the fact remains that the entire college of cardinals which had elected Urban pronounced, however insincerely, his election invalid because not free. It is not surprising that many Catholics took them at their word. The legitimacy of the rival claimants to the papacy was and continued to be doubtful. It was not indeed settled when the schism ended. For Martin V carefully refrained from any pronouncement on the subject. He even recanonised a saint canonised by Boniface IX. Nor, apart from the numeration of the later Popes Clement VII and Benedict XIII, has the Church made an official decision. So late as the present century Dom Leclercq can state 'The decision between Urban VI and Clement VII and their successors remains doubtful and probably will always remain doubtful'.[2] That is to say there was a persistent doubt, impossible to resolve, who was in truth the Vicar of Christ.

[1] St. Catherine of Siena's contemporary letters state the Urbanist claim cogently. But her violent invective against the Avignonese cardinals was not calculated to win her a fair hearing.

[2] In his French edition of Hefele's *Konzilien Geschichte*.

To defeat their adversary the rival popes refused no weapon spiritual or temporal. Not only did they excommunicate their rival's obedience and bid for the support of secular rulers by bribes of church property or ecclesiastical power, they even provoked wars against the territory of the other obedience and invested them with the quality of an indulgenced crusade.[1] The weight of evidence suggests that Gregory XII to raise funds sold papal territory to the Duke of Durazzo.[2]

Perhaps the most serious feature of the schism was the fact that the choice of allegiance was made by the secular ruler whose motives were political. France, as we should expect, declared for Clement who established himself at Avignon, also the Spanish kingdoms, Portugal, and Scotland, always the ally of France. The Emperor and England elected for Urban. To implement the decision of the Archbishop of Canterbury and his suffragans, an Act of Parliament declared Urban not Clement the true Pope and made it treason to acknowledge the latter. Religious orders were divided into conflcting obediences, occasionally two bishops disputed the same See. In practice the French Church was governed by national synods meeting in the presence of the King or his representative. Their decrees were submitted for royal approval and promulgated by royal ordinance.[3]

We must not, however, exaggerate the impact of the schism on the simple Catholic, the uneducated flock of parishioners. Services and sacraments continued as before, their local pastors informed them who was in fact Christ's Vicar and the State deprived his rival's followers of a hearing. Their religious practice was unaffected.

So the years passed. Urban VI was succeeded in turn by Boniface IX (1389-1404), Innocent VII (1404-1406) and Gregory XII (1406-1415); Clement by 'Benedict XIII (1394-1423). Neither rival would resign. Benedict XIII in particular, the

---

[1] Such was the crusade richly indulgenced by which the English would attempt to expel Clementine French from their Flemish market for imported wool, a crusade therefore primarily supported by the city magnates.

[2] Peter Partner: *The Papal State under Martin V.*

[3] See Valois, *La France et le schism d'occident*, final summary Vol. II.

Spaniard Peter de Luna, used every device to evade solemn pledges to do so.

What way could be found out of the impasse? From 1398 to 1403 the French Government, royal dukes, acting for the lunatic King, Charles VI, tried the experiment of rejecting provisionally all papal government and transferring the government of the Church to the national hierarchy. Since, however, the French rulers did not possess the strength and determination of a Henry VIII, above all because unlike him they did not reject papal authority as such, the experiment broke down and France returned for a few years more to the obedience of the Avignonese Pope.

As the schism proceeded and the rival popes dug themselves in, their offers of resignation patently insincere, Catholics everywhere reached the conclusion that in such an emergency there must be in the Church an ultimate authority able to impose its will on the recalcitrant popes, even though one of the two must be legitimate—either the College of Cardinals or a General Council. This, moreover, was not a wholly novel conclusion invented for the occasion. As Bernard Tierney has shown[1] the traditional teaching of the canonists had not been consistent. Interspersed among assertions of absolute papal power amenable to no human judgment, were affirmations by canonists since the twelfth century that for manifest heresy, insanity, wanton dilapidation of ecclesiastical property, abuse of his spiritual authority, even manifest incompetence, different canonists allege different reasons, a pope might be deposed. This ultimate power was commonly attributed to an Ecumenical Council, though some canonists, notably Jean le Moine (the Monk) himself a cardinal, ascribed it to the College of Cardinals. John of Paris, a publicist writing about the beginning of the fourteenth century, had been particularly emphatic. If a pope became, like Urban VI of unsound mind 'the College of Cardinals, as representing the entire Church, would have authority to depose him', as they could also do, if he

[1] See Bernard Tierney: *Foundations of the Conciliar Theory,* indispensable for understanding the Conciliar movement.

proved incompetent. If a pope is an incorrigible simonist or teaches what is contrary to the faith or morals, the Emperor may depose him. It is not therefore surprising that, faced by the emergency of the continued schism, Catholic cardinals, bishops and theologians and the Church with them determined to give practical effect to these theoretical propositions. *Salus ecclesiae suprema lex.*

This moderate view of conciliar authority that a general council possesses jurisdiction over a pope uncertainly legitimate, who may or may not be Christ's Vicar, to restore unity and provide a certain pope is entitled, if necessary, to depose him and arrange an election—I shall call it the moderate emergency thesis—must not be confused with the view widespread at this time that a general council as such possesses jurisdiction over a pope certainly legitimate—I shall call it the extremist normal thesis. The latter subverts the government of the Church divinely ordained substituting for the monarchy of St. Peter's successor an episcopal oligarchy. It has therefore been officially condemned. The former on the other hand affirms that a persistently uncertain pope cannot claim the authority of a pope certainly legitimate, that under such abnormal circumstances the papacy is, to use Cardinal Zabarella's apposite term 'quasi-vacant', vacant for practical purposes. As we have seen, in the view of many eminent canonists even a certainly legitimate pope may in an emergency—variously specified—be deposed by a General Council. A fortiori a pope whose legitimacy is uncertain may be deposed. Moreover, whereas the sovereignty of a pope whose legitimacy is certain, secures the unity of the Church, the sovereignty of a pope whose legitimacy is uncertain destroys it. 'On this *rock* I will build my Church'. No stronger rock than a papal monarch, be he personally weak or wicked, who is certainly legitimate. A succession of popes dubiously legitimate is a rock split from top to bottom. And this precisely was the situation confronting the Church during the Great Schism.

By 1408, thirty years after the schism, both popes had been deserted by almost all their cardinals. Fourteen cardinals from either obedience taking the initiative into their own hands, summoned a General Council to meet at Pisa in 1409. The French Government, meanwhile, had once more thrown off obedience to Benedict XIII, pronounced a heretic.[1] He was left at Perpignan with no more than three cardinals still faithful. On the other hand, England and the Emperor Wenzel deserted Gregory XII (1406-1414) who, left with no supporters save Venice, Ladislas of Naples and Carlo Malatesta, Lord of Rimini, was also deserted by his cardinals. Wenzel's rival Emperor Rupert, however, held by Gregory.

The Council met at Pisa on 23rd March, 1409, where it held 23 sessions, the last on 7th August. It was well attended, by over 500. There were 22 cardinals, 84 bishops, 102 other bishops represented by proxies, 87 abbots with 200 proxies, the Generals of the four orders of friars, two deputies from cathedral chapters, deputies from 13 universities, and some 300 doctors of theology and canon law, now for the first time given the right to vote. Seventeen Governments sent ambassadors, all in fact except Scandinavia, Scotland, Spain and Naples. The President was Guy de Malesset, the sole surviving cardinal who had elected in turn Urban VI and Clement VII.

On the 5th June, the Council pronounced Angelo Corrario (Gregory XII) and Peter de Luna (Benedict XIII) heretics which they were not and perjurers which in effect they were, for both had pledged their resignation, deposed and excommunicated them. On 26th June the cardinals unanimously elected Peter Philargi, Archbishop of Milan—he was a Greek, a foundling picked up by the Franciscans—and he became Pope Alexander V. In vain did Gregory hold an opposition Council, almost unattended. Venice went over to the Pisan pope and Gregory was now wholly dependent on Malatesta and Ladislas (1409-1410). Despite its initial success Pisa was not finally endorsed by the Church. On the contrary, a few years sufficed to discredit it.

The following May, Alexander died and was succeeded by

---

[1] Their doctrine that pertinacious schism was equivalent to heresy had been put forward as early as the 12th century.

Baldassare Cossa who took the name of the present pope, John XXIII. Within a short time the new pope lost the Pisan popularity by his refusal to tackle the question of reform or yield to the rulers' demands.

In May 1413, attacked by Ladislas, John appealed for help to the new Emperor[1] Sigismund. Sigismund demanded the convocation of a General Council. Unable to refuse, John consented. He issued a bull summoning a Council to meet at Constance, on the lake of that name between Switzerland and Germany. Sigismund in effect, though John canonically, convoked the Council. Those who cannot admit any motive even in a Christian ruler other than political advantage tell us that Sigismund called the Council to increase his imperial prestige and obtain for his imperial coronation a pope universally acknowledged. My belief is that his primary motive was in truth religious, to save the Catholic Church in which he undoubtedly believed, from the inveterate schism which had divided her so long.

The Council opened at Constance on 1st November, 1414.

The Council of Constance lasted longer than any previous Council—some three years and a half—during which time 45 sessions were held.

Wellnigh the whole of the Catholic Church accepted and welcomed the Council. Sigismund invited all rulers and almost all sent envoys, among them the Greek schismatic Emperor Manuel II Palaelogus who sought help against the Turkish peril. The most eminent churchmen attended, cardinals, bishops, abbots, doctors, and many lay representatives. There were present five patriarchs, twenty-nine cardinals from all three obediences, thirty-three archbishops, over 150 bishops, 100 abbots and 300 doctors of divinity. A contemporary chronicler estimates the clergy at 1800, at 50,000 the laymen who settled in the city. As E. I. Jacob has pointed out,[2] the Emperor's presence at Constance made it a centre of international secular diplomacy, much as the United Nations at New York today. Hence the enormous influx of lay-

---

[1] Technically only King of the Romans.

[2] *Essays on the Conciliar Epoch.*

men.[1] Among the participants were no less than seven future Popes. Gregory XII was represented by Cardinal John Domenici.

These prelates in overwhelming majority were convinced and would proclaim either with Cardinal Zabarella that *in case of emergency* an Ecumenical Council could judge and depose a Pope though normally superior to a Council, or, and they were a majority, with Gerson, the eminent French theologian, that even under normal conditions a General Council is superior to the pope who must obediently execute its decrees. At the second session, held on 7th February, 1415, it was decided that voting should be by nations, each to count equally. The numerical superiority of the Italians was thus discounted. Of these nations there were four, Italian, German, French and English; Spain as yet held to Benedict XIII. Each was to appoint a committee of deputies to prepare the decisions to be taken by the nations. The national state was well on the way to produce the national Church. John XXIII found the Council intensely hostile. His personal character was denounced and on 15th February, 1415, the Council demanded his abdication. On 1st March he pronounced a resignation conditional however on resignation by the two rival popes and therefore worthless. On 20th March he escaped in disguise to Schaffhausen and the protection of Duke Frederick of Austria. Several cardinals joined him. He revoked his resignation as extorted by fear.

At the third session on 26th March, the Council adopted Cardinal D'Ailly's pronouncement that it was entitled to conclude its work despite any papal opposition and could not be transferred elsewhere, still less dissolved without a good reason and its own consent. Nevertheless, D'Ailly and Zabarella professed allegiance to John as lawful Pope.

A congregation of three nations, English, French and German, prepared a number of decrees. The first a declaration of principle affirmed the supremacy of the Council even over a pope. A second decree pronounced penalties for the contumacy of anyone even

---

[1] This fact should have been remembered by critics who regard the large supply of prostitutes at Constance as an index of clerical immorality.

a pope who refused to obey this or *any other general council*. A third forbade on pain of invalidity a transference by Pope John to another place of his curia or any officials, the translation or deposition of prelates or other actions detrimental to conciliar authority or the creation of new cardinals.

The cardinals however and the Italian nation took strong exception to these decrees as they stood and protested to Sigismund. A compromise was reached and when the 4th session opened on 30th March Cardinal Zabarella read and put to the vote only the first decree the declaration of the Council's supremacy even over a pope and three of the disciplinary decrees. The decree extending by a side wind the supremacy claimed by Constance to all ecumenical councils was omitted.

The first decree thus passed ran as follows:

'This synod lawfully assembled in the Holy Spirit constituting a General Council and representing the Catholic Church militant derives its authority immediately from Christ and everyone without exception of whatsoever position and dignity, even a pope, is bound to obey it in all matters concerned with faith and the abolition of the schism.'

A further clause 'and the general reformation of the Church in head and members' was omitted by Zabarella. Whatever the view of the members of the Council this declaration confined as it is to the particular council called to an end a disputed papal succession and as such presuming the absence of any pope *certainly* legitimate—the quasi-vacancy of the Apostolic See— enunciated only the moderate emergency thesis of conciliar supremacy.

At the next session, the 5th, however held on 6th April the indignation produced by John's repudiation of his promise to resign enabled the extremists to carry through their full programme. Four cardinals, among them D'Ailly, stayed away from the meeting. Seven others attended and Cardinal Orsini, as on the previous occasion, presided. But before the meeting the cardinals assembled in a different apartment, protested privately that, although they attended the Session, it was to avoid scandal, not to approve the decisions that would be taken. Cardinal Fillastre refused to read the decrees. They were no doubt overawed by Sigismund present in his full regalia. The decrees against attempts by Pope John to nullify the Council's work were re-enacted also the doctrinal decree affirming the supremacy of the Council, this time with the extension of its scope omitted by Zabarella. The decree he had omitted denouncing penalties for disobedience even by a pope to *any* general council was re-introduced and duly passed. A final decree solemnly attested the complete freedom of the Council, all its members and Pope John. Thus for the first and only time the Council affirmed the extremist normal thesis of conciliar supremacy. But it was indirectly, by insertion in a disciplinary decree and in the teeth of the cardinals.

Seventh Session. 2nd May

John was charged with notorious heresy, fostering the schism, wasting the goods of the Church, contumacy, obstinacy and misconduct. Though he appears in early life to have been a pirate after the fashion of Chaucer's shipman from Dartmouth, John was innocent of the charges now brought against him and which have blackened his character ever since. For when all was over and he had submitted to Pope Martin V, he was not only reinstated as Cardinal but appointed Dean of the Sacred College, the second rank in the Church, unsuitable treatment for a convicted villain.

The proceedings against John continued. Abandoned by Duke Frederick, he was brought back to Constance a prisoner.

Eleventh Session. 25th May

John was tried on no less than 54 charges, accused of every infamy a man may commit.

Twelfth Session. 29th May

Despite Cardinal Zabarella's opposition, he was formally deposed by the Council which had recognised his authority to summon it. On 31st May, he humbly submitted to his sentence.

Imprisoned until 1419 he was, as I have just said, reconciled and honoured only to die a few months later.

Thirteenth Session. 15th June, 1415

Carlo Malatesta arrived at Constance as plenipotentiary for Gregory XII.

Fourteenth Session. 4th July, 1415

Bulls were read from Gregory investing with full power to represent him Carlo Malatesta and Cardinal Domenici and bidding them in his name convoke the Council, already assembled by the Emperor, to receive his resignation, and to invest it with the authority of a General Council. This Cardinal Domenici proceeded to do: 'I, John, Cardinal of Ragusa, by the authority of my said Lord the Pope ... convoke this Holy General Council, authorise and confirm whatever *it will do* for the reformation of the Church and the extermination of heresy'.

Gregory ended his days as Cardinal Bishop of Porto and papal legate. The Council however did *not* officially recognise Gregory as legitimate Pope. He was designated simply as 'recognised Pope by his obedience'.

Henceforth, the Emperor resigned the presidency to the Archbishop of Ostia. If the Urbanist line, to which Gregory belonged, was to the end the line of legitimate popes, and that is the opinion today commonly received, his action, though the majority of the Council did not see it in that light, conferred on the Council of Constance the canonical status of an Ecumenical Council. The earlier sessions however would later be legitimated by the future Pope (see below p. 159).

Almost two years and a half elapsed before a new Pope was elected. Meanwhile, the Council continued in session, passed decrees, even doctrinal, and governed the Church. This indeed Pope Gregory had authorised it to do. On the other hand, the Council would undoubtedly have acted in any case in the same way and a majority of the members of the Council, did not regard Gregory as the legitimate pope. The delay was due in part to a fruitless attempt made in person by Sigismund to prevail upon Benedict XIII to resign. He would do so only on condition that as the sole surviving cardinal created before the schism he should appoint his successor!

Canonically his contention was strong. For cardinals created by an uncertain pope cannot possess the status of cardinals created as Benedict had been, by a pope certainly legitimate. On the other hand if he were not the legitimate Pope he was under sentence of excommunication. In any case Sigismund refused. The Spanish kings and the King of Portugal thereupon withdrew their allegiance and Benedict retreated to a fortress, Peñiscola, on the Spanish coast. There with two or three cardinals and a following of not more than 2,000, he dug himself in until his death (1424.[1]) A Spanish nation was added to the nations at Constance.

Thirty-seventh Session. 26th July, 1417

The Council formally deposed Benedict as an inveterate fomentor of schism, perjurer, schismatic, and heretic who denied the article of faith 'I believe in *one* Holy Catholic Church'. Heresy, be it remembered, was the one offence for which *all* the canonists agreed a pope might be deposed. The election of a pope was, however, long held up by stormy disputes as to whether or not decrees of reform should first be passed. Finally the Council accepted a compromise proposed by Bishop Beaufort of Winchester—King Henry IV had sent the English representatives instructions no longer to vote en bloc with the Germans. He carried a three fold motion. A declaration shall be made that the newly elected Pope will at once take in hand the reformation of the Church. Decrees of reform already agreed upon by all the nations shall be promulgated forthwith. A committee shall be appointed to arrange the papal election.

Thirty-ninth Session. 9th October, 1417

Five decrees were accordingly published. (1) General Councils

---

[1] He was in fact succeeded by two shadow popes of Peñiscola 'Clement VIII' and 'Benedict XIV.'

must be held frequently and at fixed intervals, the first, five years after the close of the present Council, the second, seven years later, then every ten years. (2) In the event of a disputed papal election a General Council shall meet to which the Emperor and other rulers shall be invited and shall judge of the election. (3) Every newly elected pope must make a profession of faith. Two of the three rival popes had just been pronounced heretics. (4) Bishops cannot be removed from their sees without their own consent or a very grave reason. (5) Certain abuses connected with episcopal vacancies are condemned. The first of these decrees was inspired by the extremist conciliar thesis, *though it did not state it,* the transference of supreme authority to a General Council. The second expressed the more moderate thesis, that in an emergency a Council could and should assume the authority necessary to save the Church from schism.

Fortieth Session. 30th October

This session promulgated a general decree demanding reforms in the financial administration of the papacy, the composition of the College of Cardinals, appeals to Rome, tithes and the traffic in indulgences.

On 23rd October, 1417, the election of a pope had been, for this occasion only, committed to a mixed body, the 23 cardinals and 30 other prelates, 6 from each nation. The conclave which opened on 8th November did not last long. On the 11th November, 1417, Cardinal Odo Colonna was unanimously elected and took the name of Martin V (1417-1431). He was a man of good character and mild temper, above all what was most needed at such a juncture, a diplomat.

During the interval before his election the Council had condemned 45 propositions extracted from the writings of the Lollard leader Wycliff. Wycliff has been termed by his admirers the morning star of the Reformation and indeed much of his teaching was what was later termed Protestant, for example, his denial of Transubstantiation, the institution of the Mass by Christ, and the necessity of confession, his condemnation of reli-

6

gious orders, the statement that 'the Roman Church is the synagogue of Satan', an Erastianism as thorough-going as Henry
VIII's. Peculiar however to Wycliff was the doctrine that no
authority or right to property can belong to any man in mortal
sin—a doctrine which cuts at the root of all authority and property temporal or spiritual though Wycliff applied it only to the
clergy. It also renders all sacraments uncertain. Moreover
Wycliff's views were changeable and inconsistent.

Wycliff's heresy had spread to Bohemia (modern Czecho-
slovakia) brought into close touch with England by Richard II's
marriage to Anne of Bohemia. The Czech leader was John Hus,
seconded by Jerome of Prague. They were both summoned before the Council and obeyed the summons, Hus indeed eager to
defend his faith. Among other tenets of these Czech teachers
were the Protestant doctrines of salvation by faith only and Scripture the sole rule of faith. Sigismund had given Hus a safe
conduct, not, as Mgr. Baudrillart argues in the *Dictionnaire de
Theologie Catholique,* solely against molestation en route. For
in fact he received it only on arrival. On 6th July, 1415 (15th
Session) Hus was condemned by the Council, handed over to the
secular arm and burned at the stake. However erroneous his
teaching, as a man he deserves our admiration. Convinced of his
beliefs, he went to his fiery death, so a spectator, the future Pope
Pius II, recalls, as gaily as a man invited to a banquet.[1]

His disciple Jerome recanted at first but recovered his courage
and died bravely. By order of the Council Wycliff's corpse was
exhumed and burned.

The Council did not long survive Martin's election. The new
Pope concluded three concordats—the first known of these
agreements with particular governments—with Germany,
England, and the three Latin countries. They were endorsed by
the Council at its 43rd Session on 20th March, 1418, which also
passed seven decrees of more or less superficial reform.

[1] It is good to know that Bishop Robert Hallum of Salisbury, a luminary of the
Council at which Hus died, was opposed to the death penalty for heresy.

Unwarrantable papal dispensations particularly to hold several benefices were condemned and revoked. There was a general decree against simony. The pope renounced his claim to the revenues of vacant sees, monasteries or benefices, the vacancy to be filled within a year at most. The pope must not impose a tithe on any national clergy without the consent of the majority of bishops. Clerical costume was regulated. These provisions bear out the justified criticism which has been made that the reforms were in effect designed to relieve prelates from excessive papal taxation, but left their own procedure and finances untouched. Nevertheless Martin consented. He could hardly do otherwise.

On 22nd April, Martin concluded the 45th and final Session with the pronouncement: 'Everything the Holy Council here assembled has decreed *conciliariter*'—that is to say, in full session as contrasted with decisions by separate nations, *nationaliter*, 'must be believed and observed and I confirm whatsoever has been done *conciliariter* concerning the faith but no other declaration'. So the Council ended.

The majority of theologians today limit the period during which the Council of Constance should be regarded as ecumenical. Some have even denied entirely its ecumenical character. They are not however agreed as to the period during which it was ecumenical. The commonest opinion restricts it to the sessions held after Pope Martin's election and therefore with his co-operation, namely the last three of the 45 sessions. Others date its ecumenical character from its convocation by Gregory XII, the 14th session. The pope however in this confirmation made no such distinction and we may surely, with Dom Leclercq, regard the entire council as ecumenical. There can be little doubt that this was in fact Pope Martin's view.

What then was the significance of the Pope's confirmation of what had been decreed in full session concerning the faith? His language is studiously vague. For he must avoid a conflict with the Council fatal as it would have been to the exercise of his authority and the newly restored peace and unity of the Church.

It is not surprising therefore that theologians have restricted its scope though disagreeing as to its nature. Jedin would confine the confirmation to the Council's condemnation of a pamphlet by a Dominican, Von Falkenbergh, advocating tyrannicide, others to the condemnation of the Hussites. Baudrillart extends it, surely with good reason, to decisions concerned with the abolition of the schism and ecclesiastical reform, Leclercq to all decrees not prejudicial to the prerogatives of the Holy See. Pope Martin however does not state that there were any such decrees but so far at any rate as his language is concerned confirms all doctrinal decrees enacted in plenary session conciliariter.

What then of sessions 4 and 5 both affirming the supremacy of the Council over the Pope, the latter the supremacy of every general council? That the decree of the 5th session affirming the normal jurisdiction of a general council over a pope even certainly legitimate was not a direct declaration of doctrine but introduced in a disciplinary decree may seem a quibble. What is more decisive is the fact that all the cardinals in one way or another protested against the decrees of this session. Passed against their opposition they cannot reasonably be regarded as passed conciliariter in the Pope's understanding of the term. Moreover Martin explicitly condemned this extremist normal view of conciliar supremacy when in a bull published on 10th March, 1418, he forbade appeals from the Pope to a future council. Baudrillart concludes without further ado that the Pope cannot have confirmed the doctrinal decree passed in the 4th session which affirms the jurisdiction of the particular Council of Constance over a pope on the ground that the 4th session is indissolubly bound up (solidaire) with the 5th. The facts however, as he states them, do not support his assertion. For the decrees passed at the 4th session were accepted by all the cardinals who remained at Constance, were indeed the product of their agreement with Sigismund. It is reasonable therefore to conclude that Pope Martin did in fact confirm the decree then passed (Sancta synodus) affirming the sovereignty of the Council of Constance even over a pope. And this conclusion is supported by the fact that he did subsequently attempt to implement the decree Frequens ordaining frequent convocations of a general council. For this surely implies approval of the decree passed at the same time which arranges for the intervention and jurisdiction of a general council in the event of a disputed papal election, a decree which though not directly doctrinal implies the emergency jurisdiction of a council over an uncertainly legitimate pope. In 1446, it is true, Eugenius IV confirmed only those decrees of Constance which did not derogate from 'the prerogative, dignity and pre-eminence of the Apostolic See'. Though the decree of Session 5, the extremist normal thesis, is undoubtedly condemned by this restriction, it does not condemn—whatever was in the Pope's mind—the decree of the 4th session affirming the moderate emergency thesis. For that decree does not prejudice the prerogatives of a pope certainly legitimate.

Nor should this conclusion constitute a difficulty. The successful action of the Council of Constance in restoring unity to the Church was based upon the moderate emergency view of its authority—however unnecessarily and unfortunately extended by so many of its members to the extremist normal thesis. Only such emergency jurisdiction empowered the Council to compel the resignation of John XXIII by a previous deposition, to depose Benedict XIII, either a possible pope. Only such emergency jurisdiction can justify the Council in adding for this abnormal occasion conciliar representatives to the conclave reserved by previous popes to the college of cardinals.

Can we indeed believe that if Gregory XII had refused to resign the Council would have yielded and the schism continued? Surely not. Or if Benedict XIII had been the legitimate pope and it has never been officially determined that he was not, that the Catholic Church would have shrunk to a handful of Catholics living in the neighbourhood of Peñiscola, Noah's Ark as Pope Benedict termed it? Surely not. It was not convincing evidence of Urban's lawful election in 1378 which induced for example

St. Vincent Ferrer to withdraw his allegiance from Benedict.[1] It was because Benedict's obstinacy threatened a permanent schism and in view of the emergency thus created that he and others convinced themselves that the Church acting through an Ecumenical Council could and should depose him—the thesis of moderate conciliarism. Dietrich of Niem, a curial official having faithfully served Urban VI and Boniface IX turned in despair to the Council of Pisa first, then to the Council of Constance as the Church's only saviour. Were these men and all who thought and acted as they heretics or mistaken? Surely not. Were in fact the overwhelming majority of Catholics who acknowledged the authority of Constance and its action to restore unity heretical or even mistaken? Surely not.

It is easy today to maintain that if a pope has been in fact legitimately elected, though the Church may be unable to ascertain it, and in consequence is rent asunder, unable to distinguish her divinely ordained head, even if such a pope a legitimate 'Benedict XIII' is reduced to a few thousand subjects confined to a minute area there is no remedy, no authority capable of intervening to end the schism, depose a persistently doubtful claimant and restore the unity of the church. For today, as for centuries past, the problem is and has been academic. When, five centuries ago, the Church was faced in practice by such a situation her response was otherwise. Acting through a general council which deposed the claimant who refused resignation she restored her unity. That is to say she acted upon the moderate emergency thesis of conciliar supremacy. Surely she was right.

It may be objected that if this thesis is accepted, it follows that the Council of Pisa was ecumenical, the two Pisan popes Alexander V and John XXIII the legitimate popes. Subsequent repudiation by the Council of Constance and lack of confirmation by a certainly legitimate pope condemn any claim of Pisa to be ecumenical. Was it not however sufficiently representative

[1] St. Vincent defied and rebuked Benedict to his face. In conjunction with St. Collette, foundress of the Poor Clares (Colletines) also formerly of Benedict's obedience he addressed a letter to the Council of Constance on the method of ending the schism an appeal to the Council as superior for the emergency to a pope whose obstinacy was wrecking the unity of the Church.

of the Church to arrange the election of a pope? There are, I submit, strong reasons for regarding the Pisan popes as legitimate. They had been elected by cardinals of either obedience. Though the numeration of the present pope rejects their claim, the numeration of Alexander VI accepted it. Leo X declared that the Council of Constance had been convoked not by Gregory XII but by John XXIII. Valois accepts at least the possible legitimacy of the Pisan line and points out that when he wrote about 1902 the Gerarchia Cattolica an official publication of the Vatican still reckoned Alexander V and John XXIII legitimate popes.[1] The arguments I have put forward for the moderate emergency thesis are arguments in their favour.

Despite the failure of the Council of Basel which maintained it obstinately (see p. 164 seq.) and papal condemnation even the extreme conciliar thesis that Ecumenical Councils are normally and as such superior to a pope was an unconscionable time in dying. St. Thomas More on the eve of giving his life for papal supremacy declared: 'never thought I the Pope above the General Council'.

---

[1] Somewhat dishonestly however it informs us that Gregory XII resigned at Pisa in 1409. The list of popes in Westminster Cathedral oddly enough accepts Alexander V the first Pisan pope but not his successor, John XXIII.

18

THE SEVENTEENTH GENERAL COUNCIL:
(BASEL), FERRARA—FLORENCE—THE LATERAN
1438 TO UNKNOWN DATE 1445-7

THE period immediately following the Council of Constance was marked by conflict between the conciliarists and the papacy for supremacy over the Church. The conciliarism which confronted the popes was not the moderate conciliarism which attributed sovereignty to a General Council only in an emergency such as that produced by the Great Schism. It was the conciliarism which would invest in a General Council the normal government of the Church, to transfer that government from the papal monarchy to the episcopate. Since many, perhaps at first most, contemporaries were disposed to support the claim, the Pope was compelled to resort to finesse, to make all possible concessions to the conciliarists hoping in the end to wear down the opposition.

Meanwhile, the Bohemian Hussites had taken up arms against the Church for many years with striking success. On 23rd April, 1423 in accordance with the decree of Constance a Council was opened at Pavia by Martin V. It was transferred on account of the plague to Siena. It was a farce. Prelates naturally enough had no taste for such frequent journeys abroad. When the papal legates arrived to open the Council they found only two abbots. There were never more than some 250 bishops. No work was accomplished. The Council, never accepted as ecumenical by the Church, was dissolved on 7th March, 1424.

The second Council for which the Constance schedule provided, opened in 1431 in Basel. Its President was the legate

Cardinal Cesarini appointed by Martin's successor Eugenius IV (1431-1447). The opening session was held on 5th December. The episcopal attendance was small. There were three cardinals, 19 bishops, 29 abbots. But there were 303 doctors and proxies. Eugenius who intended to call another Council in Italy to meet the Greeks in view of reunion ordered the dissolution of the Council at Basel. Cardinal Cesarini, however, knowing that dissolution would provoke open schism, did not publish the Pope's bulls but wrote to the Pope urging him to withdraw or suspend them. Meanwhile, the Council affirmed its supremacy over the Pope. In December, 1433, Eugenius yielded and issued a bull formally continuing the rebellious Council in session. By this time there were some 500 members. Since the extreme Hussites had at last been defeated, the Council was able to conclude an agreement with the moderate Hussites. In return for acceptance of Catholic doctrine they would be permitted to receive communion under both kinds, a concession to which was attached considerable importance. The agreement, however, was little honoured in Bohemia where for many years Hussite rebels continued in the field. The Council acted as though it were Pope, even attempted to persuade the Greeks to come to Basel instead of to the Pope's Italian Council.

On 18th September, 1437, Eugenius issued a bull formally transferring the Council from Basel to Ferrara where he would receive the Greeks. Canonically, therefore, the Council at Ferrara was a continuation of the Council of Basel before its formal breach with the Holy See. The Council of Basel however was not the same body as the Pope's Italian Council. It is therefore truer to the facts to regard the Council of Ferrara-Florence as a distinct Council.[1]

The Council of Basel replied by condemning and suspending Eugenius on 13th January, 1436, and annulling his bull. Cesarini now left for Italy. For many years to come the Council of Basel

---

[1] Père Congar, O.P. writing in Una Sancta (August 1959) reckons these opening sessions at Basel as an additional Ecumenical Council, thus adding a Council to the generally accepted numeration. This surely is to press a technicality too far. Basel should be eliminated from the list of Ecumenical Councils.

continued in session, an anti-Council now, the centre of resistance
to papal authority. King Charles VII of France adopted an attitude of neutrality as between Pope and Council. It was expressed
by the Pragmatic Sanction of Bourges (7th June, 1438). The
German princes and the new Emperor Albert accepted the conciliar supremacy enunciated at Basel, though not submitting to
the Council's authority. In 1439 Charles VII accorded a half
hearted recognition to Eugenius. But the German Church was
henceforward divided between supporters of Council or Pope.
England, however, reacting against the Lollard heresy was
staunch in support of the Pope. On 16th May, 1438, the Council
defined the superiority of General Councils to the Pope, that is
to say the extremist normal doctrine of conciliar supremacy and
on 25th June deposed Eugenius. On this occasion no more than
seven bishops, in all 20 prelates were present. Only one cardinal,
Louis Alleman, Archbishop of Arles, supported the Council.
The same year it defined the doctrine of Mary's Immaculate
Conception more than 400 years before its definition by Pius IX.
On 5th November, a conclave composed of Cardinal Alleman
and 32 electors designated by the Council elected an anti-pope, the
last anti-pope in the history of the Church. He was Duke Amadeus
of Savoy, layman, widower and father of two living children.
He took the name of Felix V. Elected on 5th November, 1439,
he accepted the election on the 8th January, 1440. Neither France
nor Castile would acknowledge Felix. He was supported only
by his own Duchy of Savoy, Switzerland, Scotland, Aragon,
Milan, Sardinia and Sicily. The German Emperor Frederick III
was neutral. The Council held no public session in 1442, its 45th
and last on 16th May, 1443. Aragon and Milan returned to
Eugenius. Germany was on the point of submission when papal
action against the Archbishops of Cologne and Trier provoked
a league of German princes against the Pope. A compromise was
finally arranged and the German princes swore allegiance to
Eugenius on his death bed. The Pope obtained recognition of his
prerogatives, the princes his ratification of appointments to bene-

fices and other usurpations upon his jurisdiction committed
during the state of schism.

In 1448, the Emperor's pressure upon the city of Basel expelled the Council from the city and it withdrew to meet its Pope
at Lausanne. Savoy and Switzerland still acknowledged Felix V.
The newly elected Pope Nicholas V (1447-1455) however nego-
tiated an agreement in 1449. Felix V abdicated and received in
return a Cardinal's hat and second place in the hierarchy with
legatine authority over Savoy and Switzerland. He died in 1451.
All censures against his supporters were removed. His cardinalate
was restored to Alleman.[1] The Council was even permitted to
elect Nicholas and dissolve itself. The settlement was wise,
generous and Christian, therefore most honourable to the Pope.[2]
The Council thereupon dissolved itself, affirming its supremacy
with its last breath. Conciliarism as a practical danger
died with it. Anti-papal conciliarism had been decisively
vanquished.

From this anti-Council we can now return to Eugenius's truly
ecumenical council of Ferrara-Florence—the Seventeenth.

Ever since Constance, the Byzantine Emperor, Manuel II,
Palaeologus, had been in touch with the papacy. For the Ottoman
Turks were at the gates of Constantinople and only unexpected
diversions had delayed the final fall. The Emperor therefore was
in urgent need of Western aid. Manuel, it seems, intended to
keep reunion dangling before the Latins but always shelving it.
His son, John VIII, on the other hand was determined on reunion and not merely for political motives. An initial journey of
exploration (1423-4) however led to no results. Finally however
after protracted negotiations, despite efforts by the Council of
Basel to attract the Greeks, the Emperor, the Patriarch of Constantinople, Joseph II and chosen Greek bishops embarked on
27th November, 1437, for Italy on a fleet despatched by Pope

[1] He died in 1450 and for personal holiness received after death an honour greater
than red hat or papal tiara being beatified by Clement VII in 1527.
[2] We may contras tthe petty minded spite shewn by Innocent II against former
supporters of a rival with far stronger claims than Felix. (See above p. 102).

Eugenius en route for the Council he had summoned to meet him at Ferrara.[1]

The Council opened on 8th January, 1438, before the arrival of the Greeks, as 'the Ecumenical Council in which union of the Western and the Eastern Churches should be discussed and, with the Lord's help, brought to a conclusion'. The Pope himself reached Ferrara on 27th January. Sessions were held to counter the hostility of Basel and arrange procedure. The members were to be divided into three estates: the first cardinals and bishops, the second religious superiors, the third doctors of universities, dignitaries of churches. The assent of all the estates would be necessary for any decision. Learning, that is to say, was given a vote as well as prelacy.

72 bishops and abbots were present at a solemn Mass on 15th February. On 8th February the Greeks had reached Venice where they were received with the utmost pageantry of Venetian power. A contemporary letter from Venice reports that in all 650 Greeks had arrived including 25 archbishops and bishops. The Emperor reached Ferrara on 4th March, the patriarch three days later. His arrival was marred by a dispute about the customary kiss of the Pope's toe, which he refused. A compromise was reached but cordiality suffered. On Sunday, the Patriarch celebrated his liturgy. Though Eugenius wished the official deliberations to proceed forthwith, the Emperor asked for time to allow representatives of the Western monarchs to attend. Four months' delay followed to no purpose for, except the Venetian Signory, the rulers did not send ambassadors, though England and France had agents in attendance. The papal purse was heavily taxed. Eugenius was obliged to defray the expenses of the Council and the Greeks could not but chafe at prolonged exile in a foreign land.

[1] We are fortunate in Fr. Gill's recently published account of the Council of Florence. It is the only satisfactory history of the Council, based on the work of a fellow Jesuit Fr. George Hoffmann in editing and publishing relevant material. The Latin minutes of the Council have been lost, the so-called Latin acts being an account by Andrea de Santa Croce, a papal protonotary present at the Council. The Greek minutes are reports of speeches to which an early copyist has added an account of events taken from the now lost narrative of a Greek archbishop and the memoirs of a deacon Syropoulos who took part in the Council but was opposed to the union. His account is not only biased but actually misleading.

Nevertheless, the solemn opening of the combined Council took place on 9th April, 1438. There were some 160 Latin prelates. The exact number is uncertain. Estimates differ. Facing them were the Greeks. Joseph II was too ill to attend. Throughout the Council he was largely confined to a sick bed. John VIII attended with his brother, Demetrius, 20 archbishops, 8 abbots, also 2 archbishops representing the Armenian patriarch. Prominent among the Greeks were Mark Eugenicus, Archbishop of Ephesus, the uncompromising foe of union, and Bessarion, Archbishop of Nicaea, among the Latins, Cardinals Cesarini, Archbishop Andrea of Rhodes, and the Dominican theologian John of Tor- quemada.

During the delay, discussions took place between committees of Latin and Greek theologians. The subject was purgatory which had become another point of difference between the Churches. For, whereas a definite doctrine of purgatory and its pains had been developed in the Western Church, the Greek theology of the intermediate state was undeveloped and vague. In particular, the Greeks objected to the doctrine of purgatorial fire, then generally accepted by the Latins. The discussions petered out for the moment inconclusively. Meanwhile, Latin prelates and theologians were swelling the numbers at Ferrara.

The first doctrinal session was held on 8th October, 1438. Some 360 Latin ecclesiastics were present and Greeks to the possible number of 700. The Russian Archbishop Isidore of Kiev had arrived with 14 subjects. The scene was the chapel of the Duke's palace. Bessarion opened the proceedings with an eirenic speech, followed for the Latins by the Archbishop of Rhodes.

The chief doctrinal difference remained the Filioque (see pp. 129-30). Was the doctrine true? Was it legitimate to make an addition to the Creed? The latter point was debated, Mark Eugenicus taking the lead against the Latins. It is noteworthy that in these debates the Latin speakers defend doctrinal de- velopment, though as yet only in the sense of an improved statement of what has always been *explicitly* believed and taught. Fourteen Sessions were held, the last on 13th December. Though Mark and his supporters held out obstinately, the Latin arguments convinced and impressed many of the Greeks, Bessarion in particular. From the first he was open minded, ready to hear and weigh arguments.

For greater security and for reasons of health the Pope wished to transfer the Council to Florence. The Greeks on the other hand, thoroughly restive, wished to break off proceedings and return home. The Emperor, however, bent on success and reunion, persuaded Joseph and the other Greek representatives to acquiesce in the Pope's wish. On 10th January, 1439, at a solemn session, the bull of transference was read. Eugenius entered Florence on 27th January; the Patriarch and five of his metropolitans on 11th February, the Emperor on 15th February, his brother Demetrius on 4th March. The debates, resumed on 26th February, discussed the doctrinal aspect of the Filioque dispute, does the Holy Spirit in fact proceed from the Son as well as the Father?

Fr. Gill who has given us a detailed analysis of these doctrinal debates, remarks on the inferior theological equipment of the majority of Greek representatives. Indeed, with the Empire in dissolution, the Greek Church could not have developed the Universities and teaching Orders which had maintained the higher theological level of the West. Moreover, as Fr. Gill also points out, the Greeks had as a body little taste for the theological method of the Latins to interpret revealed doctrines and deduce their implications by applying philosophical terminology and argument. An angry protest against Aristotle is recorded at this Council. They preferred to confine themselves to the strictly theological authority and statements of the Fathers, as alone of weight. Nevertheless, this attitude cannot justify Mark of Ephesus in replying to quotations from Latin Fathers which affirmed the two-fold procession of the Holy Spirit, by the entirely gratuitous statement that their text had been corrupted. The less obstinate, on the other hand, were convinced by these patristic quotations. For they were sure that the Saints could not err and must therefore have taught all the same doctrine, the more so when the Latins made it plain that they did not teach two distinct sources or two distinct processions. Bessarion and others were converted by the Latin arguments, Mark and his supporters held out. Time passed and no agreement was reached. On 15th April, three cardinals visited the Greeks to urge acceptance of the Latin doctrine. Bessarion pressed for it. On 27th May the Pope addressed the Greek delegates and urged union upon them. Finally at a meeting on 3rd June the Greeks decided to accept the Latin doctrine of the procession. There were four opponents, among them of course Mark of Ephesus. Though the Emperor undoubtedly insisted on a definite decision, he did not impose the agreement actually adopted. A doctrinal statement was drawn up not without difficulty and presented to the Pope on 8th June, who received it with joy.

The major difficulty thus removed, minor differences were more easily settled. Unleavened and leavened bread alike were declared fit matter for the Eucharist. A difficulty arising from the Greek canon which, after the Words of Institution, invokes the Holy Ghost to consecrate the bread and wine, was settled by a Greek affirmation of belief that the Words of Institution do in fact consecrate. Purgatory the Greeks were prepared to accept, and the Latins did not insist upon fire as its punishment. The decree on union further declared that even before the Last Day, souls enter the state of perfect bliss or suffering and, in opposition to an opinion held by many Greek theologians, pronounced that the blessed behold God himself, not merely an energy or light distinct from his Essence.

On 10th June the Patriarch died suddenly. A paper professing submission to the Holy See is said to have been found on his desk. This, however, is uncertain. In any case his acceptance of the Filioque was taken as proof of submission to the Holy See and his burial by the Greeks according to their own rite was attended by cardinals, Latin prelates and the Florentine Government.

Still formal reunion hung fire despite papal insistence. A deadlock seemed to have been reached. On 6th July, however, a decree of union was passed and promulgated at a solemn Mass sung by Pope Eugenius. Once more, as in 1274, the Latin and the Greek Churches were formally reunited. The Emperor's name was introduced as assenting. The decree affirmed the double procession of the Spirit, the legitimacy of the addition to the Creed, the matter and form of the Eucharist, purgatory and what in fact determined belief in the other articles, papal supremacy. Mark Eugenicus alone refused assent and claimed successfully the imperial safe conduct to return home. About 21st July the Greeks began to depart, the Emperor on 26th August.

Long before the schism, the Greeks under the influence of the imperial law, permitted divorce and for several reasons. There is no record of any protest by a Pope nor, to our knowledge, at the first reunion of 1274. Nor is there any evidence that the issue was raised in the negotiations preceding the union of Florence. After the union, Eugenius protested to the Emperor, to be met with a blank refusal. Divorce, replied John, 'is not allowed without reason'.[1] The Pope wisely let the matter drop, unprepared to jeopardise the union, and, like his predecessors, aware that where the civil as well as the ecclesiastical law was concerned, he could effect nothing against imperial opposition. That is to say, he tolerated without approving the practise of divorce by Greek Catholics. We must remember that divorce among the oriental Christians has always been exceptional, abnormal. It did not, as in the secularised modern countries, seriously affect the stability of marriage. No one, surely, but a legalist zealot could suggest that the popes would or should, rather than ignore what they could not have prevented, endanger the union had it otherwise subsisted, that is to say have risked

[1] *The Council of Florence,* Joseph Gill, S.J., p. 297.

cutting off millions of Catholics from visible membership of the Church.[1]

The departure of the Greeks did not involve the conclusion of the Council. It continued in being to ratify by its assent further reunions effected by Eugenius with the 'Nestorian' Armenians and the 'Monophysite' Copts. To the former he addressed a dogmatic bull, *Decretum pro Armenis,* reaffirming the decrees of Chalcedon, and the Fifth and Sixth Councils also treating of the number, form and matter of the sacraments. Whether the Pope was able to evade the barrier interposed by the Moslem rulers of Egypt and communicate with the Negus of Abyssinia is uncertain. There is some evidence that he was successful and that his overtures met with a favourable reception. These unions however were short lived. The Council of Florence also condemned the Basel anti-pope Felix and his adherents on 23rd March, 1440. On 24th February, 1443, the Council was transferred to Rome to the Lateran. Its first Roman session was held on 14th October. Here it slowly petered out, issuing no decrees but accepting papal pronouncements, notably a reconciliation, also temporary, of Monophysite Syrians in Mesopotamia, and a reconciliation of Maronites in the Lebanon and Cyprus. Some at any rate of the Lebanese Maronites had already been united to the Church and the Maronites have remained Catholics to the present day, though their Cypriot communities were forcibly Latinised by the Venetians.

Surprisingly, we do not know when the Council terminated. There is no record of a concluding session nor any extant bull of dissolution. The Council must have come to an end between

[1] Divorce had even made a sporadic appearance in the West. The *Canones Gregorii* permit divorce for adultery and if the husband is emancipated but his wife remains a slave. Similarly, the Penitentiale Cummeani and the Confessionale attributed to Egbert. Though many bishops protested against these penitentials, they were widely influential. The Council of Verberie (756) admits several grounds for divorce, also the Council of Compiegne (757); the presiding papal legate however at the latter Council assented to only one of these canons, that by which the religious profession of one partner freed the other for remarriage. Pope St. Gregory II (715-71) in a letter to St. Boniface permitted divorce for post-nuptial impotence, and a Council at Rome (827) permitted divorce and remarriage in case of infidelity, as is clear from Mansi's text followed faithfully by Hefele but 'edifyingly' mistranslated by his translator-editor Dom Leclerc. Even as late as the 16th century, Luther's opponent Cardinal Cajetan taught in Rome that the prohibition of divorce for infidelity was merely an ecclesiastical law like the celibacy of the clergy.

7th August, 1445, when the union with the Cypriot Maronites was celebrated, and Eugenius' death on 23rd February, 1447.

Isidore of Kiev, created a cardinal, returned to Russia in the hope of establishing the union of Florence. The ruler, however, Basilii, determined upon a national Church independent alike of Constantinople and Rome, rejected the union and Isidore was driven into exile. A few years later, however, Kiev, though not Moscow, was temporarily in union with Rome. Bessarion also received a cardinal's hat. He remained in Italy.

The reunion effected in 1439 was as short lived as the earlier union of 1274. The Emperor, it is true, did not repudiate it, nor his successor, Constantine, nor his prelates, and until in 1453 Sancta Sophia became a Mosque it was a Catholic Church in union with the Holy See. But the opposition, led until his death by Mark's obstinate sincerity, repudiated the union, and its opponents were undoubtedly a majority. The Orthodox would not even set foot in Sancta Sophia while the union was acknowledged and the Pope mentioned in the liturgy. Many even of those who had signed, repudiated their signatures on the plea that they had been extorted against their will. The Greeks, it was alleged, had been starved into surrender, though in fact the Pope had done all he could, admittedly not enough, to provide adequate maintenance. Turkish conquest was widely preferred to union with Rome. 'Better' so a spokesman is reported 'to see the turban of the Turk ruling us . . . than the Latin mitre'.

The year before the end, as a result of a firm letter from Pope Nicholas V and a visit to Constantinople by the Russian Cardinal Isidore, at a solemn liturgy celebrated before the Emperor on 12th December 1452, the decree of union was publicly proclaimed. In 1444, a Crusade organised by Pope Eugenius at great cost of effort and expense had suffered a crushing defeat when King Ladislas of Hungary was killed on the battlefield of Varna. The Pope could do nothing more to save Constantinople and a few months later than the solemn proclamation of union (29th May 1453) it was captured by Sultan Mahomed II. Henceforward the anti-unionists were triumphant and in 1484 at a synod held in Constantinople, the Greek Church formally repudiated the Council of Florence.

Where hostility and prejudice have taken root, nothing but the strength of charity can eradicate them. With few exceptions, even the Greeks more or less convinced by theological argument remained alien in spirit, reluctant, grudging in their own assent. Pope Eugenius, from first to last utterly conscientious and loyal to truth, leaves nevertheless an impression of coldness, even *hauteur*. With much provocation and the best intentions he scolded and pressed where a spontaneous and unconditional manifestation of love would have been more persuasive. On both sides there was much bickering over questions of etiquette and procedure, as among the quarrelling apostles at the Last Supper, and here also Christians should have imitated their Master. Except for a handful of orientals, Isidore certainly and Bessarion, there was no union of heart. When that union is wanting, a union of minds is not likely to stand firm. The lesson alike of Lyons and Florence surely must be first to establish this union of hearts, by mutual love and a powerful sense of brotherhood in Christ. Then but not before can doctrinal and ecclesiastical union be profitably undertaken. Our present Pope's loving heart and wide humanity argue favourably that this first and indispensable union at any rate may be achieved at the approaching Council. Such a gesture as Mayor La Pira's visit to Russia should do much to melt the ice frozen hard by centuries of estrangement. If Lyons and Florence display the goal to be reached, their ultimate failure warns us against an insufficient method of reaching it.

19

THE EIGHTEENTH GENERAL COUNCIL:
LATERAN V 1512-1517

MANY years ago, the priest of the parish where I lived let a house to a parishioner. Holy and devoted though he was, the combination of pastor and landlord ended disastrously. 'Which thing is an allegory' or an example of the impossible combination attempted by the papacy until the loss of temporal power in 1870. Throughout these centuries, the popes sought to combine the incompatible positions of spiritual shepherd and ruler of an Italian state, as such involved in the power politics of Western Europe. The attempt to exercise a political supremacy over Christians had, it is true, apart from Pius V's impracticable deposition of Elizabeth now become outmoded. All the more tenaciously, perhaps, did the popes cling to their possessions as Italian princes. Inevitably their action in the one capacity interfered with their action in the other. The cornelian found on beaches often combines transparent portions and opaque. Such has been the papacy. Transparency to the divine Light, opacity of secular politics, these have in various degrees been combined in the papacy, and the latter has diminished the former. From the Counter-reformation, the spiritual aspect of the papacy, transparent to the divine Light, has predominated over the opaque, the worldly and political. Even so, the latter has interfered with the former and to a considerable extent restricted its testimony and action. In the period immediately preceding the Reformation, the opaque progressively gained upon the transparent, the pope became less and less the shepherd of souls, more and more the Italian prince. Everywhere bishops also were temporal princes or government officials. Well may Père Bouyer[1] speak of 'a Christianity which had become confused with the institutions of a secular society (cité) and a society utterly decadent as was the Christian society at the close of the Middle Ages. . . .' Or 'the grave menace to the survival of genuine Christianity presented by the habitual acceptance of a religious facade, a religious respect perhaps wholly exterior, for an institution acknowledged by society'.

This was the radical evil affecting the Church, this the true scandal. I am, I must confess, irritated and bored by the stupid historical cliché which represents the second Borgia pope, Alexander VI (1492-1503) as the typical wicked pope. In fact he was by nature warm-hearted, tolerant, kindly, human. In another age and environment he might well have left behind him the reputation of an admirable pope, a true father of souls. It is a just maxim of our law that a man must be accounted innocent until proved guilty, and a pope surely is entitled to the same justice. It has *not* been proved that after his succession to the papacy, Alexander VI broke his implicit vow of chastity, that his relation to Giulia Farnese was more intimate than the affection of an old man for a charming young girl.[2] In fact, his sin as pope was Eli's complacency towards the crime of his sons, Cesare in particular, the desire to endow them with an Italian principality, in fact simply the combination of paternal love, in itself an admirable sentiment, with the temporal power politics common more or less to all these popes and evil in them all. Julius II (1504-1513) was a worse pope than Alexander. For, taking his very name from the pagan Julius Caesar, he led armies into battle for his temporal sovereignty, an activity diametrically opposed to the function of Christ's Vicar.

On the other hand, the patronage extended by these popes to the literature and art of the Renaissance, as they understood and

---

[1] *Du Protestantisme à l'Eglise*, pp. 120-1.

[2] There are even historians so obtuse as to take seriously the papal threat in a letter to excommunicate her if she did not return to Rome.

intended it, the furtherance of a Christian humanism, was altogether admirable. That the spiritual capital of Christendom
should be also its intellectual and artistic capital was no ignoble
or unchristian ambition. The poison of religion is not the human,
as such, intellectual or aesthetic values, but secular power, force,
latent or in operation. 'The sword' Dante observed 'has been
joined with the pastoral staff, wherefore both must go astray.
By confusing in herself two forms of government, the Church of
Rome falls into the mire, defiling herself and her burden' (Pur-
gatorio XVI, 109-11, 127-29). His words were fulfilled only
too truly in the Renaissance papacy. That in mediaeval Christendom the pope must dominate the Emperor or be dominated by
him was, as we have seen, inevitable. That he should be subject
to no temporal ruler, possess therefore, as today he does, an
independent statelet of no political importance, is highly desirable. That he should govern an extensive state in central Italy
was a disaster.

Amid the spiritual decadence of the official hierarchy, and the
splendours of an artistic and intellectual humanism springs of
genuine and profound religion never failed—the preaching, for
example, of St. Bernadine, the *devotio moderna* in the Netherlands one sidedly individualistic perhaps, but pure and deep,
Gerard Groote's Brethren of the Common Life, and the Canons
of Windesheim, the religious philosophy of Cardinal Nicholas
of Cusa, Marsilio Ficino's Christian Platonism, the Imitation of
Christ for so many souls Protestant as well as Catholic, a source
of true and interior Christianity.

In such an environment, an Ecumenical Council would accom-
plish nothing in the sphere of practical reform. It could but bear
its witness to Catholic doctrine which, after all, is a valuable
service to the Church.

The pursuit of political aims by Julius II had not unnaturally
aroused against him the hostility of the King of France, Louis
XII, and the Emperor Maximilian. Encouraged by their support,
a knot of rebellious cardinals blew upon the dying embers of
radical conciliarism and summoned an anti-papal council to meet

at Pisa. It was opened on 1st November, 1511, by four cardinals, two archbishops, one bishop and five abbots, all French. Once more it affirmed the supremacy of a Council even in normal circumstances. Local hostility compelled a transference to Milan. It finally petered out at Lyons. Julius was officially condemned.

In reply, Julius had summoned a council to meet at the Lateran. It met on 3rd May, 1512, the Eighteenth Ecumenical Council. It was attended by fifteen cardinals and some hundred prelates, mostly though not exclusively, Italian. The number of bishops never exceeded 150. The General of the Augustinians preached. A sermon was a regular feature of every meeting, indeed its staple constituent. We do not hear of a sermon by the Pope, hitherto usual at Councils where he was present. Julius' *forte* was soldiering rather than preaching. The first session was held on 10th May, when the Archbishop of Spalato addressed the Council on the Turkish peril and Church unity.

The second session, 17th May, was addressed by the Dominican Master General, the great Thomist philosopher and theologian Thomas de Vio Cajetan. His theme was councils and in particular the usurpation by the Council of Pisa-Milan. The Emperor Maximilian who had rallied to the Pope, sent as his representative a councillor Matthew Lang, Bishop of Gurk. He arrived on 4th November and was created a cardinal. The outlandish and unecclesiastical dress he insisted on wearing was an occasion of ridicule.

At the third session on 3rd December, Maximilian's letter of adherence to the Pope was read, France placed under an interdict. At the fourth session on 10th December, the address was delivered by Christopher Marullo of Venice. He attacked the Pragmatic Sanction (Charles VII's ordinance arrogating to himself power to dispose of the appointments and revenues of the French Church, and now revived by Louis XII) and pronounced a panegyric of Julius in the most flamboyant language: 'Thou art shepherd, physician, governor, cultivator, in brief a second God on earth'.

At the fifth session on 16th February, 1513, a bull was promulgated against simony in papal elections.

On the night between the 20th and 21st February, Julius died. On the 11th March he was succeeded by Leo X (1513-1521), the first Medici pope—pre-eminently a humanist. At the sixth session, 27th April, the Bishop of Modruscha spoke of the Turkish peril and of Church reform. At the seventh session, 17th June, two of the schismatic cardinals were reconciled.

At the eighth session, 19th December, the patron of Pisa, Louis XII, accepted the Pope's Council. A doctrinal bull (*Apostolici regiminis*) was promulgated, a papal decree, that is to say, accepted by the Council not a pronouncement by the Council. Neo-Aristotelian doctrines about the human soul were condemned, that, at any rate so far as philosophy can inform us, man's intellectual soul common to all men is to be distinguished from an inferior animal soul individual and mortal. The contrary teaching of the Council of Vienna (see above p. 139) was reaffirmed. That the condemned doctrine is probably good Aristotelianism does not make it compatible with the Christian faith. A constitution was adopted on peace among Christians, the Crusade against the Turk and the reconciliation of Hussites.

At the ninth session, 5th May, 1514, a bull was promulgated against various abuses. Bishoprics are not to be given to minors or the ignorant, nor may bishoprics or abbacies be given in commendam—that is, to be held by someone, often not in orders, who does not exercise the office. These abuses, however, continued to flourish and Leo X himself would continue to practise them. The cardinals are exhorted to curtail their expenditure. Clerical concubinage is once more condemned though recognised as in fact widespread. Penalties were imposed for blasphemy. Old laws against simony, against violation of the Church's rights or property, or of clerical privilege were repeated once again. Provincial councils must be held once every three years. The privileges enjoyed by the friars were curtailed.

The tenth session was not held until a year later, 4th May, 1515. It issued a decree on control of the press. During the past century, to save peasants and craftsmen from the moneylenders' clutches, the Franciscans had set up institutions to provide credit, which lent money at the interest necessary to defray running expenses. They were called monti di pietà. This had been attacked as immoral. The Council formally sanctioned the practice.

Another and even longer delay followed before the eleventh session on 19th December, 1516. A concordat was then concluded with the French crown on terms extremely favourable to it. The King could appoint to all sees and abbacies.

The ruler of the now united Spain would receive the same power. And although the Spanish Inquisition was the creation not of the State but of the Church since it was established by Pope Sixtus IV (1471-1484) at the request of Ferdinand and Isabella, it was controlled by the State, and therefore became a powerful instrument by which the Spanish monarchy secured an effective share in the government of the Spanish Church. That the State should thus appoint the pastors of the Church and employ them in her service as civil servants and diplomats, was another aspect of the secularisation and infection of the Church by politics.

Preachers, the Council decreed, must be authorised by the Bishop. No preacher must foretell the future, the date of anti-Christs' coming, or of the Last Judgment. This prudent measure which was, in part at least occasioned by the prophecies issued quite recently by Savonarola, though applicable to St. Vincent Ferrer's vaticinations of a speedy end of the world, has resulted in the banishment of such vagaries and delusions to what may be termed the Left Wing Protestant sects. Hitherto they had been too frequent in Catholic pulpits. Papal supremacy over Councils was reaffirmed, though without reference to the entirely abnormal conditions under which the Council of Constance had met. The union with the Maronites, formerly concluded at the Council of Florence (see above p. 173) had no doubt been partial and insecure. It was now cemented by a letter from their patriarch, Simon Peter, read at this session.

It accepted the supremacy of the Pope, and complete Catholic orthodoxy.

The twelfth and final session, on 16th March 1517, imposed tithes for three years to finance a Crusade against the Turks. The practice of looting cardinals' houses during a papal vacancy was forbidden. Little in the way of practical reform emerged for the time. To make this possible, nothing less was required than the long-gathering storm—preluded already by Waldenses, Lollards and Hussites—the tempest of the Protestant Reformation. Seven months after the close of the Council it would break.

20

THE NINETEENTH GENERAL COUNCIL:
TRENT 1545-1564

Period 1: 1545-1547 (last two sessions at Bologna)

Period 2: 1551-1552

Period 3: 1562-1563

'THE way of spiritual childhood,' wrote St. Therese of Lisieux, 'is the way of *trust* and complete surrender.... Holiness consists not in any particular pious practice but in a disposition of the heart [spirit] which makes us humble and tiny in God's arms, aware of our weakness but confident even to the point of rashness in the Father's goodness.... To be little is not to take credit for any virtues we may practice in the belief that we are capable of any good of our own, but to recognise that the Good God places this treasure of virtue in the hand of His little child'. What St. Therese taught, Luther sought, even caught sight of. Since, however, his temperament, character and theological environment were so utterly different from the Saint's, he could not focus his vision clearly or give it fitting expression. On the contrary, from the outset he understood and stated his insight amiss. Père Bouyer himself a convert from Protestantism, in his important study 'Du Protestantisme à l'Eglise' has shown that the positive teachings of Luther and the other reformers—that in the order of salvation God's grace is all in all, man is powerless to do anything of himself, that we are saved by a faith which is a surrender to God's saving gift of himself in Christ, the absolute sovereignty of God, the supremacy of Scripture as a source of revelation—were true and profoundly Catholic. In an age when Catholic religion, to a very large extent though *by no means completely,* had become externalised, a matter of those devout practices in which St. Thomas has told us holiness does not consist, Luther uncovered deep wells of personal religion largely choked. Influenced, however, partly by a faulty philosophy and theology, but more by the deficiencies of individual Catholics and their practices, he concluded that Scripture is the sole doctrinal source, that tradition and the doctrinal authority of the Holy See and her Bishops must be rejected. Moreover he rejected many Catholic doctrines among them the Sacrifice of the Mass, indulgences, purgatory, prayer to our Lady and the Saints, the veneration of images and relics, monasticism and in general the value of religious celibacy. Had Luther's errors been due, as Père Bouyer maintains, solely to the presuppositions of a nominalist philosophy he might well have been disabused of them. For at an early stage of his revolt he was personally confronted with a Catholic theologian and philosopher, Cardinal Cajetan, who far from being a nominalist was an eminent and vital exponent of Thomism. Moreover, Luther could have learned from the liturgy with which he daily worshipped, a doctrine wholly adequate to his deepest and truest intuition. It is evident that in fact Luther's denials and misstatements were largely due to his personal disposition and its reaction to the more or less violent and often ill-informed attitude of Catholic authority to him. From complete adherence in 1517 to Catholic sacramental teaching Luther moved in a few years to whole-hearted opposition to it. The Reformers saw the Catholic sacramental system, above all the sacrifice of the Mass not, as they are, as sovereign operations of God's unmerited grace, but perversely as human substitutes for it, human attempts to force God's hand.

The rapid spread of Protestantism—within two or three years of Luther's revolt, Zwingli was propagating an even more radical reformation in Switzerland—was due throughout to a combination of factors of wholly different nature and value. The source and mainspring of Protestant religion was mis-stated and misinterpreted insight of spiritual truth. The Reformation nevertheless was assisted by the widespread dislike of a foreign religious control, particularly when exercised for political ends and making considerable financial demands, by the ambition of rulers brooking no papal control of their subjects' religion and of the established Church, their greed which found in the new doctrines a welcome pretext for robbing the Church and in particular for confiscating the possessions of religious orders since the religious life was declared superfluous, ascetic practices powerless to promote holiness. Without the sincere though fanatical zeal of a minority of Protestants and *the support of temporal rulers*, the Reformation must have failed. Where these two forces were united it succeeded.

Official condemnation of Luther's theological statements was not long delayed. In the bull *Exsurge Domine* (1520) Leo X condemned Luther's doctrines.[1]

What in Luther was still a somewhat amorphous lava flow of emotional convictions, was crystallised into a more coherent theological system by his disciple Melancthon. He had much to do with compiling the Confession of Augsburg which has remained the official creed of the Lutheran Churches.

A little later the French John Calvin (1509-1564) strengthened Protestantism by elaborating a veritable Summa of Protestant theology, the whole dominated by the conviction of God's absolute sovereignty. By requiring for salvation sanctification as well as justification, he restored the Catholic emphasis obscured by Luther on an interior holiness, effected by divine grace. Above all, he rejected Luther's complete subjection of Church to State. Having constructed a system of church government such as he mistakenly believed to be that of the New Testament, he struggled, not without a considerable measure of success,

---

[1] Not all these however were condemned as heretical condemnations which alone can claim infallibility. We can therefore agree with Luther against Leo X that to burn heretics *is* contrary to the will of the Holy Spirit, Divine Love.

to make this reformed Church independent of State control. Taking over the leadership of Swiss Protestantism—Zwingli had fallen in battle at the height of his activities—Calvin built up at Geneva a veritable theocracy, austere, bleak, legalist, in many respects the reverse of Luther's initial assertion of Christian liberty, but not without the grandeur due to his devotion to God's sovereign will. Even at Geneva, however, the secular authorities frustrated his desire to establish a weekly celebration of the Lord's Supper. There can be little doubt that the strength of Protestantism has lain chiefly in the Calvinist churches.

On the other hand, in many respects, Calvin was more radical than Luther. He rejected the real objective presence of Christ's Body in the consecrated elements, and the Lutheran survivals of Catholic liturgy. He was also, most unfortunately for Catholic art, unlike Luther, a thorough going iconoclast. The combination in early Protestantism of powerful factors, good and evil, insight and misconception, faith and fanaticism, zeal and selfishness, reformers and rulers, proved well nigh irresistible. Like wildfire the Reformation swept Western Europe. Before the century closed the Scandinavian countries, Great Britain, Holland, a great number of German states including the former territory of a military order, the Teutonic Knights, which became the nascent Kingdom of Prussia, many Swiss Cantons, were Protestant. For long the religious allegiance of France, the Southern Netherlands which finally remained Spanish and Catholic, Bohemia, Poland, many, perhaps most of the German States finally Catholic, even Austria, had hung in the balance. Calvinism had even penetrated into Italy when it obtained a foothold in the Court of Ferrara. Catholic priests and bishops as well as laymen fell away en masse. So externalised had Catholicism become, a matter of social conformity and the ruler's will. Though Catholic worship in the Middle Ages was as splendid, as worthy of God as any human service may be, no steps had been taken to teach the people Latin and thus enable them to understand and appreciate the liturgy they witnessed as ignorant spectators. Enough for them a few set prayers, the rosary, private devotional practices.

Catholic theology they need not know, ought not to know, the Spanish Dominican Melchior Cano held. A Catholic government enforcing religious conformity was sufficient, and now in country after country the government turned against the Catholic Church. Under the aegis of the remaining Catholic governments, notably the Spanish-Austrian Hapsburgs, in Spain, the Netherlands, Austria, the Catholic German States, Italy and later France, a Catholic revival began, the movement known as the Counter-Reformation. Though it did not restore to the Catholic laity their lost liturgical inheritance, it taught them the doctrines of their faith, fostered a life of prayer and mortification. It was led by religious orders which sprang up on many sides. There were the Barnabites, Theatines, Capuchin Franciscans who played a leading part in the activities of the Counter-Reformation, a little later the Oratorians, the reformed Carmelites founded by St. Teresa and St. John of the Cross, centres of contemplative prayer, who developed and propagated mystical theology, reformed houses of the older orders and above all, the Jesuits. Ignatius Loyola, converted from the life of a Don Juan, forged the strongest yet most flexible weapon in the hands of the Church to spread and defend her faith. The Society of Jesus was formally sanctioned by Paul III (1534-1549) in 1540.

Adaptability combined with unity was the hallmark of the new order. Entire obedience was demanded to a General—himself and his order bound to a particular loyalty and obedience to the Holy See. The end would justify not all means, but all means morally lawful. The Jesuit could adjust himself to his social and cultural environment, to the manners and outlook of men of the world, yet so as to sanctify it and them. The Jesuits almost from the first became skilful educators in Europe, their schools extorting the unwilling admiration of their enemies. Contemporary architecture and art served their aim, expressed in the Society's motto *Ad Majorem Dei Gloriam,* To The Greater Glory of God. The Jesuit St. Peter Canisius became an Apostle of Catholic Germany successfully holding back the Protestant

advance. St. Francis Xavier, one of Ignatius' original com-
rades, carried the Gospel to Japan.

For some centuries, apart from a few sporadic and ineffective
attempts by early Franciscans, the mission to the heathen though
the first charge imposed upon his Church by her Founder had
been neglected. In the negative as well as the positive understanding of Belloc's ambiguous phrase, Europe had been the faith,
the faith Europe. Now, as though to compensate the mounting
losses at home, foreign missions revived. Spanish and Portuguese
American conquests had brought Christianity to heathen popula-
tions of Central and South America. The Jesuits carried the
mission over the world. Jesuit missionaries reached the Congo,
Brazil, India, Malacca, Japan, where until it was all but extinguished by the best organised persecution yet known, there was
a flourishing Christian Church. And the Jesuits would shortly
establish themselves in China. Had not European prejudice prevented the institution of a native clergy and the adaptation of
Catholic ritual and customs to local conditions, their missions
would undoubtedly have been far more successful than they were.
Nevertheless, they effected much and the missionary endeavour
has never since ceased.

Nevertheless the labour and devotion of individuals or orders
was not enough. The Church must set forth in monumental
fashion the doctrines denied by the Reformers, must adopt
measures of practical reform. Certainly the papacy possessed
authority to perform the task alone. There were, however, many
Catholics who still attributed even greater authority to a Council
or at any rate to the Pope with a Council. Moreover, the theological discussions necessary to hammer out the most satisfactory
doctrinal formulas required the deliberations of a Council. A
Council should therefore have been called in the early days of
the Reformation. Years passed. The Reformation marched forward triumphantly. No Council was summoned. The popes were,
in fact afraid and not without reason, that the Council might
prove another Basel, might attempt to establish its sovereignty,
defy their commands, possibly even add to the disastrous Pro-

testant revolt another anti-papal schism. Memories of conciliarism had rendered popes shy of ecumenical councils. An obstacle
even more serious was the rivalry between the Hapsburg Emperor
and the French King, the Catholic monarchs, without whose
goodwill no Council sufficiently representative could in fact be
held.

The union under the sole authority of the Emperor Charles V
of Burgundy, the Netherlands, Austria, Hungary, Bohemia, with
Spain and her American dominions, the Milanese and the kingdom of Naples, his inheritance from his father's marriage with
the heiress of Ferdinand had once more rendered an Emperor a
menace to papal independence. Imperial troops had indeed conquered and sacked Rome (1527). Even when the division of the
Hapsburg possessions between Charles' son Philip and his brother
the Emperor Ferdinand had somewhat reduced the threat, the
danger of Hapsburg domination by no means ceased, particularly
since Spain possessed a firm foothold in Italy. Although Charles
V pressed for a Council, he expected from it such reforms as, he
hoped, would satisfy legitimate Protestant demands and thus
effect the reunion for many years his cherished aim. He had
misconceived both Protestantism and Catholicism, an error
typical of the statesman little studied in theology. Valuable, possibly decisive years were lost, pledges given, a Council summoned
only to be postponed indefinitely.

It was not until May, 1545, that a handful of bishops met at
Trent and it was not until 13th December, in the same year, the
third Sunday in Advent, that the three legates representing Pope
Paul III finally opened in the Cathedral the Nineteenth Ecumenical Council.

A city of the Italian speaking Tyrol, Trent as a meeting place
was a compromise between the papal desire for an Italian, the
Emperor's for a German city. Further, as a territorial bishopric
it was ecclesiastical territory. There were now present four cardinals, the legates, Cadinal Del Monte, Corvino and Pole, and
Cardinal Madruzzi, Bishop of Trent. There were four archbishops, twenty-one bishops, five heads of religious orders. There

were also present, though without a vote, forty-two consultant theologians, among them the eminent Catharinus and Soto, four secular priests from Spain, thirty-eight regulars (members of religious orders).

By the second session, the bishops were twenty-eight—truly a small number to inaugurate one of the most important Councils in the history of the Church. Procedure was arranged. A limited number of votes was allotted to members who were not bishops. Between the sessions many informal meetings were held for discussions and preparatory work.

Second Session. 7th January, 1546

A legatine address was read to the Council. Rules of conduct were prescribed for members and for the inhabitants of Trent. The voting members were now forty. There were representatives of the Emperor, the King of the Romans and the King of Portugal, thirty-nine theologians, six canonists. It was decided to proceed simultaneously with doctrinal definition and practical reform.

Third Session. 4th February, 1546

The Council made a formal profession of faith. It emphasised papal supremacy and ended with the 'Nicene' creed.

Fourth Session. 8th April, 1546

The doctrinal work of the Council was opened by a decree on Scripture. These decrees were not passed without debate, largely as to the most suitable formulas to be adopted. There is little place for these debates. We must, however, always bear in mind that, like the text of a law, a doctrinal decree is not and cannot be fully intelligible apart from its interpretation in the schools of Catholic theology.

The supreme doctrinal authority of Scripture was affirmed but also the authority of tradition. Nor may Scripture be interpreted in a sense contrary to ecclesiastical authority or the consent of the Fathers. The Canon of Scripture was fixed and for the first time the Church officially defined that the Deutero-Canonical books are truly and fully canonical. These are Old Testament books revered by the Jews but not accepted by them as canonical scripture—in fact almost all the books printed as 'the Apocrypha' in Anglican bibles. Hitherto, Catholic theologians had been divided on this matter, many following St. Jerome in denying their canonicity. It is noteworthy that before the decree passed, Seripando, General of the Augustinian Hermits defended the negative view. This suggests that Luther, once a member of his Order, had never regarded these books as canonical. In any case, the allegation, too commonly made by ill-informed Catholics, that the Reformers arbitrarily excluded these books from their Canon is unjustified. What they did was to accept an opinion widely current which the Church would shortly reject. At the same time, the Vulgate was declared the authentic and authoritative version of the Bible. The precise significance of this decree is not easy to determine. For not only has the Church permitted for private use translations made directly from the original Hebrew and Greek, Pope Pius XII has issued for permissive use in the recitation of the liturgical office a version of the Psalter and Canticles made directly from the Hebrew and differing widely from the Vulgate.

At all these doctrinal sessions, decrees of practical reform were enacted. A censorship of religious books was established.

Fifth Session. 17th June, 1546

A decree was issued on Original Sin. It is incurred by all Adam's descendants and can be removed only by baptism or the desire for it—a desire now generally understood as the will to do whatever God has ordered, therefore, if that were known to be His will, to be baptised. In ordinary parlance, sin means the commission of what is known or believed to be morally wrong or the omission of what is known or believed to be a duty. Obviously, original sin cannot be sin *in this understanding of the word*. It may be described perhaps as an undue alienation from God, a lack of that supernatural union with Him for which mankind has been created. The Council condemned the doctrine that concupiscence, the desire to do what is morally wrong even if rejected by the will, is sin.

The Council excluded Our Lady from the scope of its decree on the universality of original sin—but left it open, after debate between defenders and opponents of the Immaculate Conception, whether or not she had in fact been conceived without original sin. The papal definition of 1854 would settle the question in the affirmative. Theological schools must be established, unauthorised and ignorant preaching suppressed.

Sixth Session. 13th January 1547

A lengthy decree was published on Justification,[1] one of the issues on which Luther first broke with Catholic doctrine. It was a carefully balanced statement condemning alike Pelagianism and Protestantism. A theological tractate in itself it is impossible to summarise it here. It concludes with 33 doctrinal anathemas. They affirm, inter alia, man's free acceptance of grace, that the will of fallen man is still free, that the good works of a sinner are not sins, that men are not justified by a merely external imputation of Christ's merits, or by confidence that we are so justified, that a soul in grace can keep God's law, that not only faith is required of the Christian, that a man once justified can lose grace and cannot completely avoid venial sin (even indeliberate), that temporal punishment will be exacted even when the guilt of sin has been removed, that good works done in grace, though God's gift are also man's merit, that the adult is not justified by faith alone—he must freely accept the grace which justifies him and cooperate with it. It is widely and, I am convinced, truly held that mystical or infused prayer is the experience of union with God effected by a loving will. This belief seems to run counter to a decree which appears to deny that man can be certain of being in a state of grace, united not opposed to God. The Council, however, admits that by 'special revela-

---

[1] 'Justification' is the passage from the state of alienation from the supernatural life of union with God into the state of supernatural union with Him; 'not only pardon of sin' but 'a sanctification and renewal of the inner man'.

The Nineteenth General Council

tion' a man can be certain that he will persevere to the end and
be saved. This special revelation surely may be understood as
the supreme but extremely rare experience termed by the mystics
the mystical marriage or transforming union which St. John of
the Cross, though not all mystical theologians, regards as precisely this inamissable grace. Surely then we are justified in
regarding the lowest degree of infused prayer, a degree granted
sporadically at least to large numbers who seriously pursue interior prayer, as a special that is to say individual, revelation;
not that the subject will be finally saved or even remain in a state
of grace when the experience has passed, but simply that here and
now he is not in a state of mortal sin i.e. of deliberate and radical
enmity with God. Any other view would make God a deceiver and
deny the evident fact that when A is conscious of love for B, for
the time at least A does love B.

Bishops were required to reside in their diocese. Too often
they had been absent on the service of the State. Priests must
reside in their parishes, religious in their convents.

Seventh Session. 3rd March, 1547

The Reformers had rejected the sacramental theology of the
Church. The Council now began a detailed exposition of Catholic
sacramental doctrine and practice. Thirteen canons were passed
on the sacraments in general, affirming that they are effective in
themselves *ex opere operato* not merely as exciting faith, that
the minister must have at least the intention to do what the
Church does, denying that all Christians lay as well as clerical,
can be ministers of all the sacraments, that mortal sin deprives
a minister of his sacramental power, that without her authority
the ritual of the Church can be lawfully changed or omitted.
Fourteen canons condemned errors concerning baptismal theology or practice, e.g. that only adults should be baptised, three
dealt with errors concerning Confirmation.

Pluralism, the accumulation of benefices by one man was
strictly limited. Other reforms enacted were concerned, among
other things, with episcopal vacancies, with the relation between

7*

the bishop and religious exempt from his diocesan jurisdiction.

Eighth Session. 11*th March,* 1547

The Council is transferred to Bologna. Plague had broken out at Trent. But a menacing political situation may well have been a further motive. For Charles V still intent upon his chimera, a compromise with the Protestants, was showing hostility to a Council so uncompromising in its opposition to Protestantism. He forbade bishops subject to him to leave Trent for Bologna.

Ninth Session, Bologna. 21*st April,* 1547

No more than 44 members were present, three cardinals, thirty-six bishops, four generals, one abbot. Discussions took place regarding the sacraments, and canons were passed on the subject of the Eucharist which, however, were finally shelved.

Tenth Session, Bologna, 2*nd June,* 1547

The same subjects were considered. The attendance had now risen to three cardinals, eight archbishops, sixty-nine bishops, six generals, two abbots. The sacrament of Penance was discussed at an informal meeting. On 13th September, in consequence of the political situation, the threatening attitude adopted by Charles, the Council was prorogued indefinitely. During these months valuable material was prepared for a possible resumption of the Council.

On 10th November, 1549, Paul III died. He was succeeded by one of the Tridentine legates, Cardinal Del Monte, Julius III (1550-1555). He revived the Council which was solemnly reopened with the *Eleventh Session,* 1st May, 1551. The presiding legates were Cardinal Crescenzi and two assistants, Pighini and Lippomano. The attendance was scanty. Thirteen bishops accompanied the legates. The session adjourned till the autumn. No business was transacted. King Henry II of France was hostile, refusing to send bishops.

Twelfth Session. 1st September, 1551

Even now the attendance consisted of no more than two cardinals, seven archbishops, twenty-six bishops, twenty-five theologians. The theologians were ordered to examine the Protestant doctrines about the Eucharist with a view to the issue of a doctrinal decree.

Thirteenth Session. 11th October, 1551

The numbers had increased, though the number of archbishops was still small. There were 52 voting members, among them five archbishops and five heads of religious orders. There were three episcopal electors from Germany, forty-eight consultant theologians. An important decree concluding with eleven canons was issued on Eucharistic theology. Thus the Council continued where it had left off four years earlier, defining Catholic sacramental doctrine. The objective presence of Our Lord's Body and Blood in the consecrated species, and, in particular, transubstantiation were reaffirmed. It was defined that Christ is received wholly under either species, bread or wine, and should be adored in His Eucharistic presence, that the communicant must previously have confessed mortal sins, that communion should be frequent. Eleven canons condemned errors to the contrary.

The reforming decrees were concerned with episcopal courts and appeals from them, and the procedure against criminal prelates.

Fourteenth Session. 25th November, 1551

A decree was issued treating of the sacraments of Penance and Extreme Unction to which were appended 19 canons condemning errors. The sacrament of penance, confession and sacramental absolution, is the normal means by which mortal sin committed after baptism is forgiven. All remembered mortal sins must be confessed. Even perfect contrition, that is sorrow for sin for love of God, though it restores God's grace even before confession, must include the purpose of subsequent confession. Imperfect contrition (attrition), sorrow for sin for some good but inferior motive, cannot restore grace until sacramental absolution has been received. Though the confession of venial sins is good, it is not strictly necessary. For their guilt can be removed in other ways. Absolution is not merely a declaration that God has forgiven sin, but a judicial sentence. The penance imposed should be proportionate to the gravity of the sins confessed.

The decree and canons concerning Extreme Unction affirm its sacramental character and two-fold effect: spiritual grace and remission of sins conferred in view of a good death, bodily healing.

The reforming decrees concerned clerical dress, criminous clerks, patronage and the like.

Fifteenth Session. 25th January, 1552

Since a handful of Protestants had appeared at Trent, the Council, not to bar the door upon a reconciliation however improbable, postponed the publication of doctrinal decrees already prepared, to allow time for more Protestants to arrive. Letters of safe conduct were issued. They would not have been dishonoured as in the case of Huss (see above p. 158).

Meanwhile, Henry II had allied himself with the Protestant princes and Augsburg had fallen into their hands. Since the Council seemed no longer safe, at the *Sixteenth Session, 28th April*, 1552, a papal decree was published suspending it. The second phase had closed.

When Julius III died (1555), after the 22 days' reign of Marcellus II, Cardinal Caraffa, co-founder of the Theatines, became Pope Paul IV (1555-1559). Autocrat and fanatic, scenting heresy everywhere and obsessed by hatred of Spain, he provoked the last war waged by a Catholic monarch, Philip II, against the Pope. He was not the man to favour a Council where his policy might be criticised and the Spanish episcopate would be represented. The suspension therefore remained. It was not until the Pontificate of his successor, Pius IV (1559-1565) that the Council would resume and complete its work. Pius IV, of the Medici family, was a man of diplomatic skill and conciliatory temper, large-hearted and wide-minded. To the states of the Empire he granted lay communion under both kinds and to the end of his life was prepared to sanction, as the Emperor desired, a married priest-hood. Philip II, however, tenaciously opposed the concession.

The Council was summoned for Easter, 1561. When, however, the four papal legates, Cardinal Hercules Gonzaga, Hosius, Seri-pando, Simonetta, arrived at Trent on 16th April, 1561, they found so few bishops present that no official session could be held. Catherine de Medici, now Regent in France, for political reasons was favouring the Huguenots whom for political reasons she would ultimately massacre. The Lutherans were determined to boycott the Council. Cardinal Mark Altemps, Bishop of Con-stance, was appointed a fifth legate.

Finally, the *Seventeenth Session* was held on 18*th January,* 1562. There were 113 voting members, fifty-three consultant theologians. No decrees were passed.

Eighteenth Session. 25th February, 1562

There were 133 voting members and more than fifty theo-logians. A decree was issued reviewing condemnations of books and inviting Protestants.

Nineteenth and Twentieth Sessions. 14th May and 4th June, 1562

The numbers had risen further but nothing was accomplished.

This third period of the Council was disturbed by disputes concerning the authority and status of bishops in respect of the Pope. In particular, the delicate question of reforming abuses in the Curia where the vested interest of so many cardinals was involved, gave rise to violent dissensions, so violent indeed that the continued existence of the Council was in danger. It required all the Pope's tact and moderation to enable it to weather the storm.

Twenty-First Session. 16th July, 1562

At last the Council was able to continue its task of doctrinal statement interrupted ten years earlier. A decree was passed with four canons attached, concerned with Holy Communion. Communion under one kind is sufficient and the Church has authority to prescribe it for all but the celebrant. The primitive practice, still preserved by the Greeks, of communicating infants, though not condemned, is declared unnecessary.

Reforms were promulgated concerned, among other things, with the conferring of benefices and the administration of endowments. The hawking of indulgences was forbidden.

Twenty-Second Session. 17th September, 1562

A decree was passed on the sacrifice of the Mass, concluding with nine canons. This aspect of the Eucharist had been from the beginning the object of the Reformers' vehement hatred. For Protestants regard the Eucharistic sacrifice, as it is taught by the Church, as a sacrifice additional to the sacrifice of Calvary and therefore derogating from its sufficiency. The Mass is declared to be the sacrifice of the New Law—a true sacrifice of propitiation. But the victim and priest are identical on Calvary and in the Mass. On the Cross and in the Mass the same sacrifice is offered but after a different fashion. Mass may be offered for the dead and in honour of saints. The canon of the Mass is free from error, the ceremonies prescribed by the Church are valuable incentives to devotion. The language used about them 'stemming from the practice and tradition of the Apostles' reflects the unhistorical perspective, which saw the primitive Church as identical even in the externals of practice and ritual with the Church of the 16th century, a perspective unfortunately which played into the hands of Protestant critics.[1] Private Masses are approved but with a reserve as to the term 'private' which anticipates its formal rejection today. Water must be mixed with the wine in the chalice and, although Latin must be retained as the liturgical language, explanations of the liturgy should be given.

The question whether, in fact, the laity might be permitted the

[1] This false historical perspective was supported by the belief to which Catholics long held tenaciously that the writings of the pseudo-Denys, which comprised mystical interpretations of the elaborate ceremonial used in the writer's day (late 5th or early 6th century) are the genuine work of St. Paul's convert.

chalice was left to the Pope's decision. A number of regulations were passed dealing with ecclesiastical finance.

Between this session and the next, dissensions all but wrecked the Council. Throughout, the Spanish bishops displayed a markedly anti-papal attitude. A contingent of French bishops led by Charles de Guise, Cardinal of Lorraine, seemed a further threat to papal authority over the Council, though they proved more amenable than had been expected. Cardinals Gonzaga and Seripando died and were succeeded as legates by Cardinals Morone and Navagero. The Emperor Ferdinand I assembled a small Council of his own at Innsbruck to prepare a scheme of reform to be presented at Trent. In a personal interview, Cardinal Morone arranged a compromise with him.

Twenty-Third Session, 14th July, 1563

There were present 235 prelates. among them six cardinals, 12 ambassadors and 133 theologians. The Council had at last gathered numerical strength. A decree was passed on Holy Orders followed by eight canons. There is a sacrificial priesthood deriving its sacerdotal power from its apostolic succession. There are four minor orders. The subdiaconate is to be accounted a major order. Orders is a sacrament. Bishops are the highest order, the sole ministers of confirmation[1] and ordination. The consent of the people or the secular government is not required for ordination. Nor can secular authorisation supply for a lack of orders.

Bishops must reside in their dioceses. Only thus can they fulfil their duty to know their flocks.

Before the next session opened, violent dissensions once more broke out during the work of preparation. The Spanish and French bishops were particularly intransigent. Once more the diplomacy of Pope Pius restored peace.

Twenty-Fourth Session. 11th November, 1563

A brief decree was issued on matrimony followed by 12 canons.

[1] Parish Priests however are today not only permitted but commanded to confirm dying persons who have not received the sacrament, even infants. But it must be with oil blessed by a bishop.

Marriage is an indissoluble union and a sacrament. Polygamy is prohibited by divine law. The Church may dispense from the prohibitive degrees of consanguinity and affinity laid down by Leviticus—Henry VIII had denied this power—and from degrees not mentioned in Scripture. She may ordain diriment impediments to marriage, that is impediments which render marriage not only unlawful but null and void. The marriage bond cannot be dissolved even by infidelity. The Protestant Churches, except the Church of England whose attitude on this question has from the outset been ambiguous, permitted divorce for infidelity. The canon against divorce was drawn up in an unusually indirect form to spare the susceptibilities of the Greeks many of whom admitted and admit that the Latin practice is in conformity with the teaching of Christ, their own a concession to human weakness. It does not therefore define the indissolubility of marriage, though this is the logical conclusion to be drawn.[1] The ecclesiastical judge may, however, pronounce separations. Clergy in major orders and vowed religious are incapable of contracting a valid marriage. Virginity is a higher state than marriage. The Church rightly forbids marriages to be solemnised, celebrated with full ceremonies and Mass, at certain seasons. The Church is the judge of matrimonial cases. At the same session clandestine marriages, that is to say, marriages contracted without the presence of a priest and two witnesses—always unlawful and therefore sinful, were declared null and void. The decree however would take effect only where the Council's decrees were promulgated. In England it did not come into force until St. Pius X in 1908 issued his decree *Ne Temere*.

A number of reforms were enacted concerning the status, appointment and revenues of the clergy.

Twenty-Fifth and Final Session. 3rd and 4th December, 1563

A decree was passed on purgatory. 'There is a purgatory and the souls there held captive can be assisted by the prayers of the faithful, above all by the sacrifice of the altar.' Preachers are for-

[1] See the article *Adultere* in the Dictionnaire de Theologie Catholique.

bidden to indulge in theological subtleties or speculations. Superstitious or unfounded descriptions of purgatorial pains are forbidden or anything that savours of money-making.

Since 'purgatory' means a place or state of purification, the definition, as Baron von Hügel pointed out, favours the view of those theologians who hold that the souls in purgatory are in fact still impure and being purified, rather than the view which denies this and maintains that these souls, though from the moment of death sufficiently pure for the beatific vision of God, are detained in exile to satisfy an unpaid debt of punishment.

A further decree declares that the Saints should be invoked and their relics venerated. The decree of the *Second Nicene Council* prescribing the veneration of images is renewed, in face of the Lutheran neglect of images and the far more deplorable iconoclasm of the Calvinists. The honour paid to the image, so it is defined, is referred to the subject it represents. 'No trust is to be placed in an image for its own sake.'

The Reformation began with Luther's protest not only against the unquestionable abuses of an indulgence particularly scandalous for its commercialisation and the preachers' unwarranted affirmations, but against the very principle of indulgences. The last word of the Counter-Reformation statement of Catholic doctrine at Trent affirmed their efficacy and value. The reforming decrees were concerned with the observance of fasts and feasts, monastic life, relations between the regulars and bishops, further regulations for the life and work of the clergy, forbidden books. A revision of the liturgical books, Missal and Breviary, was discussed and left in the Pope's hands. It would be effected by the next Pope, St. Pius V (1566-1572). Cardinal Morone thereupon dissolved the Council now composed of four cardinal-legates, two other cardinals, three patriarchs, 25 archbishops, 167 bishops, seven generals, seven abbots, 19 procurators for absent bishops.

On 26th January, 1564, Pius IV confirmed the Council's decrees. The following November he issued the Creed known as the Creed of the Council of Trent because it was based upon its decrees. It is publicly professed by converts from Protestantism.

The so-called Catechism of the Council of Trent was the work of Pope St. Pius V who issued it in 1566. It was intended not for the laity but for the instruction of priests.

The Council of Trent, despite obstacles which time and again threatened to destroy it and in fact dragged out its existence over many barren years, had enunciated the Catholic religion against Protestant denials. Such a statement of necessity is defensive and conservative, above all in its maintenance of existing usage. The Council of Trent set its seal on the post-Tridentine type of Catholicism such as has endured into our days, a Catholicism of a beleagured Church, the Church, as they say, 'in a state of siege'. Emphasis has inevitably been laid on those aspects of Catholic faith, practice and worship which are anti-Protestant, to the neglect of those aspects common to Protestants and Catholics, of truths for example the non sacramental priesthood of the laity, the value of bible reading, which Protestants have mis-stated or placed out of due perspective. As regards the liturgy in particular, the Counter-Reformation as Père Bouyer has pointed out, cherished 'a rigid and unintelligent traditionalism' which however was 'the providential means whereby the Church managed to keep her liturgical treasures safe throughout a long period when scarcely anyone was capable of understanding their true worth'.[1] To conserve entire the treasure handed down, doctrinal, sacramental and devotional was indeed the accomplishment of Tridentine Catholicism, restricted, it is true and therefore restricting, but indispensable and of primary importance. The doctrinal deposit thus secured could develop and today we witness the beginnings of this new growth.

That Catholicism cannot remain for ever Tridentine does not alter the fact that only as Tridentine and largely as the achievement of Trent could it have weathered the 16th century storm, halted the Protestant advance, inspired Baroque culture and art.

[1] *Liturgical Piety* by Louis Bouyer, p. 8. Unfortunately, however, Père Bouyer fails to appreciate the distinctive beauty of Baroque art, despite the liturgical blindness.

Protestant historians cannot forgive the Council of Trent because it did not make the Catholic religion Protestant or at least become, though some of its members displayed a tendency in that direction, a second Basel. Catholic historians recognise with gratitude and admiration its achievement of doctrinal statement and practical reform.

Nevertheless, below the surface of conceptual theology, the expression of doctrines in terms of intelligible statement, lies the deep spring of personal communion with God, a communion which, however differently they may interpret it in theological concepts and terminology, is experienced by the devout Catholic and the devout Protestant. To both alike it is the same experience. It has been well described by an anonymous Carthusian[1]: 'the "exercises" of the spiritual life are reduced to a single act *received* rather than produced, of incalculable worth because belonging to the divine order. It consists in letting God be in ourselves. You may term it charity, faith, trust, adoration, propitiation, thanksgiving. At this point all these words seem to mean the same, the ideas they express to fuse like burning substances in the crucible of a heart [spirit] ... wherein the Person of Love is aflame. ... The Life of the soul is consumed in the Life of God. ... By consuming her, God has transformed her. Every instant the soul is born of God, she lives with the divine life, knows God with the knowledge with which he knows himself, loves him with the love with which he loves himself'. The soul's action, that is to say, is God's and is experienced as such. Yet man abides throughout the recipient of God's action within him. Doctrinal statement maintains and expresses the Catholic faith, but only from this depth can reunion proceed—because at this depth union already exists.[2]

---

[1] See *Le Paradis Blanc.*

[2] An Austrian Jesuit indeed, Fr. Kung having expounded the theology of the neo-Lutheran Karl Barth with the guarantee of Barth himself has argued that it is identical with the teaching of Trent. Barth and Trent *mean* the same. *If* he is right the Protestant heresies on justification and grace must be accounted like the Monophysite and Monothelite, heresies not of doctrine but doctrinal terminology.

21

THE TWENTIETH GENERAL COUNCIL:
THE VATICAN COUNCIL 1869-1870

THREE hundred years, the longest interval since Councils began with Nicaea, elapsed before the Council of Trent found a successor. The experience of Trent, its factions and interruptions, had proved how difficult it was to carry through an ecumenical Council in face of conflicting and more or less Erastian Catholic governments. Moreover, Trent had developed the Catholic answer to Protestantism and until the Revolution Protestantism remained the organised opponent of the Church in Western Europe. Meantime however a more radical foe had come into the field, a foe whose first social and political victory was the French Revolution. It was secularism, the total rejection of Christianity, rationalism, atheism or at best a vague deism. Despite a temporary reaction provoked by the excesses of the Revolution, this current of ideas prevailed in the nineteenth century. Protestantism became largely a liberal Protestantism often amounting to no more than Unitarianism. The world was breaking away from the Church and Christian doctrine, with a positive hostility to the Church which did not stop short of such measure of persecution as the liberal regard for toleration and the rights of conscience could, without too flagrant a contradiction, admit. Hard pressed by this new foe in those countries moreover which had rallied to the Counter-Reformation, the Church entered what may be termed the Maccabean period of her history. She will concentrate her energies in defence of her doctrines, rights and privileges against the secularist invasion, using when possible the support of conservative governments whose authority also was threatened by the liberal movement. Uncompromising opposition on every issue, blindness to all that was good in the liberal ideals, obstinate defence of outworks not truly defensible, refusal to yield the least whit of political privilege or temporal government; such was the Catholic war of defence. Between the liberalised, rationalist and increasingly secularised world that had come into existence and the Church lay a gulf of mutual incomprehension. This too was historically inevitable.

It was to concentrate the Catholic strength and deploy the Catholic front in this war against a secularist liberalism that Pius IX decided to convoke a Council which would do for the Counter-Revolution what Trent had done for the Counter-Reformation. On June 29, 1868 he issued a bull convoking the Council.

'The Catholic Church,' says the Pope, 'with its saving doctrine and venerable power and the supreme authority of this Holy See, are by the bitterest enemies of God and man assailed and trampled down.... Wherefore we have judged it opportune to bring together into a general Council all our venerable brethren of the whole Catholic world.... In this Ecumenical Council must be examined ... and decreed all things which in these difficult times relate to the greater glory of God, the integrity of the Faith, ... the eternal salvation of men, ... the observance of ecclesiastical laws, the amendment of morals and the instruction of Christian youth.... Care must be taken that all evils may be averted from the Church and from civil society.'

As Abbot Butler comments,[1] too wide and too vague a programme. But it was the Christian counter-offensive against secularism. Nothing is said of papal infallibility, the doctrine which is particularly associated with the Vatican Council. Even when the Council met, Pius expressed his intention of leaving the matter to the decision of the bishops. Nevertheless he soon became its active champion, exerting all his influence to secure its early definition. Before the Council met it was generally believed that

---

[1] *The Vatican Council*, by Abbot Cuthbert Butler. An invaluable history, objective and balanced.

to define papal infallibility was the primary objective of the Council. Bishop Ullathorne of Birmingham, for example, wrote to a correspondent 'the Pope, I believe, is bent on the definition, if he can, as the crowning of his reign and I think it will in some shape probably pass'.[1] It was not duplicity on Pius's part. He no doubt expected that the bishops would as a body spontaneously bring forward and define his infallibility.

The Council was solemnly opened by the Pope at St. Peter's on December 8, 1869. Never had an ecumenical Council gathered so many bishops, moreover from so many parts of the world, together with bishops of Eastern Christians in union with the Pope, the Uniats. If the large number of Italian bishops gave them a voting strength disproportionate to that of other national hierarchies, this was due not to papal machinations packing the Council, but to the historical fact that in Italy the primitive system of a bishop for every Christian community of appreciable size still continued. At a general congregation held on December 10 there were present 679: 43 cardinals, 605 bishops, 31 abbots and generals of religious orders. According to Clement Raab 'the highest number present at any time was 774: 49 cardinals, 10 patriarchs, 10 primates, 127 archbishops, 529 bishops, 22 abbots, 26 generals of religious orders, 1 apostolic administrator'.

The meetings of the Council were divided into General Congregations and Public Sessions. The former discussed propositions brought before them, the latter made a solemn pronouncement in accordance with decisions already reached in the Congregations. A draft already prepared by a committee of theologians and canonists was submitted to the Congregations and debated. After prolonged debate in the Congregations— speeches by individual bishops unrestricted in time and often wandering from the point—the drafts if, and in fact they were, materially altered were referred back to a committee or deputation elected by ballot to deal with the subject in question, faith, discipline, the Regulars, the Eastern Churches, the missions, to which they belonged. Obviously the important deputation was

[1] The Vatican Council, p. 143.

the deputation for Faith. The leading champions of infallibility, of whom Archbishop Manning of Westminster was the informal leader, managed to pack it with their supporters, as Abbot Cuthbert Butler admits, an unfair manoeuvre. He also says that it was contrary to the Pope's intention. This however I venture to doubt. Pius could so easily have rectified the departure from his wishes. It is more likely that he was converted to approval.

The Congregation met for the first time on December 16 debating a general constitution on Faith. The Second Session on January 6, 1870 was formal, confined to a solemn profession of the creed of Pius IV. The recital of a creed was a regular formality at an ecumenical council.

The proceedings of the Council were unfortunately subject to an oath of secrecy. With so many hundreds cognizant, this did not prevent leakage. It did however leave scope for a host of rumours, many of them absurd, which circulated from the beginning and were collected in reports of the Council circulated by its enemies notably that of 'Quirinus' the work of the anti-papal theologian, Dr. Friedrich and 'Janus' the work of a German anti-papal Catholic historian, Doellinger who drew on reports by Friedrich and Lord Acton. It was not until years later when the harm had been done and Quirinus's story had been generally accepted that a detailed account of the Council's proceedings including every speech made, was published.

At this point we must consider the two parties in opposition, the majority in favour of defining papal infallibility, the minority against it. Apart from a handful of bishops, the minority agreed with the majority in accepting the doctrine as true. Their objection was to the advisability, the 'opportunity' of defining it as an article of faith. They were afraid that the definition might be understood and in practice applied to cover a wide field of papal utterances as was desired by the extreme papalists, Manning for example, his henchman W. G. Ward, and in France Veuillot, the editor of the Univers. These men maintained that papal infallibility extended to all public utterances by a pope, a claim historically untenable. The inopportunists also feared that to affirm papal prerogative might in fact diminish the divinely given commission and authority of the bishops. Moreover they feared not unreasonably that the definition would place a further obstacle to the return of Orientals and Protestants to the Church. Though from the first decidedly a minority, they included many of the most learned and eminent prelates. One of their leaders was Bishop Dupanloup of Orleans, undoubtedly the most outstanding French bishop. Among some 36 French inopportunist bishops there was Archbishop Darboy of Paris. The majority of the German and Austrian bishops were inopportunist among them the Church historian Hefele,[1] and Ketteler one of the earliest bishops to interest himself in social problems. There were four Irish bishops among them Newman's friend and correspondent Moriarty of Kerry, two Hungarian bishops Simor and Haynald, and Strossmeyer of Bosnia, a particularly forceful personality. Many bishops from the United States were inopportunist, two English bishops decided inopportunists. The majority of the English hierarchy were in favour of a carefully guarded definition. The Archbishop of Milan and some other bishops from northern Italy were inopportunists. On the other hand the Spanish, Spanish-American, South Italian, Belgian and Polish bishops supported the definition. Both parties have been the object of calumny. The infallibilist majority were not a body of ignorant yes-men. Nor were the inopportunist minority disloyal Catholics. There was no doubt much intrigue outside the Council on both sides. And the Pope undoubtedly exploited the veneration due to his office, the affection inspired by his personality and sufferings, to influence the bishops in the direction he desired. What is more regrettable, he gave his warm approval to writings calumniating the minority and advocating extreme views of papal infallibility. But no man is free from faults. The statement so frequently made that the Council was not free is untrue. Bishops spoke their mind on all subjects, particularly on what was called 'the question' with entire freedom and almost, though not quite, always received a respectful hearing. Every statement proposed

[1] Hefele in fact did not believe the doctrine of papal infallibility.

for definition was debated and carefully weighed. Only towards the close when arguments on all sides had been fully heard, the heat of a Roman summer was proving a severe strain and the threatening political horizon urged haste, were the proceedings speeded up. The closure found indispensable in the most democratic of parliaments was applied only once and with the general approval of the Council. Proceedings at Trent had been far more stormy. In any case the procedure of a Council is but human. The Church claims a divine sanction only for its final decisions.

Moreover in the most important respect the Council enjoyed untramelled liberty. Since the relations between Church and State were on the agenda and this had become known, there was a threat of intervention by England urged by Acton's friend, Mr. Gladstone. Manning however through the British envoy in Rome was able to avert it. And a similar threat from the French Government, more serious because the Pope depended on French troops for defence of Rome against the Italian government, was also averted. No government attempted to interfere in the Council even by envoys making protests, suggestions or threats in the course of its proceedings. Caesar, though his motive was a secularist indifference, respected completely the things of God.

The draft on faith was submitted to the Council and debated in several Congregations. In consequence it was sent back to the deputation to be entirely recast. It is noteworthy that, in spite of the outcries of bigoted disapproval which greeted Bishop Strossmeyer's assertion that vast numbers of Protestants loved Jesus Christ, his protest was not made in vain. The statement that secularism, atheism, rationalism, and pantheism were products of Protestantism was removed from the draft. Bishop Ullathorne of Birmingham, a moderate who refused to participate in lobbyings outside the Council, successfully carried through an important change of wording. The original draft of the decree on faith spoke of the 'sancta Romana Catholica Ecclesia': the holy Roman Catholic Church. Ullathorne supported by other English and American bishops, fearing lest this wording should be construed as support for the Anglican branch theory that the Catholic

Church could be and was divided into branches, one of them the Roman Catholic, asked for a change of wording. The formula 'Holy Catholic Apostolic Roman Church' was finally carried. It does not however follow that in itself the appellation Roman Catholic i.e. Roman and Catholic is objectionable. It had been in fact commonly used by English Catholics since the Reformation.

Meanwhile petitions for and against defining papal infallibility were sent to the Pope. He transmitted them to a special Congregation of 26 appointed to report to him on proposals made by bishops for conciliar action. With one dissentient, the Committee reported in favour of the proposal. On March 1st Pius confirmed its decision and on March 6 it was publicly announced that the doctrine would come before the Council. Outside, a war of pamphlets was being waged, the champions of both parties active in canvassing for their respective views. Lord Acton then resident in Rome was an unofficial leader of the inopportunists supplying them with historical ammunition against the definition.

Third Session. April 24, 1870

677 voted. The Constitution on Faith was decreed. To it were appended 18 canons condemning errors on God as Creator, revelation, faith and the relation between faith and reason. It was a defence of the fundamental principles of Catholic Christianity. There is 'one true God, Creator and Lord of all things visible and invisible' which He has freely created out of nothing: materialism and pantheism in any form are condemned. The existence of this divine Creator can be known by the natural light of human reason. Nevertheless a revelation is necessary primarily because man has been called by God to a supernatural union with himself above the plane of natural reason. The sources of this revelation are Scripture and Tradition, and the former must be interpreted by the Church. This, as is pointed out in the decree, reaffirms the previous decrees of Trent. The canon as fixed at Trent is also reaffirmed and the authenticity of the Vulgate. This revelation, made credible by external signs, is to be

received by divine faith, itself the effect of a free choice accepting divine grace. Though faith is a source of knowledge distinct from reason and concerned with mysteries beyond the scope of reason, it can never be opposed to reason which establishes 'the foundations of faith' and is in turn enlightened by faith. Alleged scientific conclusions which contradict revelation are thereby shown to be erroneous unless indeed a dogma of faith has been misunderstood contrary to the mind of the Church.

This Constitution should in the normal course have been followed by constitutions on the Church, her nature, unity, and infallibility, her hierarchical constitution and the relation between Church and State. Indeed the draft had been published with its annexed canons. It was evident however that, if this procedure were followed, the crucial matter of papal infallibility could not come before the Council for at least a year. Who could be sure that the Council could meet in a year's time? It proved in fact impossible. Under these circumstances and in view of the tension within the Council, the heated controversies outside it, all turning on the question of papal infallibility, it had become desirable to settle it without delay. A petition signed by nearly 100 bishops[1] asked the Pope to order the immediate discussion of the draft constitution on the papacy. He agreed and on April 29 it was officially announced that the papacy, the Pope's primacy and infallibility would be discussed without further delay. In vain did Dupanloup write to the Pope entreating him not to force forward a measure which, in the writer's view, threatened an extensive schism. The Pope in his reply, not content with refusal, charged Dupanloup unjustly with intellectual pride. The bishop however of course had not only the right but the duty to act, however mistakenly, as he thought the good of the Church required.[2]

On May 14 the draft of the constitution on the papacy, remodelled by the infallibilist deputation *de fide,* came before a

---

[1] So the official record in Mansi. Bishop Moriarty however writing on April 28 to Newman speaks of a deputation on the part of 400 bishops.

[2] I am surprised that Abbot Cuthbert Butler should call this unfortunate letter 'truly paternal.'

general Congregation and the debate opened. Bishops spoke freely on both sides, Hefele in particular from his unrivalled knowledge of ecclesiastical history urging historical objections. His arguments, it must be said, for example criticisms made at Chalcedon of Pope Leo's dogmatic letter, Honorius and the Monothelites, went beyond a mere inopportunism and called in question the doctrine itself. On May 25 Manning, as he said, the only member of the Council brought up outside the Church, made a most impressive speech in favour of the definition—which, he erroneously predicted, would produce a multitude of English conversions. Every argument on either side was ventilated, indeed at too great length and with much repetition.

On June 3 the debate on the Constitution generally was ended by the application of the closure, the only time it was applied at the Council. Enough surely had been said.

The chapter on Papal Primacy was now discussed. The minority objected, not to the statement of papal primacy but to what seemed to them insufficient recognition of episcopal authority. A minority leader, Cardinal Rauscher of Vienna, secured a modification of wording. The discussion ended on June 14. On July 13 this part of the constitution, concerning the papal primacy, amended by the deputation in view of criticisms, was carried by a large majority. From June 15 onwards the proposed definition of papal infallibility, the second part of the Constitution of the papacy, was debated. Many of the bishops wished to introduce into the definition words of St. Antoninus[1] 'the successor of St. Peter using the Council and seeking for the help of the universal Church cannot err'. In point of fact the Pope does consult the episcopate before issuing an *ex Cathedra* decision. To make such consultation a condition of infallible utterance or to pronounce such consultation indispensable, would however, it was objected, introduce an element of doubt and provide possibility of evasion. A decree professedly an infallible pronouncement was, it might be argued, invalidated by lack of sufficient consultation. Once more the two parties debated. Cardinal Guidi,

[1] Dominican Archbishop of Florence, died 1459.

Dominican Archbishop of Bologna and a distinguished theologian, though not an inopportunist, expressed his fear that infallibility might be claimed for irresponsible personal utterances by the Pope. He therefore wished consultation with the bishops and investigation of the dogmatic tradition to be defined as conditions of infallibility. The Pope, most regrettably, sent for the Cardinal and lectured him for disloyal opposition. The same day, June 19 Cardinal Cullen of Dublin proposed the form of definition derived from Cardinal Bilio which was in the event adopted and passed. Of 57 speakers 35 spoke in favour of the definition as proposed, 22 against it. Finally the intense heat and weariness of endless oratory induced many bishops to renounce their right to speak and on July 4 the debate ended. On July 11 the deputation on Faith brought before the Council the amended definition. Its spokesman Bishop Gasser of Brixen introduced and defended it in an able speech. On July 13 with the addition of a historical preamble stating that in fact Popes had consulted the Church either by a Council or in some other way and with four amendments, the definition in its final form was put to the vote. 601 voted, 451 in favour, 88 against, with conditional approval i.e. on condition of further amendment 62. 76 other bishops in Rome were absent from the Congregation. Two further amendments were in fact adopted. On July 15 a deputation of six minority bishops pleaded passionately but fruitlessly for such alteration of language as would satisfy their objections, for words requiring for an infallible pronouncement consultation in some form or other with the bishops.

On the eve of the fourth and final session when the constitution would be finally enacted, the minority bishops, at first determined to record their adverse vote, were persuaded by Dupanloup not to resist the Pope to his face but to leave Rome before the session.

On July 18 the session was held. In the Pope's presence and amidst thunder and lightning, interpreted by the superstitious in terms of their theological beliefs, the Council solemnly defined the Constitution on the Papacy. 533 voted for the definition, two

Riccio of Cajuzzo and Fitzgerald of Littlerock against it.[1] Many
bishops apart from the inopportunists had already left Rome.

The greater part of the Constitution is a reaffirmation of the
papal supremacy bestowed by Christ on St. Peter and his successors. The concluding definition runs as follows:

'Faithfully adhering to the traditions received from the beginning of the Christian Faith, for the glory of God our Saviour,
the exaltation of the Catholic Religion and the Salvation of
Christian peoples, the sacred Council approving, we teach and
define that it is a dogma divinely revealed that the Roman Pontiff
when he speaks ex Cathedra, that is, when in discharge of the
office of Pastor and Doctor of all Christians, by virtue of his
supreme apostolic authority he defines a doctrine regarding the
faith or morals to be held by the Universal Church, by the divine
assistance promised to him in blessed Peter, is possessed of that
infallibility with which the Divine Redeemer willed that his
Church should be endowed for defining doctrine regarding faith
or morals: and that therefore such definitions of the Roman
pontiff are irreformable of themselves and not from the consent
of the Church.

'But if anyone, which may God avert, presume to contradict
this our definition, let him be anathema.'[2]

All the inopportunist bishops even Hefele submitted and accepted
the definition. But a schism of 'Old Catholics' rejecting it arose
in Germany and Switzerland encouraged by the State. It obtained
episcopal consecration from the schismatic Church of Utrecht
and continues, though it cannot be said to flourish, until the present day.

Since the definition there is one and only one papal pronouncement which certainly and professedly fulfils the prescribed conditions for infallibility, a definition by Pope Pius XII of our
Lady's bodily Assumption.

Though many bid us receive as infallible pronouncements—
encyclicals and the like—admittedly fallible, no-one today expects
as did Manning, Ward and Veuillot to receive a multitude of
infallible definitions on every question of faith or morals on

[1] They immediately submitted.
[2] This translation is Abbot Cuthbert Butler's.

which a Pope may wish to speak his mind. Among others Bishop Fischer, secretary to the Council and therefore in the best situation to know its mind, published an explanation of the definition careful and moderate. In effect the infallibilists secured the definition of infallibility, the inopportunists its interpretation. And in this connection we may do well to remember the judgment of Eduard Meyer an historian with no Christian belief. He finds in a text of the fourth Gospel: 'it will be for him, the truth-giving spirit ... to guide you into all truth (John XVI, 13) 'already present, however little the writer was aware of it, the doctrine of the infallible Church. And the entire development of the Catholic Church *down to the Vatican Council* is pre-formed in these words.'[1]

It was the Pope's intention that the Council should resume its labours that winter with the remainder of the Constitution on the Church. The withdrawal of French troops, followed on September 26 by the entry of the Italian army into Rome, made this impossible and on October 28 the Pope suspended the Council indefinitely. It was an intervention of Providence. The time was not ripe for an anti-secularist Trent, an authoritative and comprehensive statement of Catholic doctrine in regard to the issues raised, evolution for example, by the new world of scientific and humanitarian advance, metaphysical and theological decadence. Has it come even now?

The Vatican Council has never been formally dissolved and none of the bishops subscribed its decrees. The forthcoming Council almost a century later will not however be regarded as its continuation. It is long since defunct. With the definition of papal infallibility its work was done.

Anfange des Christentums, Vol. III, pp. 646-7.

EPILOGUE

ALMOST a hundred years after the Vatican Council, another ecumenical council is in preparation. Were it but a matter of promulgating one particular doctrinal definition, the more expeditious method of taking the sense of the episcopate would be by writing to each. If however comprehensive statements on doctrine or discipline are to be promulgated in terms hammered out by personal discussion a council is indicated. Such comprehensive statements are envisaged for the forthcoming council. For all the Bishops over the world, Catholic Universities and others have sent into Rome their suggestions for conciliar discussions and decrees. Only some of these could possibly be adopted. Too wide a programme would demand too much time. It may be that the subject of episcopal jurisdiction and rights, the cause at Trent of acrimonious debate and left untouched at the Vatican Council, will once more be brought forward. Pope John has spoken of adapting Canon Law to changed conditions of the modern world. The Council has been preceded by a synod of the Roman diocese occupied with disciplinary enactments. Many of these, applicable universally, will perhaps be extended by the Council to Western Catholicism as a whole. The Pope has also spoken of Christian reunion as an objective of the Council. To speak, as we must, according to the human probabilities of the situation, for we cannot exclude unexpected interventions of divine Providence, there seems little prospect of corporate reunion on any considerable scale as a result of the Council. Separations and hostilities rooted in the tradition of centuries are not quickly overcome. The failures of Lyons and Florence testify that reunion cannot be imposed on aversion or ignorance. Before any further steps can be taken, an atmosphere of mutual understanding and Christian charity must be created. This at least we should and may confidently expect from Pope John's Council. And this alone would be valuable fruit of its labours. Catholics watch with interest, sympathy and prayer the work and meetings of the ecumenical World Council of Churches, though for doctrinal reasons the Catholic Church cannot officially participate. Orientals, Anglicans, Protestants will surely watch with the same sentiments the sessions of the Council.

Other possible subjects are a permanent diaconate of married men, liturgical reform, the liturgical use of the vernacular. For some years now work has been done in Rome on a revision of Breviary and Missal. The result may perhaps be submitted to the Council for criticism or approval. For our present Pope has shown himself a man to welcome suggestions. The Roman synod, he has informed us, was a suggestion made to him.

Many are hoping for an authoritative declaration upon the morality of warfare under the conditions introduced by the atom bomb. The difficulties, I fear, are insuperable (see above p. 103). But the accepted teaching of Catholic moralists such as Vittoria sufficiently condemn participation in any war in which nuclear weapons are employed or threatened.

Some are hoping for what may be called definitions of devotion, for example that our Lady is co-redemptress and mediator of all graces. But are not co-redemption and universal mediation functions which in due proportion to personal holiness are exercised by every living cell in Christ's mystical Body? Others are opposed to definitions of this kind. If there is uncertainty here, there can be no ground for anxiety. The worse party may win a General Election, a false doctrine cannot win a general Council. Of this the Vatican Council is an apt illustration. It was not won by the extremists of the Manning, Ward and Veuillot school for all that their mistaken loyalty pleased Pio Nono.[1]

---

[1] This is not to deny that ecumenical councils in the past have anathematised individuals unwarrantedly e.g. the sixth Council's personal condemnation of Honorius and Sergius.

Of this at any rate we may be assured. The prospective Council will present the Catholic religion for what it is in fact but has too often failed sufficiently to appear, the integration rather than the negation of all that is true and valuable in religious beliefs outside the pale, of insights which, however partial, may have been more clear and powerful among their adherents than among Catholics, of truths and values which though contained at least implicitly in the deposit of Catholic faith, may not yet have been sufficiently developed by Catholics, the reconciliation in the Catholic synthesis of what is partial, one-sided, excessive, defective outside the Church. This positive approach put forward in a spirit of Christian charity to all, especially to fellow Christians, should enable the approaching Council to take the lead in mustering throughout the world the positive against the negative forces, tendencies and ideologies, against all that would restrict human knowledge and endeavour to one department or level of human experience, or to fewer than all, to levels lower than the highest. This struggle between the darkness which excludes spiritual light and the light of comprehensive truth divides mankind today. In that struggle surely the forthcoming Council could play a leading role. God or no God, whether His existence is denied, doubted or merely ignored, spirit illusory or more real than matter, man an animal like the lower animals, enslaved to animal instinct and wholly mortal or an immortal spirit incarnate —these supreme issues in debate throughout the world confront the massive social affirmation of God, spirit, man's spiritual nature and destiny, which is the Catholic Church. In the twenty-first ecumenical Council her voice of affirmation—the everlasting Yea in face of the persistent Nay—will speak out loud and clear to the world.

INDEX